MW01002747

HARVEST
of a DECADE

HARVEST of a DECADE

Disraelia and Other Essays

WALTER LAQUEUR

Transaction Publishers
New Brunswick (U.S.A.) and London (U.K.)

Copyright © 2012 by Transaction Publishers, New Brunswick, New Jersey.

All rights reserved under International and Pan-American Copyright Conventions. No part of this book may be reproduced or transmitted in any form or by any means, electronic or mechanical, including photocopy, recording, or any information storage and retrieval system, without prior permission in writing from the publisher. All inquiries should be addressed to Transaction Publishers, Rutgers—The State University of New Jersey, 35 Berrue Circle, Piscataway, New Jersey 08854-8042. www.transactionpub.com

This book is printed on acid-free paper that meets the American National Standard for Permanence of Paper for Printed Library Materials.

Library of Congress Catalog Number: 2011009837
ISBN: 978-1-4128-4232-7
Printed in the United States of America

Library of Congress Cataloging-in-Publication Data

Laqueur, Walter, 1921-
Harvest of a decade : Disraelia and other essays / Walter Laqueur.
    p. cm.
Collection of previously published articles.
ISBN 978-1-4128-4232-7
1. Jews—Europe—History—19th century. 2. Jews—Europe—
History—20th century. 3. Zionism. 4. Holocaust, Jewish (1939–
1945) 5. Jews—Russia—History. 6. Terrorism. I. Title.
DS135.E83L325   2011
940'.04924—dc22

                                                        2011009837

Contents

Preface   vii

Acknowledgments   xiii

Part 1: Israel and the Jews   1

    Disraelia: A Counterfactual History, 1848–2008   3

    How to Solve the Conflict—Israel and the Palestinians   25

    Zionism Revisited   35

    The Terrible Secret   45

    No Ease in Zion: Herzl and Lohengrin   57

    The Jewish Century?   65

    Abuse of History   69

Part 2: Whither Russia   73

    Russia: The Years to Come   75

    Russia's Muslim Strategy   87

    The Cold War: Two Histories, Two Narratives   103

Part 3: Europe, Our Great Hope   109

    Better Fifty Years of Europe?   111

    Europe's Long Road to the Mosque   117

    Islamic Fascism, Islamophobia, Antisemitism   125

    Islamophobia   131

Part 4: Terrorism   135

    Postmodern Terrorism   137

    The Terrorism to Come   147

    The Ticking Clock   163

Underestimating Terrorism   169

Suicide Terrorism   177

Fanaticism   183

Part 5: Heroes and Antiheroes   187

Hans Paasche: Eccentric and Martyr   189

Ernst Nolte   199

The Orientalist   203

Arthur Koestler   207

Victor Serge: The Revolutionary   215

Burckhardt and the Red Cross   221

Montefiore—King of the Jews   227

Three Witnesses: The Legacy of Viktor Klemperer,
Willy Cohn, and Richard Koch   231

Index   247

Preface

This is a selection of essays written during the first decade of the twenty-first century, the ninth decade of my life. We spent most of this time in Washington, but there were long stays in the UK, Germany, and other European countries. Some of my publications during this period were in languages other than English but with two exceptions, are not included here. Those I have selected deal with a variety of topics but even so, they do not entirely reflect my interests during this period, which were more in the cultural field than in politics. However, politics obtruded themselves quite irrespective of the predilections of the individual.

Why feel an urge to comment on world affairs beyond a certain age? One does know from long experience that the worst does not always happen, and if it does happen, probably not in one's lifetime. It has obviously to do with a feeling of unhappiness, perhaps even foreboding with the way things are unfolding. It has to do with watching dangerous developments and decisions taken that are wrong, perhaps fatally wrong—but the number of warners is small and their voices may be shrill sometimes, but they are usually unheeded. Ideas and intellectual fashions emerging from the groves of academe, particularly in America, seem wrongheaded and often out of touch with the real world. This growing isolation causes growing bitterness, alienation, and a feeling of impotence that turn into greater radicalization and even more far-fetched thinking.

But has it not always (or very often) been like this? Not, I believe, to this extent. In my lifetime, there have been more acutely dangerous situations such as the coming of a world war or the seemingly unstoppable march to victory of totalitarian regimes. Such immediate dangers seem not to exist at the present time. But there are long-term trends equally or even more threatening—the decline of the West and the ability of small groups of people, unprecedented in history, to inflict enormous damage. The decline of the West would be less of a tragedy—history after all is a constant sequence of decline and fall and rise of powers and civilizations—if one could see other centers willing and able to replace them. But with all the shortcomings of the Old World, it is difficult to see *lux ex oriente*. For me Tennyson's words still ring true: "Better fifty years of Europe than a cycle of Cathay."

Perhaps such visions are too pessimistic; history has been replete with unforeseen events, positive and negative, but this is not a strong hope at the present time. How to explain that these prospects are so often ignored? I wish I had an answer. There is a psychological mechanism inducing us to suppress unpleasant truths, but this cannot be the whole explanation; throughout history, there have been men and women overcoming such self-censorship.

Israel and the Jews

It was clear to me since the aftermath of the Six Days' War in 1967 that trouble was brewing. Policies that might have been successful when carried out by big powers could not work in the case of a small country, surrounded by enemies, bereft of important mineral resources such as oil fields. It was not that Israeli politics such as the expulsion of hundreds of thousands in the wake of a war and the settlement of occupied territories were particularly evil; these things have taken place in time all over the globe. In "Disraelia," an essay in counterfactual history, published on April 1, 2008 (the date was overlooked by some readers), I tried to describe what would have happened if many more European Jews had emigrated to Palestine in the nineteenth century. But they did not do so, and when Israel came into being in 1948, it was a very small country even after the absorption of large numbers of immigrants from North Africa, the former Soviet Union, and other parts of the world. It had neither the demographic nor political strength to hold on to the territories acquired after the war of 1967. It did not take long for the fatal consequences to be seen all too clearly: *et asher yagorti ba li*—"For the thing which I greatly feared is come upon me" (Job 3:25, KJV).

There is no certainty that the hostility facing Israel would have been much less even if it had acted more wisely. Arab countries facing deep internal crises needed an enemy to explain to themselves and the rest of the world their own weaknesses and shortcomings. But the demonization and isolation of Israel would have been much more difficult, just as the turning of a national conflict into a dangerous religious conflict might not have happened but for Israeli insistence on its exclusive rule in Jerusalem (a city *de facto* divided)—a city holy to three world religions.

The outcome of the war in 1967 generated a mystic-nationalist wave of enthusiasm, which was by no means shared by all, perhaps not even by a majority, but which many found impossible and perhaps unnecessary to resist. It was not only a matter of the mistaken policies of successive Israeli governments. The country or, to be more precise, the ethnic composition and the political mood changed. The Israel I had known between 1938 and 1955 no longer exists; when Lova Eliav died in 2010, one of the last Mohicans of a generation I had known and often admired, verses from Yeats (*September 1913*) obtruded themselves:

Romantic Ireland's dead and gone
It went to its grave with O'Leary

It was not Romantic Israel that disappeared but a pioneering elite, which with all its shortcomings had laid solid foundation for the state, without which it would never have come into being. (To claim that it was a failed generation because of its lack of enthusiasm for a free market society is to invite ridicule.)

And yet I wrote on Israel and Middle Eastern affairs only with great reluctance at a time when attacking Israel had become a favorite sport and when so often it was difficult to say whether the element of malice was stronger or the ignorance underlying. Attacks on the part of Palestinians I found perfectly understandable; how could it have been otherwise in view of a conflict between two peoples? But how to explain the fact that Israel alone was singled out from all the evildoers in the world by people who had no immediate stake, emotional or material, in this conflict? It would have perhaps been understandable if the number of victims in this case would have been greater than elsewhere or if the atrocities committed would have been even more horrible. But such claims were not made. If so, why was Israel singled out for condemnation, sanctions, and boycott?

The explanation seemed obvious—a small and weak country could not behave like a great power, which few dare to criticize let alone attack. This basic truth has not been understood in Israel—there was a pained outcry that their country was treated unjustly, as if there was one justice in international affairs for the strong and the weak.

I also suspected that the resentment against Israel would sooner or later turn into criticism of Jews, who were making too much noise about the Holocaust. This has now come about not just from Iranian leaders, but also from Hollywood moviemakers and some historians. I was not sure that it was a good idea to press the remembrance of the mass murder in Europe too much on people who had not directly suffered or did not want to be reminded. Would this have an educational or political effect or would it on the contrary cause a reaction? It was bound to generate resentment: Why did the Jews mourn so ostentatiously, so intensively, and for so long after the event? Did they think that their tragedy was unique? Other peoples too had suffered and showed their mourning more discreetly. There had been no Nobel Prizes or big museums connected with these other crimes. Did Jews think their tragedy was unique?

Their tragedy was unique, but it became politically incorrect to say so. True, the Nazis had killed millions of Russians and Poles, but they never intended to exterminate these people. Millions had been murdered in Cambodia, in Africa, and in other genocides, but nowhere else in recent centuries had there been a plan to make whole peoples disappear from the face of the earth.

I was not greatly surprised when the anti-Holocaust reaction came. The motives were as usual complex: A mixture of bad consciences, the suspicion that Israel would use the Holocaust argument to justify some of its policies, anti-Semitism, and hyperactivity on the part of some Jewish officials to press their days of mourning on others not directly affected.

Whither Russia?

After the defeat in World War I, it took Germany less than fifteen years to become again a major power. It took Russia even less time after the breakup of the Soviet Union. True, it owed this spectacular return to the export of oil and gas, and the base on which the new power was based is quite narrow, whether one applies economic, demographic, or other measures. Expansion may not be on the Russian agenda, but it certainly is again in a position of influence in world affairs especially to counteract Western interests if it feels so inclined. For a long time, well preceding the revolution of 1917, Russia has seen the West as the main threat facing it. There has been a neo-Eurasian party in Russia, more recently an orientation toward BRIC (China, India, Brazil, sometimes with the addition of Turkey). But this is not a very real-istic perspective. Russian policy certainly wants to leave as many options open as possible, but there has been growing awareness that a great deal of modernization is needed to put Russia on a more stable basis and that such modernization can be achieved only with Western help. Hence the recent moves toward rapprochement and a new détente with America and Europe. But there have been many such initiatives in Russian history, and their results have frequently not been what was desired. Will it be more successful this time, and will it be possible to achieve modernization with a minimum of concession as far as political freedom is concerned?

These are important political questions, and the answer may not be forthcoming very soon. Intellectually Russia has become considerably less interesting than even during the post-Stalin era. The Russian intelligentsia has shrunk, and cultural let alone philosophical issues are not on top of the agenda of the regime. There was a time when the extreme right (*Zavtra* and beyond) could be counted upon for some outrageous but entertaining state-ment. However even from these circles, there is now little but repetition and tiredness. There must be somewhere remnants of the Russian intelligentsia, but it becomes more and more difficult to discover these traditions.

Europe, Our Great Hope

At the beginning of the decade, books and articles about Europe's brilliant feature were quite common, but after a few years, they disappeared and those who had announced that the twenty-first century would be Europe's quite sensibly turned to other topics. Those in the United States like the present writer who had doubted and even ridiculed such optimism acquired the reputation of Europhobes, which was of course ludicrous. Europe could play an important indeed vital part in world affairs at a time of American global retreat. But there was no willingness even to think about the future.

It was not that the famous "European model" was wrong, that the welfare state should be abolished, and so on. The real problem was Europe's weakness, the fact that it retreated from its own values and ideals, that it talked a great deal about human rights, but that in view of its weakness, it counted for less and less in world affairs. This weakness I found far more disturbing than its economic crisis from which sooner or later it was bound to recover, wholly or in part. It gave America a great deal of good advice what not to do, but hardly any positive guidance.

Should Europe have any foreign policy at all given its reduced state in the world? A case could perhaps be made for opting out of world affairs, adopting the Latin American model, but there was no willingness to ponder the consequences of European abulia.

I had written in the early 1970s an optimistic history of postwar Europe, and there was much ground for such sentiments. A late translation of this book appeared under the title *Europe on the Road to World Power*. But after 1973—always with some notable exceptions—European progress came to a halt, and the few steps forward such as the introduction of the Euro were not decisive. My history of Europe after 1945 was followed by the late Tony Judt's *Postwar*, a fine book that contained everything but made no mention of the main issue—that the Europe he loved was gradually disappearing.

It has always been a mystery to me how otherwise astute observers could be blind to the changes that were taking place in Europe. Even if they did not walk the streets of Europe, even if they did not use public transport, or visit schools and kindergarten, they cannot have been blind to what was going on around them.

This obliviousness is a fascinating phenomenon, again. To my regret, I have no wholly convincing explanation for it.

Terrorism

Terrorism continued to be a major issue in world affairs even though there had been no major terrorist incidents after 9/11—the attacks in Madrid, London, Bali, Kampala, and other places did not really belong to the category of mass destruction and megaterrorism. Terrorism continues to change in character and motivation and will do so in future. To give but one example, when I wrote *Post-Modern Terrorism* in 1996 (two years before Bin Laden and Zawahiri proclaimed their jihad), the issue of religious-fanatic terrorism was much less in the foreground than today.

Some new theories of terrorism made their appearances such as the idea that terrorism occurs wherever foreign invasion had provoked it. There are now "critical studies" of terrorism tending to blame the victims rather than the perpetrators; there are attempts by governments to change our terminology—"man-made disaster" instead of a terrorist attack. There is no apparent limit to human ingenuity as far as misguided interpretations are concerned.

It has been my feeling for a long time that the present period in the history of terrorism is one of the transitions. There have been several major terrorist attacks during the last decade, but the age of megaterrorism has not yet arisen. Perhaps it will never come, but this would be a great surprise, for so far in history, weapons once invented have always been used. Very little thought has been given to what could be done to prevent and counteract the coming attacks; it will be infinitely more difficult than counterterrorism at the present time because such attacks will be carried out by very small groups of people.

I have had for a long time strong doubts about the wisdom of the war in Iraq and especially in Afghanistan, not because it is (or was) an unjust war, but because if such a war had to be fought, it should have been conducted much more relentlessly and with much greater force, not accepting the lack of rules of asymmetric warfare. But the readiness to do so did not exist, and in such circumstances, it would have been better not to get involved in the first place. There were other reasons as well. One was that Afghanistan is by no means unique as a potential base for preparing dangerous future attacks—such conditions now exist also in Somalia, Yemen, and probably one or two other countries. Furthermore a Taliban-ruled Afghanistan will be a danger even more for Russia, India, and China than the United States, but as long as NATO and America will be in Afghanistan, these countries will not accept responsibilities that are in their own national interest.

It is probably unrealistic to expect Western public opinion to fully realize the threats that may be ahead; such a realization will come only following disasters on a heretofore not experienced scale. There is the danger that in such a case the pendulum will swing too far in the opposite direction, from excessive tolerance to panic and hysteria. There may be bad days ahead for those complaining about the violation of their privacy because of the installation of cameras in streets, airports, and airplanes and similar such measures; "You ain't seen nothing yet" in the words of the rock song. Miracles, after all, do happen, and perhaps we shall be spared such horrors and the inevitable reaction.

Heroes and Antiheroes

A few of these I knew in person, most of them I did not. Some of the names will be unfamiliar to readers, but I believe that they deserve to be remembered.

In view of the structure of the book, a certain amount of repetition was inevitable for which I apologize. I tried to reduce it to a minimum. Hence the need for deletions in some cases and of updating in a very few others.

Acknowledgments

"Disraelia: a Counterfactual History 1848–2008" and "Russia's Muslim Strategy" were first published in the *Middle East Papers* series of the Middle East strategy project at Harvard University in 2008 and 2009 respectively; both essays appeared in French in *Commentaire* in 2009 and 2010 respectively as well as a number of other languages. They are reprinted with permission. The same applies to the following.

"Exodus" ("How to Solve the Conflict") was first published in the *National Interest* (2009).

"Zionism Revisited" appeared as the preface to a new edition (2003) of my *History of Zionism from the French Revolution to the Establishment of the State of Israel.*

"Bombing Auschwitz" is part of *The Bombing of Auschwitz. Should the Allies Have Attempted It?* Edited by M. J. Neufeld and Michael Berenbaum (New York, 2000).

"Suicide Terrorism" (2002), "Fanaticism" (2005), "Koestler" (2005), and "The Orientalist" (2005) were published by the *Times Literary Supplement.* "Koestler 2" is the postface to a new edition of *Scum of the Earth* (London, 2006).

"Terrorism to Come" in *Policy Review* (August 2004).

"The Terrible Secret" is the preface to a new edition of the French Edition of *Le Terrifiant Secret* by Gallimard (Paris, 2010).

"Russia, the Years Ahead" (November 2010) and "Postmodern Terrorism" (October 1996) were published in *Foreign Affairs.*

"Two Histories of the Cold War" in *World Affairs* (September 2010).

"A Crisis of Wishing" in *American Interest* (July/August 2010).

"Europe's Long Road to the Mosque" and "The Ticking Clock" were published in *Standpoint* (2010).

"Islamofascism" appeared as *The Origins of Fascism, Islamophobia, Antisemitism* on *OUPBlog*, the Web site of Oxford University Press.

"Hans Paasche," "Carl Burckhardt," and "Ernst Nolte" are published here for the first time.

"Jewish Century" appeared in the *Los Angeles Times* (2004).

"Moses Montefiore" in *Wall Street Journal* (2010).

"Three Witnesses" in *Holocaust and Genocide Studies* (1996).

"How Dangerous Is Terrorism?" in *Debating Terrorism and Counterterrorism*, edited by Stuart Gottlieb. CQ Press (Washington, 2009).

Part 1

Israel and the Jews

Disraelia: A Counterfactual History, 1848–2008

Counterfactual history is . . .

> a reaction to the extreme depersonalization and determinism of current historical studies, with their emphasis on social history opposed to events and personality-driven history.—*Wikipedia*

Heinrich Graetz, *History of the Jews*, Volume 8, Preface

Great were the hopes and expectations of European Jews when the walls of the ghettos came down. It was a long drawn-out process, and conditions varied from country to country. In Britain it began with the readmission of the Jews under Cromwell. In France, the Revolution and Napoleon proceeded with the emancipation of the Jews which had come under way at the time of the absolutist kings and the Enlightenment. In Eastern Europe, the decline and eventual disappearance of Poland hastened the process—but it did not go very far. Jews were limited to a Pale of Settlement in Russia and to certain professions, they could not study and own land, and many professions were closed to them.

The number of Jews greatly increased between 1750 and 1850 and their life expectancy was considerably higher than that of non-Jews. They streamed to the major towns from the countryside where they had only a very meager living; even in Germany about one-third were peddlers and about the same number had no known source of income but depended on alms given by their coreligionists who were better off. The economic situation of the Jews in Poland and Russia actually deteriorated during this period, hence the increasing migration to the West.

As the Jews moved to the cities, they came into conflict with the merchants and artisans, and this created new tensions. The educated classes advocated in principle the emancipation of the Jews, but the great majority would still have favored that they left Europe. The Jews were aliens in Christian societies. Among the thinkers of the Enlightenment, anti-Jewish feeling was quite

3

strong, and the great philosophers of the later period were not quite sure whether the Jews, being a miserable people, could be rehabilitated. Fichte suggested cutting off their heads and giving them new ones. The attitude of the Romantics yet one generation later was equally negative.

Among the Jews, many of the educated embraced Christianity in Western and Central Europe. This affected not only outsiders like Heinrich Heine but large sections of the Jewish establishment, the leading members of the community.

Soon after the Napoleonic wars had ended, a great many books and pamphlets were published in Germany and France, but also in Eastern Europe, discussing what could be done about the Jews, and in 1819 there were the first sporadic anti-Jewish riots.

The attitude of the Churches was ambivalent. They welcomed the baptism of so many Jews, but a growing number of influential churchmen began to resist it. They doubted whether the conversion was genuine; the Jews did not truly believe in Christianity, but regarded it (as Heine had put it) as the entrance ticket to European civilization. They still felt solidarity with other Jews all over the world; Jews still looked like Jews and behaved like Jews. Their character could not be changed by the act of baptism. Some churchmen suggested making intermarriage mandatory (the philosopher Schopenhauer had also suggested this).

Others believed in the purity of Christian blood, just as Catholicism in Spain had in the 16th and 17th centuries. There was something in Judaism beyond the religion which could not be changed by baptism—except perhaps over many generations. According to them, Judaism was a tribe, a race, perhaps even a nation of sorts. And so anti-Judaism (the term anti-Semitism was to be coined only three decades later by Wilhelm Marr) became a major force in European politics and public opinion. In Western Europe, Jews were hated because a growing number was getting rich; in Eastern Europe where most of them lived, they were hated and despised because they were poor and useless.

Anti-Judaism manifested itself in steadily spreading pogroms beginning with the Hep Hep riots in Germany in 1819. They were mostly locally confined but they continued on an ever-growing scale year by year. They spread to Austria, Hungary, even upper Italy and above all to Poland, the Ukraine and Rumania. Local police forces did not at first intervene but advised the Jews to stay indoors as much as possible, especially on Sundays and Christian holidays. This approach worked for a while, but in 1823 bigger and more aggressive mobs attacked Jewish houses and shops and put them on fire. The number of fatalities was relatively small but in some instances (Frankfurt and Budapest 1823, Kalisch, Poznan and Galatz 1824) the fires went out of control and caused considerable damage to non-Jewish houses and businesses. As a result, smaller Jewish communities were advised to move to bigger cities where, the authorities argued, it would be easier to maintain public order. However, there was growing opposition to this influx on the part of the city councils and other interest groups. They suggested that the only reasonable way was the return of the Jews to the ghettoes, but there was much dissension over where the ghettos should be located. Other heated debates concerned the fate of the Jews who had been baptized: Should they be kept for at least a generation or two in special ghettos as a kind of purgatory?

Britain and France (with the exception of Alsace) were relatively free of pogroms in view of the small number of Jews in these countries, but the mass attacks in Szegedin, Regensburg, Homel, Kishinev and various towns in Galicia kept the Jewish question at the top of the European political agenda. The intellectual debate raged all over the continent. A number of philosophers, liberal churchmen and professors called the new anti-Judaism a relapse to the Middle Ages, a nasty blot to be removed as speedily as possible.

But the anti-Judaic literature, albeit on a much lower level of sophistication, was far more widely read. It ranged from relatively mild attacks to unbridled incitement and demands for the expulsion of the Jews. The moderates argued that European Jews, while small in number, had acquired within the last generation unprecedented political and financial power in a variety of fields—in banking as well as the media. Many of the new newspapers and publishing houses were in the hands of Jews, many of the writers were Jews or of Jewish origin. They were trying to hide. Why did the editor of the *Golden Treasury*, the best-known anthology of English poetry, call himself Palgrave whereas his real name was Cohen? Why Boerne and not Baruch? These attacks came from the political right as well as from the left. The left-wing anti-Judaists argued that the superrich Jews were bloodsuckers and should be expropriated. The great bestseller of the decade, Toussenel's *Les Juifs, rois de l'epoque,* which appeared in many tens of thousands of copies in all major European languages, was written by a disciple of the Socialist Fourier.

The extreme anti-Jewish literature made no bones about its conviction that there was no room for the Jews in Europe. *The Protocols of Satan and the Sanhedrin,* published in 1836, described in detail the giant Jewish conspiracy which threatened to enslave the Christian people of Europe. The Jews were secretly establishing an army headed by the chief Rabbi of Bratislava seconded by the chief Rabbis of Filene, Lissa and Ostrowo. But since their numbers were insufficient, they were preparing terrible weapons of mass destruction, especially poisonous substances. According to their master plan, some of the non-Jews would be corrupted and bought by them, the others would be cowed into submission by threats of the spread of horrible epidemics, and the leading anti-Jews would be arrested and put away in concentration camps. A particularly insidious new weapon was the new net of railways established all over the continent. Most of them were in the hands of the Jews (or would be acquired by them); this would eventually do away with national borders (and national traditions). It would lead to internationalization (occasionally the term globalization was used), the end of religion, patriotism and all the sacred values of the nations of Europe. An East German nobleman, von Hundsfott, in a widely-read pamphlet entitled *The Anti-Jewish Manifesto*, suggested that one-third of the Jews should be baptized, one-third deported to the Arctic region and one-third to the Sahara desert.

The wilder accusations and speculations of the radical anti-Judaists were studied but not taken very seriously by the authorities. But the governments were still heavily preoccupied by the "Jewish Question," and this not so much out of humanitarian considerations but because there was the danger that the anti-Jewish pogroms would turn into general attacks against the established order. There had been already many cases of peasant unrest. Not only Jewish shop owners had been attacked and their shops devastated, but also their Christian competitors who were accused of "foul Jewish practices."

To return the Jews to the ghettos seemed impractical, and it was in this context that the idea of a Jewish mass evacuation first occurred.

From a letter written by Sarah Austen in London to her friend Lady Anstrutter in Berkshire, 1842

Dizzy came for dinner last night and the conversation was sparkling as always. He was alone, his new wife suffers from a head cold as many in London do at this time of the year. The talk was about literature, politics and of course the latest gossip. Dizzy was in excellent form, and those who do not know him well could easily gain the impression that he could not care less that Peel passed him over when his recent government was formed. But I have the impression (and my female intuition has seldom been wrong), that our friend is deep down quite unhappy. He faces a crisis. He is now thirty-eight years of age, a man of great talents and great ambitions. But he has not really settled down and in his own eyes he has been a failure—in literature as well as in politics.

For most of our countrymen, he has remained a stranger; a few may admire him but they do not trust him. They are willing to forgive him his foppish-ness, the strange way he dresses and behaves—we are most tolerant towards eccentrics. But many think he is too clever by half. He gets along with women much better than with men. This may one day help him with the Queen if he decides to pursue his political career. But the politicians think him too inconsistent, he has switched parties too often. And he has been hurt even though he does not show it. He was rejected or defeated as a candidate four times, he was jeered and booed after his maiden speech. He adores England and everything English, but there is too much in him that is not English.

What surprised me most last night was his constant harping on Jews and Jewish affairs. You may remember that some ten years ago, when he was not in good health, his doctors advised him to take a long trip to a warmer climate. He went to Greece, Palestine and Egypt and the impressions gained on this trip seem to preoccupy him to this day. Everyone I know who went to Jerusalem returned with all kind of horror stories about the sad state of the holy city. But Dizzy thinks it is wonderful, inspiring, the center of the world and the greatest promise for the future of mankind. He wrote a few books at the time such as *Contarini*, which I don't think were among his best, and mentioned that he now works on yet another about a character named David Alroy of whom I never heard but who seems to fascinate him endlessly. It seems that this was a Jew in 12th-century Persia, a messiah of sorts who was called King of the Diaspora and who promised to lead the children of Israel back to their promised land. He was apparently also a great magician what could make himself invisible and enlisted the warlike mountain Jews of Azerbaidjan who were going to help him to recapture Jerusalem. The adventure ended badly but our Dizzy got carried away and seems to think that he may succeed where David Alroy failed. Can you imagine Dizzy engaging on a new career, king of the Jews? Is he serious—to the extent that he was or will be ever serious?

The gardens are magnificent at this time of the year . . .

From a letter by Moses Hess in Paris to Solomon Oppenheim in Cologne, February 1843

Last night we had the weekly meeting of the German Workers Club. We talked about the French socialists and their theories; it was of no particular interest. Weitling, a self-educated tailor from Magdeburg and Wilhelm Marr, his sidekick, went on and on about Fould and the other Jews who have been taking a leading role in developing a French railway net.

I went home with Dr. Charles (Karl) Marx, a young academic who recently arrived here with a wife. He married a German noblewoman and lives around the corner from me, rue Vauncy. I did meet him before and was greatly impressed, a young man of 26, erudite, sarcastic, with a sharp intellect, quite full of himself; he may go far. But in some respects he is astonishingly naïve. He truly believes that the whole history of mankind is nothing but the history of class struggles and totally underrates the importance of nationalism and religion in conflicts past, present and to come. As we walked along the Luxembourg and Boulevard Raspail I tried to talk some sense to him. But I doubt whether I made him rethink some of his views which are quite detached from political realities. He is deep into Hegelian philosophy and has only contempt for those who cannot follow his dialectical forays.

He is working, he told me, on a long essay on the Jewish question. All religion is bad, but some are worse than others. Judaism is (or in any case has become) worshiping mammon, unless the Jews get rid of Judaism they shall never be fully emancipated. When I asked him what this meant in practical terms, I did not get a clear answer. Why are the Jews disliked, why do people want to get rid of them? (And this includes, I told him, many of our own comrades including the wild Bakunin, a militant revolutionary second to none, who was also at our meeting. And Marr—I would not be surprised if one day he will be the leader of an anti-Jewish party in Germany.) I told Marx, if Jews are disliked it is not because of their religion but because of the shape of their noses. There is something beyond religion, even beyond mammon which you do not want to accept.

Do not be childish, Marx said, the whole issue is not of such great importance. With the stormy development of the economy, with capitalism as a powerful engine, borders will disappear, internationalization will make giant strides. The confrontation will be between rich and poor not between nations, peoples and races. Weitling and Marr are well-meaning but they are simpletons, not very intelligent; for some time to come we shall have to face backward and reactionary views even among some of our own comrades, but not for very long.

I gave up, the man is so sure of himself, but he knows no more about the Jews than about their enemies. The other day he called Lassalle, the agitator from Breslau who is emerging as the leader of our party in Germany, a "Jewish nigger." But if Marx would look into the mirror for a moment, he would realize that his complexion is not exactly lily-white; his close friends call him the "Moor." But I sensed it was pointless to argue with him and so I said: Marx, I wish you luck, you are one of the best minds in our movement, maybe one day you will be our leader and the whole world will know your name. But however much you will distance yourself from Judaism and the Jews, you will always remain for the others the Communist rabbi, the Jew Marx. Marx snorted contemptuously, who cares?

Note from Baron Heinrich von Buelow, Foreign Minister of Prussia, to Carl Nesselrode, Russian Foreign Minister, 1845 (Strictly Confidential)

Your Excellency will remember our discussion about the Jewish question during your recent visit to Berlin. In the meantime I had the opportunity to discuss this with Prince Metternich in Vienna.

Metternich said that while he was not in a position at the present time to take the initiative, he was very supportive as far as the promotion of Jewish emigration from Europe was concerned. The Jewish problem was of increasing concern to the Austro-Hungarian monarchy, especially in its Eastern parts. Metternich also made some interesting practical suggestions. The financial costs of an emigration project of this kind would exceed the resources of the countries of Europe which might contribute but could not carry the main burden. He proposed that the Rothschilds should be approached and asked to establish a central fond together with some other Jewish bankers.

Some of them have grown very rich in recent decades and they will realize that it is in their own best interest if at least half of their co-religionists would leave Europe, so as to prevent growing political tensions from which they, the bankers, would be the first to suffer. He also suggested Turkey as the main place to which European Jews should be directed, either to Palestine or some other part of the Ottoman Empire. They have after all a historical connection with the Holy Land. Of course, there will be resistance in Constantinople, but this could perhaps be overcome if we enlist the support of Britain and France and explain to the Sultan the great financial benefits that may accrue to the Sublime Porte.

.. I should be grateful for the comments of your Excellency and remain with profound respect etc. etc.

Stratford Canning, British Ambassador in Constantinople, to Lord Palmerston—Excerpts (the dispatch cannot be exactly dated, but was written either in 1842 or 1843)

I fully share your conviction that it is in the best interest of HM government to strengthen the Sublime Porte in every possible way against Russian pressure. However, only after my recent arrival here did the overwhelming odds we are facing became fully clear to me.

The Ottoman Empire has been stagnating since about 1700, their defeat at the gates of Vienna and the peace of Karlovats. It has been retreating at all fronts, in Europe as well as in Asia and Africa, and since the recent war (1827) stagnation has turned into rapid decline. Why did we have to follow the Russian lead in making war on Turkey on behalf of the Greeks? The Philhellenic foolishness and Lord Byron's antics proved to be stronger than the pursuance of our interests. The Greeks would have received independence sooner or later in any case. But the defeat we inflicted on the Turks, above all the battle of Navarino, strengthened Russian influence in the Near East, made the Sublime Porte appear a sinking ship and gave fresh impetus to all the separatist movements. The tribes at the Persian border have been on the offensive, so have been the Wahhabis on the Arabian peninsula, and Mehmet Ali in Egypt, while calling himself Viceroy, has virtually unlimited powers, having expanded his rule from Damascus to Khartoum.

This year we shall have to deal with a new Sultan, Abdul Mecid. He is a youngster aged 19, not ungifted (his French is quite good, no English unfortunately), his heart is in the right place and he has the full support of the Grand Vizier, Mustafa Reshid. But will he be strong enough to carry out the reforms which are so long overdue?

I have the gravest doubts. He may just push through one of his pet projects, to replace the turban by the fez, but the aversion against any new ideas, against any innovation, technical or otherwise, is so deeply rooted that I cannot envisage any major progress in the coming years and decades. This would mean further weakening of the country. The local Pashas will be either powerless, unable to collect taxes, which would lead sooner or later to bankruptcy. Or they will become more or less independent of Constantinople following the example of Mehmet Ali. The Russians, liberally distributing baksheesh in the Royal palace, would become virtual masters not only of the Bosporus but of the Eastern Mediterranean.

The situation is critical—the present agony could continue for another hundred years, but the whole edifice might collapse within a year or two following the slightest turbulence.

In these circumstances, the immigration of Jews could be a stabilizing factor.

Note Verbale, the Russian Ambassador in Berlin, to Foreign Minister von Buelow

. . . the Tsar found your and Metternich's suggestions of great interest. How to proceed? We believe that the approach to the Sultan and the Grand Vizier should come from Prussia. The Sublime Porte is notoriously distrustful, any such suggestion made by us would unfortunately be thought detrimental to Ottoman interests, an attempt to undermine the Sultan's rule etc. But if the approach is made by you, the reception could be more favorable. Ideally, the whole initiative should be kept secret, but this might be impossible for any length of time. For this reason we suggest the appointment of an international commission for the economic development of the Ottoman Empire which should study the feasibility of this project and present its findings within a year to us as well as the Sublime Porte—how many Jews could be absorbed, in which parts of the Ottoman Empire and so on. In other words, the Sultan would be in a position to reject the project if it does not meet with his approval. The members of this study committee should be appointed as soon as feasible. It might be a good idea to include a number of academics so as to disguise the true, political purpose of the venture.

Paris, December 1845 (from the Rothschild Archives)

Nathanael Rothschild opened the meeting which took place in his private home. Present were his brother Lionel from London, Lionel's brother-in-law Moses Montefiore, Solomon Maier Rothschild from Vienna, Achille Fould, Bischoffsheim, Moses Warburg, Baron de Hirsch, Oppenheim from Cologne and two others who wished to remain anonymous. Nathanael swore those present to secrecy; any premature disclosure could mean the end of a scheme which at this stage was as yet in an exploratory stage. He reported that he had been contacted by leading statesmen and even royalty concerning the emigration of about two million Jews from Europe to overseas, preferably to the Ottoman Empire, if the political preconditions could be arranged.

Montefiore opened the discussion and said that the scheme should be given serious consideration in view of the precarious situation of the Jews in many European countries and the unwillingness of both governments and the general public to push forward the emancipation of the Jews. But he foresaw enormous difficulties. The Jewish question was most acute in Eastern Europe, but the government of the Tsar was quite hostile—it wanted to get rid of the Jews but at the same time engaged in extortion. General Paskevich, Viceroy of Poland, had told him that Jews could leave Russia only if each family paid a considerable ransom—this was the law of the land and no exception would be made for the Jews.

At the same time, the Ottoman authorities were extremely opposed to any change in the status quo. The influx of so many foreigners and non-Muslims would be considered an attempt to undermine their authority. They talked endlessly about *tanzimat* (reform) but were deadly afraid of it. The Muslim population was easily inflamed against the Jews (and everyone else), as the recent persecutions in Damascus had shown. (Several Jews were arrested, tortured and killed there on blood libel accusations.) Lastly, the Sultan was no longer in full control of the southern parts of the empire, and one would have to negotiate separately with Mehmet Ali, Viceroy of Egypt, who had been for a while the effective ruler of Syria and Palestine. However, he proposed full cooperation with the investigation committee which was to be appointed.

The discussion lasted to a late hour. Most of those attending were of the opinion that if the scheme would receive massive support from the main powers, if the other preconditions existed, if there was sufficient willingness among the Jewish communities to collaborate, then those assembled and their friends should not stand aside. Several names of leading figures were mentioned to popularize the scheme at the right time among the European Jews, among them the British politician Disraeli, as well as Montefiore and a number of rabbis. The fear was expressed that the rabbis would not get along easily with each other.

Vienna, January 1847, Executive Summary of the Report of EIC (European Investigation Committee), appointed twelve months ago to study the feasibility of Jewish settlement in regions of the Ottoman Empire

We have the honor to submit our final report and want to express our particular gratitude to Major Helmuth von Moltke, seconded to the Ottoman army, to Captain Felix Jones of the Indian civil service, William Tanner Young, British Consul in Jerusalem, as well as (follows a list of twenty more names) for their invaluable help and advice.

Our conclusions, in briefest outline, are that mass settlement of European Jews in regions of the Ottoman Empire is possible if there is the willingness on the part of said Jews to settle and adjust themselves to difficult conditions, and if the necessary financial means will be at their disposal. We would rule out Anatolia and the Hejaz but also Syria which is comparatively densely populated. However, historical Palestine is relatively empty and the same is true for parts of Mesopotamia. We would except from the region of settlement Jerusalem, which should be a *corpus separandum*, an internationalized city, in view of its importance for the world's leading religions. The Pashaliks of Baghdad and Bassora should also be outside the region of settlement, even though the number of Jewish residents in Baghdad is reportedly larger than that of the Muslims.

There are only rough estimates concerning population statistics in these regions—perhaps 200-300,000 in Palestine, several Bedouin tribes in the desert between the Jordan and the Euphrates and Tigris, perhaps 400,000 in the Pashaliks of Mossul and Kirkuk. The city of Baghdad had 170,000 inhabitants, but after the recent plague epidemic which raged for three years and the flooding of the Tigris, this figure has shrunk to a mere 20,000. To quote a recent report received by the Indian government (Rawlinson to Malmesbury), "no province might be easier to govern than the Pashalik of Mesopotamia but with all its advantages the Pashalik of today is almost a desert."

We suggest Jewish settlement in Palestine, above all the coastal plain, the Esdraelon valley and Galilee. It is unlikely that this area can absorb more than a million inhabitants over a decade, but we see further possibilities for settlement in Western Iraq (Mossul, Kirkuk). It is our feeling that it will be easier for European Jews to get along with the Kurdish tribes than the easily fanaticized Sunni and Shiite population in the North. Settlement on a smaller scale should also be explored in Southern Palestine and the oases in the desert between the Jordan and the Tigris.

We do not believe that many will find work in agriculture in view of the dearth of water and other resources, but we see good prospects for industry and trade. The regions are rich in minerals which could be developed by enterprising Jews. We also see a great future for the development of railway lines crossing what is now a desert. With the development of steamships, the number of visitors and pilgrims will rapidly increase.

We suggest an administration based on a cantonal system with far-reaching regional autonomy: three in Palestine, two or three in Western Mesopotamia, one for the wide area between Palestine and the North. They should be accountable financially to central offices located in Jaffa and Mossul, and to an international committee consisting of members, of the Ottoman government and one representative each of the European powers. Overall Ottoman political sovereignty will not be affected. This system may sound complicated but it may work in our opinion. It all depends on whether the immigrants from Europe will show both enterprise, patience and tact, and whether the local population will realize the great benefits that will accrue to them from this common venture.

There will be no doubt resistance, some malcontents will argue that they prefer backwardness to sharing their country. However it ought to be born in mind that this resistance could probably be overcome with good diplomacy as well as the liberal distribution of baksheesh. Furthermore, as we have pointed out earlier on, the Ottoman Empire is a diverse polity with many thousands of Christians, Circassians, Copts, Chaldaeans, Armenians, Turcomans and a dozen other nationalities, not to mention the many Bedouin tribes. The region we have in mind is sparsely populated—perhaps a million or less—and whether yet another nationality will be added may not make a great difference, given a minimum of good will from all sides.

It is impossible to predict whether, as a result of these developments, one or several states will eventually come into being, what language will be spoken, what religion will be predominant, or whether there will be peaceful coexistence between the various religions. We have no doubt that there will be conflicts between the various parties involved, but there seems to be a reasonable chance that they might be resolved.

Berlin, March 1847, **Vossische Zeitung fuer staats-und gelehrte sachen** *and Ludwig Philippson in the* **Allgemeine Zeitung des Judenthums:** *A Report about a European Jewish meeting to discuss the future in light of EIC Report*

The meeting, which took place in the Ephraim Palais on the Molkenmarkt, was attended by leading representatives from all major European Jewish communities. It was opened by the British parliamentarian Disraeli, who was elected unanimously president with Rabbi Zvi Hirsch Kalischer of Thorn and Rabbi Yehuda Alkalai of Bosnia/Croatia as his deputies. Sir Moses Montefiore was elected honorary president.

There was a general debate about the proposal made by several European governments to promote the emigration of Jews from Europe to the Ottoman Empire. The following arguments against this scheme were most frequently voiced: While aware of anti-Jewish sentiment and action in much of Europe, the prospects were not as dire as predicted by some, especially if the governments concerned would take a more active part in removing the existing anti-Jewish legislation. This was the view taken by several radical democrats of Jewish origin. While Zion remained dear to all Jews, it was more than doubtful whether mass settlement was possible or desirable in present conditions. Widespread banditry was reported from many parts of the Ottoman Empire; it was not at all clear who would defend the defenseless Jews against such attacks.

Orthodox rabbis maintained that such a mass return should occur only in the days of Messiah, to act prematurely would be against G'd's will, it might be considered blasphemous. Some amount of emigration from Eastern Europe might be necessary, especially if the governments concerned would not take a constructive part in normalizing the conditions in which most Jewish communities were existing at the present time. However, a variety of other possibilities should be explored, above all North and South America.

The minority view was that the Jewish condition in Central and Eastern Europe was more precarious than generally assumed. If Jews would not take the initiative, others would, and the results could be lamentable, perhaps even tragic. Emigration was a necessity and the only part of the world with which Jews had a historical, religious and emotional connection was Palestine and the Near East.

Disraeli in a passionate speech reminded those assembled that social and political conditions quite apart, Jewish existence in many European countries was at present a life without dignity, self-esteem and honor, and that a return to their native country would be more than a social reform, it would be a long-overdue moral revolution restoring pride to the Jewish race. The people which had given birth to the Maccabeans and Bar Kochba would be able to defend itself in its old/new homeland. However, all Disraeli achieved was a resolution that the suggestions for the resettlements of Jews should be further studied and be further discussed in another well-prepared meeting in Vienna, in a year from now.

Mehmet Emin Ali Pasha, Ottoman Foreign Minister, to Reshid Pasha, Grand Vizier, October 1846

Your Excellency asked me to summarize very briefly my views on the suggestions made increasingly often by European powers concerning the settlement of Jews in the Ottoman Empire. The other day a member of the British parliament named Disraeli came to see me—an amusing and clever man. He tried to persuade me that we would enormously benefit from these schemes, economically and politically. He seems to be their chief diplomat, the front man of all the leading Jewish bankers. Of course, he exaggerates, but there is some truth in what he says.

Broadly speaking, I favor this initiative even though it is impossible to say at the present time whether many Jews will want to move to our country (and how many we want to accept). While East European Jewry is at present in a miserable state, many of them are quite capable and enterprising individuals and would be a positive element as far as the reforms we want to see carried out are concerned. They certainly share our views about Russia, the main threat facing our country. Would they blend in with the other religious elements in our country? In principle, no one but Muslims can be trusted, but I feel the Jews will be more loyal subjects than the Greeks, the Armenians, and even the Arab tribes with whom we share a common religion.

As for Syria, Lebanon and Palestine—this region only spells trouble (as Mehmet Ali found out at his cost when he tried to rule it). These people unfortunately understand only the language of the sword and the whip.

Whether there will be one more nationality, one more religion, does not really matter. If the Jews fail, it will be their funeral not ours. If they succeed, they will contribute to prosperity and stability in our country.

Vienna Jewish Congress, October 1848 (from *Die Presse*)

This meeting had been scheduled to take place in March, but was postponed as the result of the revolutions, riots and pogroms in several European countries. The murder of thousands of Jews in Poland, the Ukraine, Rumania, Hungary, and to a lesser extent in Prussia and other German states overshadowed the proceedings. Rabbi Alkalay in his opening speech quoted the Biblical saying from the book of Job, *asher yagornu, ba*—what we predicted and feared has come to pass. The great majority decided in favor of the proposal to promote emigration to regions of the Ottoman Empire following the suggestions of the EIC. Disraeli had been to Constantinople and had received the permission to proceed from the Grand Vizier who had transmitted instructions to the local Pashas.

Jewish applicants were to register within the next month at offices in about hundred European cities (a list is in the appendix). Time was of crucial importance. The Rothschilds together with a group of other leading bankers accepted responsibility for the financial aspect; some of the funds needed would be in the nature of a gift, but half would be a loan to be repaid within fifty years. Some of the funds would be used for transport and living costs during the first two years of the stay of the immigrants in their new homes, but half was to be earmarked for the establishment of new industries and the building of the infrastructure. Barons Hirsch and Fould would be in charge of transport—from Odessa and Trieste. At the present time it was impossible even to estimate how many immigrants were to be expected. The proposal to hire an international armed guard to protect the immigrants against banditry was defeated. Disraeli said in his concluding speech that Jews, well-trained and armed, would fulfill this function; the vicious circle of depending on the protections of others had to be broken.

From the diary of Heinrich Heine, Trieste, December 1849 (published in part in the Augsburger Allgemeine Zeitung*)*

This is the second night I have not been able to sleep. I went down to the harbor watching the embarkation of hundreds of Jews on the steamships which had been rented by Hirsch commuting between this harbor and Jaffa. Five hundred are leaving every day, even on Sabbath, the rabbis having decided that this was a case of *pikuah nefesh*—the commandment of saving souls overrides the full observation of the Sabbath laws. Another 500 are leaving daily from Odessa.

What heartrending scenes! Tears came to the eyes of an old cynic like me. The children of the ghetto leaving a continent that has wrought them so much misery, burned on the stake in the Middle Ages, pogroms in the present new Middle Ages. No one was mourning to leave this continent of suffering and humiliation, and yet who had thought that a history of almost two thousand years would end like this?

By the waters of Babylon we were sitting and weeping—from the desert we came and to the desert we shall return. Judaism is not a religion, it is an affliction. As I watch the children of the ghetto, the poorest of the poor entering the ships with their few bundles, I cannot dispel dark forebodings. It was not just the separation of families for a long period, with husbands and young bachelors traveling as an *avant garde* and their families and friends following once they will have taken care of elementary living conditions. Will they be able to survive in wholly unfamiliar, often hostile conditions or will they disappear without a trace in the deserts of Arabia? They will have to fight nature, an inclement climate and diseases. They cannot and should not transfer the ghetto but will have to begin a new life in every respect. Will they be able to defend themselves against the elements in a bandit-infested country? Sometimes I feel that there still are enormous energies in this old people which only wait to be released, at other times an inner voice tells me, "Too late."

Montefiore and Disraeli were at the harbor with words of encouragement, promising all kind of help, narrating stories about their travels in these parts. Disraeli approached me, he knows my poems and recited two by heart. He told me to be of good cheer, what do they have to lose but their chains? Montefiore, a giant of a man, and Disraeli, in his red waistcoat speaking with the help of translators to some of the departing Jews and Jewesses, sounded genuine. But they have been over there for a short time as honored guests with red carpets wherever they went. How will these poor wretches, Europe's stepchildren, fare—pale, weak, so defenseless? Perhaps this is another desert generation and whatever hope there is rests with the next generation. But the odds are against them.

I went to bed with a heavy heart, not at all sure whether I had witnessed the last act of a long tragedy or the beginning of something wholly new.

Marx in London to Heine in Paris, January 1850

. . . I share your misgivings. In fact I am certain nothing can come of this project. After so many centuries in the ghetto, the Jews are not capable of doing any constructive work. Degeneration has proceeded too far and lasted too long. You talk about new industries—but what and where? Weaving silk and carpets? The Persians are doing it better. There are no raw materials upon which new industries could be based in the Ottoman Empire, except may be salt from the Dead Sea and that stinking substance called petroleum which is good for nothing except perhaps putting tar on our streets . . .

The Admor of Sadagora to Rabbi Hirsch Ostrower in Lissa, March 1853

Blessed be you my son and favorite pupil and your house and all of Israel, Amen. I have been young and now I am old, yet have I not seen the righteous forsaken nor his seed begging bread (Psalms 37:25). You told me about the commotion in your fold and the questions you are asked—should we stay or leave? Does the house of Israel have a future in Europe? Should we move our tents to the Holy Land even though it is in the hands of strangers? Should we embark for the land of the Hurons and Iroquois where, some false prophets are saying, the fleshpots of tomorrow will be found? (Exodus 16:3) I wish I had an answer, my son, but there is no guidance in our holy books, and even the wisest of the wise among us fall silent. Let us not put our trust in princes (Psalms 146:3). Perhaps we shall see clearer in the days to come; in the multitude of counselors there is safety (Proverbs 11:14).

Peace be within thy walls.

Encyclopedia Britannica, *Eleventh Edition 1911, "Ottoman Empire" (Excerpts)*

. . . world affairs seem to have bypassed the eastern regions of the Ottoman Empire during the second half of the nineteenth century. The influx of almost two million European Jews between 1849 and 1855 caused far-reaching changes in the economy and social structure of the empire. But these took place only gradually.

The immigrants were dispersed over the eight cantons originally envisaged by the EIC, extending from Jaffa to Kirkuk. Living conditions during the first years were extremely harsh for the newcomers and they were endlessly complaining about their bitter fate. It is estimated that about 100,000 of them left the country, mostly for America.

However, beginning in the 1860s there was an impressive upswing in economic activity in manufacture, trade and transport. The decision of the Rothschild committee early on to send some 500 of the most gifted young Jews to study at European universities and technical colleges bore fruit. A number of light industries were established which gave employment to hundreds of thousands of Jews, Bedouin and Arabs. These industries caught up and in some instances overtook the United States as well as Europe. Modern cities developed in Disraelia (as the region came to be called), with modern amenities.

A few of these industries ought to be singled out: the canning of food which made it possible to export fruit and vegetables to Europe at all seasons; textile industries which produced new, cheaper and more effective fabrics such as viscose as well as synthetic dyes; a pharmacological industry which pioneered various analgesics; and various cardiac medicines based on Dead Sea salts but also synthetically-produced substances. Dr. Paul Ehrlich lived in Disraelia for more than a decade and Pasteur came for frequent visits. A whole range of new medical technologies were developed. Lastly, a photographic industry came into being which pioneered gravure and color printing, with the help of European inventors such as Daguerre and Fox Talbot, who spent years in. Also a small and simple camera, predating the Kodak Brownie (1901) by ten years, was mass-produced and conquered the world markets.

There was some agricultural development but in view of the lack of water resources it was decided to restrict it. A new set of railway lines now criss-crosses this region and several harbors have been built to modern standards. Planners now deal with the preparation of airfields, as this mode of traffic is thought likely to dominate the coming decades.

Population: This region counts now twelve million inhabitants, more than half of them of Jewish extraction. The birthrate is high (about 4.5), and infant mortality lower than in most European countries. Intermarriage, much to everyone's surprise, is fairly high. Illiteracy has virtually been stamped out and there are eight major universities and corresponding technical research institutes.

As a result, this Eastern region of the Ottoman Empire is now of greater economic importance than the Western section. Politically the Jews have been moving very cautiously. They have not pressed for independence but on every occasion profess loyalty to the Sublime Porte and friendship to the other ethnic minorities in the Empire. At the same time, the cantons have given them a great measure of independence to develop their own culture and indeed their way of life. Hebrew, Turkish and Arabic are official languages, on the same footing. In the northern cantons Kurmanji (Kurdish) is taught but also Balachi, Gilek and other dialects.

It was not easy for the Jews to gain the trust of the Kurds and Arabs, but the Jewish leaders showed shrewdness in selecting their partners, above all the heads of the Rishawi and Dulaimi tribes on the Euphrates, the leading, most dynamic figures in Kurdistan and Mesopotamia. They have solemnly sworn that there would be absolute equality in the administration of the region, and they have by and large kept their promise. They have explained to their interlocutors that separately, each for himself, they would achieve nothing, but if they stuck together, they might become one day the richest and most powerful region in the whole Near East. No one talks in present conditions about full political independence, taxes are paid to the Ottoman tax collectors. However, given the slow but seemingly inescapable disintegration of the Ottoman Empire, it seems only a question of time until Disraelia will be an independent state with its own government. Where will its capital be?

Encyclopedia Britannica, *Supplement 1932*

During the Great War, soldiers from Disraelia did not have to serve outside their own region; they persuaded the Young Turks that their economic and technical contribution to the war effort would be more important.

The state of Disraelia came into being as the result of the peace treaties of Sevres and Lausanne. It is a democratic republic with Tel Aviv as its capital, but Mosul as the second capital where the parliament is convened during the winter months. A president is elected for four years and there is the principle of alternation, by which a Jew is invariably followed by a Kurd or an Arab, unless there is an overwhelming (three-fourths) majority for reelecting the incumbent.

During the turbulent period immediately following the Great War, Disraelia was several times attacked by its neighbors, but these attacks were easily repelled owing to its own superior organization and modern equipment. More serious was the separatist strife inside the country in the late 1920s and the early 1930s. Matters came to a head with the assassination in 1929 of the president of Disraelia, Emanuel Marx (a grandson of Karl Marx, the Socialist thinker) by a group of Jewish fanatics who demanded the division of the country and the expulsion of all non-Jews. These extremists were harshly dealt with. Their crime was considered not just political murder but high treason; twenty of the ringleaders were executed following the verdict of a military court appointed during the state of emergency. About 150 of their militant followers were expelled from the country for perpetuity. Later there was an attempted coup in the Kurdish–Arab sector which also aimed at the partition of the country. This extremist group had tried to engage in terrorism during a few weeks but found no mass support. The main figures were apprehended and shot; appeals for clemency were disregarded.

Following these unfortunate events, mass meetings took place in which the unbreakable unity of the country was reaffirmed by leaders of all sides. Freedom of religion is absolute but religious incitement is severely punished. Since then calm has prevailed in the country.

Various authors, Disraelia: An Intellectual History (page 32)

Disraeli resigned from all his positions in 1860 after the survival of his project seemed assured. In his last speech to the Disraelia General Assembly he said, "If you truly want it, it won't be a fairy tale." He returned to his British career and became prime minister in 1868. He died in 1882 and is buried in the garden of his villa on Mount Carmel. After his death, this building became a refuge for distinguished political refugees from all over the world. Trotsky spent several years there in the 1930s and later also Che Guevara, Solzhenitsyn, as well as Ayatollah Khomeini and most recently the Saudi entrepreneur Osama bin Laden. On fine autumn evenings in the late 1960s one could watch these four walking in the Carmel forest, surrounded by several learned rabbis, heatedly discussing fundamentalism, pro and contra.

The impressive building also served as an Institute of Advanced Philosophical Studies. It is difficult even to imagine the intellectual history of the late twentieth century but for a number of historical confrontations which took place in this building, such as Heidegger debating Wittgenstein.

Giselher von Dirksen, German Ambassador in Tel Aviv, to Foreign Ministry in Berlin, November 1933

I saw earlier today Sleiman Abdul Hadi, the Disraelian foreign minister, at his request. He said that recent speeches by Herr Hitler, the new Chancellor, in which some unfriendly remarks about German Jews and Jews in general had been made, had provoked concern in this country. While he fully realized that every country was at liberty to deal with its subjects as it saw fit, he had to emphasize that there were considerable sympathies in Disraelia, not only among the Jews, for the Jews in Germany, and that such speeches would not contribute to a better climate in world affairs. If Germany was unhappy with the 200,000 Jews remaining there, Disraelia would be happy to receive them. At the same time, Abdul Hadi extended an invitation to the Führer to come to Disraelia early next year. What was the occasion? An interesting technical experiment would be carried out, and knowing the Fuehrer's interest in modern technology, he thought he would not want to miss this.

How to explain this somewhat cryptic invitation? I suspect I have the explanation. Last week General von Horstenburg, our military attaché, returned somewhat shaken from an event to which all military attachés had been invited. He was in a highly excitable state, almost incoherent—quite unusual, given his stolid character. He repeated time and time again that he had just witnessed the greatest revolution in military warfare in thousands of years. Pressed by me, he revealed confidentially that the Disraelians had succeeded in producing a super-bomb which they call an atomic bomb, capable of destroying a city of many square miles, that is to say the biggest cities in the world. He had watched the explosion in the desert. The Disraelian chief of staff in his short speech had stressed that the energy thus released would never be used for military purposes, but the implications were clear to all those present.

There had been rumors to the effect that Disraelian research institutes had been engaged in research in this direction (nuclear fission), but we had no idea that they had made that much progress. Moreover, this seems to be not the only breakthrough in military technology they have achieved. I am sure that this information will be checked by the proper institutions in Berlin and submitted to the Fuehrer in person. Given this breakthrough and the newly developed oil fields in the north of the country, this certainly amounts to a geopolitical revolution of the first magnitude.

"Disraelia in 2007: The Probable Scenario," The Journal of Futurist Studies, June 1967

The foreign policy of the state would be neutral (albeit not neutralist). Lobbyists on behalf of the United States and NATO would be active in trying to establish closer relations in various fields and pressing for military bases. Russian lobbyists would be trying equally hard to explain the benefits of a close rapprochement with their country. However, Disraelia would also be part of various regional defense schemes and would participate in common maneuvers with Iran.

What would be Disraelia's standing in the world? It goes without saying that it would be a key member of the United Nations, perhaps even considered for permanent membership in the Security Council and chairing the Commission for Human Rights.

In the cultural area, generous support would be given by Disraelia to struggling universities in the United States and Britain. The U.S. Association for the Promotion of Middle Eastern Studies would pass an almost unanimous resolution demanding an urgent expansion of cultural exchanges with Disraelia, as well as a more constructive attitude towards this country, to rectify past neglect by the White House and Congress. Leading political science professors of the neo-realistic school, the various Mzezinskis and Bodenheimers, would complain in their books that the lack of warmth in the relations between the two countries was not in the best interest of the United States, that there was much to be learned from the Disraelia experience. Leading Middle East specialists such as Juan Finkelstein, Rashid Massad, and Joel Judt would take the lead in founding a Washington-based pro-Disraelia lobby.

What of the attitude of leading European and American intellectuals of the left and the right, of bishops and moral philosophers? Most of them would be enthusiastic in their approach, almost embarrassingly so, holding up the achievements of this state as a shining example for the rest of humankind. One American ex-president would announce that he and his wife had decided to retire to a place in southern Disraelia to grow a new brand of groundnuts. The Disraelian government would make an unofficial approach to the British Broadcasting Corporation complaining that the one-sided laudatory reporting on all things Disraelian was unfair and embarrassing, and likely to provoke resentment among neighboring countries. (BBC correspondents had been shown weeping uncontrollably at the recent funeral of the prime minister of Disraelia.)

The International Association of Conflict Resolution would convene its annual convention in Disraelia, to discuss Robert Frost's "Good fences make good neighbors—true or false?" The majority consensus would be that putting up fences or walls has been the best solution for keeping the peace from the days of the Great Wall of China to the present (e.g., the walls between India and Pakistan in Kashmir and between Yemen and Saudi Arabia), to prevent minor skirmishes from turning into major battles. The fences (to be called henceforth Walls of Peace and Pacification) would be made mandatory by the United Nations to help peacekeepers all over the world.

True, some contrarian voices would still argue that the state, however great its achievements, however humanitarian its policies, was colonialist in nature, founded in part by settlers from Europe. But these dissenting voices would not be taken very seriously. Against them it would be maintained that Disraelia had come into being well before most other member states of the United Nations, including those in the Middle East. If as the result of this process a few had been forced to leave their original places of residence, such cases had occurred all over the world. No one would demand the return of millions of refugees from India and Pakistan of 1947 vintage; the Indian Constitution in its preamble made this legally impossible. No one would demand the return of German refugees from Russia and Eastern Europe. More than ten million had been affected at the time. To bring up such historical incidents would be morally and politically justified only in a much wider framework—if one questioned all migration in history, or at least during the last thousand years. However, such an approach, it would be agreed, would create more problems than it would solve.

Some extreme Islamic sects might engage in incitement against this secular state, but no responsible Arab or Muslim politician would dare to support such propaganda, no more than they would dare to attack China, India or Russia just because Muslim minorities are allegedly persecuted in these countries. On the contrary, Muslim theologians from Al-Azhar to Indonesia would praise the state as a model of friendly coexistence between the Muslim world and the people of the book. A minor Muslim pilgrimage to Al-Quds (Jerusalem) would be instituted, bringing several hundreds of thousand pilgrims each year to pray at the Aqsa Mosque and visit the Dome of the Rock.

Walter Laqueur, "Disraelia: A Counterfactual History," Middle East Papers, April 1, 2008

Once the state had come into being, there would be an almost unlimited number of possibilities of how it would develop; we cannot possibly know whether the Second World War would have taken place and if so what role Disraelia would have played in it. It is quite likely that a Cold War would have occurred and that it would have ended as it did. There would have been crises, domestic and external, affecting the state as has been the case with regard to all nations all over the world. There would have been setbacks; not all dreams would have ripened.

But there is much reason to believe that this state, given a high birth rate, would have some sixty million inhabitants at the beginning of the 21st century. It would have advanced industries, leading the world in fields such as nuclear and computer technologies. It would be the fifth-largest oil producer in the world, economically reasonably healthy with a growth rate of 6–8 percent, competitive with Europe, America and even Asia. It would have powerful armed forces, living in peace with its neighbors, at least to the extent that peaceful relations could be expected in this unquiet part of the world. It would not be a model state, but by the standards of time and place, considered much better than average. No one would dare to question its right to exist, and those who did would not be taken seriously.

Could such a state have come into being? Perhaps—assuming that the great anti-Semitic wave would have occurred in Europe eighty years earlier than it did, provided the Ottoman Empire would have disintegrated eighty years earlier, and provided that the Jews of Europe would have read the signs of the times correctly, and under wise leadership would have followed a policy leading them to peaceful solutions.

But Hitler appeared on the scene only in the next century, and the Ottoman Empire survived another eight decades. The Jews did not emigrate when it might have been possible, because there seemed no cogent reason to do so at the time. There is a world of difference between 1848 and 1948; what was possible a century earlier was no longer possible a hundred years later. Jewish assimilation was much more advanced; Arab nationalism had awakened.

One century could have been the difference between a strong and rich state, universally respected, and a small and relatively weak country, isolated, without important natural resources. There is a vast difference between a state of six million inhabitants and one with sixty, fortified by considerable oil fields and reserves. In terms of Realpolitik as well as moral legitimacy, six million are bad, an invitation to all kind of calamities; sixty million are beyond good and evil, other categories apply. To quote *Animal Farm*, four legs good, two legs bad. Or as Marx would have put it in a letter to Moses Hess (who never finished studying his Hegel): quantity is becoming a new quality. What is considered normal behavior in the case of a state counting sixty million is a moral outrage when done by a small country. In the circumstances, a small state was bound to be considered an intruder and an enemy. A bigger and stronger state might have been accepted.

These basic insights of political science and moral philosophy have unfortunately not yet been fully digested by many in Israel and outside it.

How to Solve
the Conflict—Israel and
the Palestinians

The Arab–Israeli conflict has preoccupied all American presidents and administrations since the 1960s out of all proportion to its intrinsic importance and this will be true, in all probability, in the years to come. The reasons are far from obvious for the region is of no particular strategic or economic importance. As far as the number of victims is concerned, the conflict ranges quite low on the list of external and internal wars in recent decades. Hundreds of thousands Muslims were killed in the Algerian civil war, the war between Iran and Iraq, many more in Darfur, Somalia, the Philippines, Chechnya, Pakistan, Yemen, the Lebanon civil war and so on. The number of Israeli Jews killed during the last thirty years was also quite small. But isn't it true that Palestine and Jerusalem are of central religious importance for Muslims and Jews alike, hence the depth of the emotions, it is the perception which counts, not the number of victims. However, Jerusalem (or to be precise, one specific place in Jerusalem-al Aqsa) appears only once in the Koran and in any case the conflict predated the upsurge of Muslim fundamentalism. When Hafez el Assad suppressed a revolt by the Muslim Brotherhood in the city of Hama in 1983 many more people were killed than in all the intifadas, the recent Lebanon wars and the Israeli invasion of Gaza.

It could be argued that if Arabs kill Arabs this is an internal affair but once non Arabs are involved, this becomes an international problem of far wider importance, Islamophobia, a crime against humanity. But this does not account for the preoccupation of Western media with this conflict. Events in Israel and Palestine figure very prominently whereas there are no TV cameras or foreign correspondents in the regions of Africa, Asia and the Middle East where mass killings are taking place affecting millions of people.

Or is it perhaps the fear that the conflict, albeit directly affecting only a small number of people, might trigger off a larger conflagration—something akin to Sarajevo, 1914? Anything could happen in the age of weapons of mass destruction, but we have not reached this stage yet and such fears certainly do not explain past and present concerns about Palestine; Pakistan is a far more dangerous place, so is Iran.

No wholly convincing answer has so far been provided for the questions asked—why the preoccupation with this tiny region in the Middle East and why the belief that this consists the main danger to world peace, the most dangerous powder keg?

No conflict, except perhaps the Cold War, has produced as great a literature as the conflict between Israelis and Palestinians. Dozens of weighty books have appeared during the last year alone. Most of the leading protagonists in the negotiations have provided their accounts. The most recent wave began with Shlomo Ben Ami, Israeli foreign minister at the time (*Scars of War, Wounds of Peace*), the leading American mediators have provided their recollections (Dennis Ross, Martin Indyk (*Innocent Abroad*), Aaron Miller (*The much too promised land*), Daniel Kurtzer and Lozensky (*Negotiating Arab–Israeli peace*), not to mention President Carter (*We can have peace in the Holy Land*).

There have been recent comprehensive, analytical accounts (for instance Lawrence Freedman's *A Choice of enemies*), books about the wars of 1948, 1967, 1973 as well as the first and second Intifada, about the Israeli settlements (Gershom Gorenberg and Idit Zartal), about the Israeli lobby in the United States, about Khamas. The Arab side found many advocates such as Rashid Khalidi. Books by Arab political leaders or diplomats are fewer, there is no tradition as in the West for Arab prime ministers or other leading officials to write books about events in which they were involved (Saddam Hussein was an exception but he wrote novels). There are some such books but they suffer from what an Egyptian writer (Tarek Heggy) has called "our culture of denial." There might be also an element of fear; an Egyptian government minister Youssef es Sibai was killed for no other reason than accompanying Anwar Sadat on his flight to Jerusalem. Writers of memoirs sometimes suffer from memory lapses. President Carter who regards the Israeli settlements beyond the 1967 as some of the main stumbling blocks to peace does not mention that it was precisely under his administration (1982–86) that many of these settlements were established or rapidly developed—and precisely those situated in the middle of Arab territory (such as for instance Ariel, Elon Moreh, Bethel, Kfar Adumim, Karnei Shomron et al.).

With all this most memoirs or other works are of some value for understanding the recent phase in this stormy conflict. They deal with the many attempts in recent decades to find peaceful solutions or at least armistices of long duration—the meetings at Camp David, Taba, Annapolis and the countless smaller meetings and exchanges.

But hardly any of these books offer solutions how to solve the conflict except suggestions of a technical nature. One of the few and a very notable exceptions is Benny Morris's *"One State Two States—Resolving the Israel/ Palestine Conflict* (New Haven, CT: Yale University Press).

Morris was born on a Kibbutz the year Israel came into being. He is the leading, most productive, and certainly most widely discussed Israeli historian of his generation. He was the first and most prominent of the new post-Zionist historians breaking with certain taboos of official Zionist historiography. He showed that it was not true that all Arabs left their homes in 1948 because their leaders had asked them to do so—and this was how the refugee problem came into being. While there were cases of panic, elsewhere Arabs were expelled by Israeli armed forces. There was cruelty and even some crimes. Morris refused to do his military reserve service in the West Bank occupied territories and for a while (in 1988) he was arrested. He became the favorite source of reference and authority of the left and Palestinian writers. The use of the terms "left" and "right" in the context of the conflict is unfortunate and misleading—well to do neighborhoods in Israel vote for the peace parties whereas poor villages and cities are solidly pro-Likud. But the use of the terms is by now deeply rooted and there seems to be no chance to revise it.

However, in the course of further studies Morris became far more critical of the Palestinians who had tried in 1948 to destroy the new state. 800 of them had been executed or massacred during the war that year (but so had hundreds of Jewish civilians), a number infinitely smaller than in any comparable conflict. There had been individual cases of expulsion, but no systematic policy of ethnic cleansing. But perhaps this had been a mistake, for on occasion ethnic cleansing (such as in Eastern Europe, the Indian subcontinent and other parts of the world) had defused conflicts and stabilized the situation. Is it not likely that the same would have happened in Palestine? In the case of an existential threat to the existence of the state expulsion seemed to be wholly justified.

As a result of such unorthodox reflections based on further studies following the second Intifada Morris came under heavy attack by his erstwhile comrades and supporters. The darling of the far left became a traitor to the good cause for seemingly no good reason, a racist, chauvinist and perhaps even a fascist. He was boycotted by the circles which had fervently backed him earlier on. But Morris was not swayed: While still favoring Israeli compromises to resolve the conflict peacefully, he saw no such readiness on the other side, their opposition to the existence of the state was fundamental and total, based on a culture of revenge and religious belief. In brief, he saw no longer a chance for peace, certainly not in his life time.

In his new book Professor Morris discusses past and present ideas by Jews and Arabs concerning the future of Palestine—should it be one state or two, and what would its character be? Following a long (perhaps overlong) discussion of recent articles in American and British literary journals (mainly by Jewish writers with strong opinions but not equally strong background in

27

the history of Palestine and its present state) he turns to the origins of the one state and two state conceptions.

The early settlers in the 1880s thought (as did Theodor Herzl, the founder of modern political Zionism) that gradually more and more Jews would come, more and more land would be bought and as a result a Jewish state would emerge. Such belief was subsequently criticized as both naïve and chauvinistic for did it not ignore the presence and rights of the (Arab) residents of the country?

But given the demographic realities at the time such belief was not really that utopian. Palestine, part of the Ottoman Empire at the time, was not empty but nor was it overpopulated. The slogan "a land without people to a people without land" often ascribed to the Zionists was in fact formulated by British Christian thinkers in the early nineteenth century. The year Herzl's *Judenstaat* (Jewish State) was published (1896) the total population of Palestine was less than half the population of Vienna, the city in which Herzl lived, and by no means all of them were Arabs. It surely seemed possible to find an accommodation for all nationalities in such a state just as national minorities more or less peacefully coexisted in other multinational states at the time. Herzl, an old fashioned liberal, believed in equal rights for all citizens; the non Jewish citizens would not only prosper in the state he envisaged but have equal rights in every respect.

The Ottoman Empire collapsed in World War I, Palestine became a League of Nations mandate under British administration and with the Balfour declaration (1917) envisaging a Jewish national home Herzl's dream seemed near realization. But the Jewish masses did not come to the national home and when they wanted and desperately needed to come after Hitler's rise to power, the British authorities had drastically restricted immigration. Furthermore Arab opposition against Jewish immigration had become intense and led to riots in 1921, 1929 and an insurrection in 1936–39. In these circumstances the efforts of the small Jewish groups advocating close rapprochement with the Palestinian Arabs and eventually a binational state were doomed. The leadership of Palestinian Arabs was opposed not only to Jewish immigration but also to the presence of recent (post-World War I) arrivals.

The concepts of the Zionist parties (except the Revisionists, the forerunners of Likud) concerning the future of the national home remained vague. When the idea of partition was first mooted by the British Peel Commission in 1937 even the Zionist left was divided and Ben Gurion who accepted it with great reluctance prevailed only with great difficulty. The Peel Report provided for the transfer of some 300,000 Palestinian Arabs living in the Jewish state to neighboring countries. Morris notes that such "ethnic cleansing" was not considered morally reprehensible at the time but endorsed by the League of Nations—such as in the case of the population transfer between Turkey and Greece after World War I. This was considered the best, probably the only way to evade the persecution of minorities and the prevention of irredentist internal wars. There were other proposals such as the cantonization of Palestine but they were never seriously discussed let alone accepted.

Peel remained a dead letter, thereafter came the Biltmore declaration by Ben Gurion in the U.S. (1942) envisaging a Jewish state in parts of Palestine and eventually the UN declaration of November 1947, which led to the establishment of the state of Israel. But a Palestinian Arab state which had also been decided upon by the United Nations never came into being and the Palestinian Arab territories were ruled by Jordan up to the war of 1967.

Morris describes the peace feelers, such as they were, during the first two decades after 1948. They were doomed from the outset. Fatah which came into being in the 1950s stood for the liberation of all of Palestine from the Mediterranean to the Jordan. It was only after the war of 1973 and the various misfortunes of the Palestine Liberation Organization that it weakened its position, expressing a willingness to make concessions.

For Israel 1967 was (or could have been) the great turning point. It had occupied virtually all the lands west of the Jordan, for the first time it was in a position to make substantial concessions. It waited for a phone call from the Arab governments indicating their willingness to make peace but this call never came. And so Israel became saddled with Judea and Samaria (in the language of the settlers) who soon began to stream into the West Bank and also in the direction of Gaza; without Gaza, some Israeli politicians (such as Israel Galili) argued, Israel could not exist. A few at first, their number swell to several hundreds of thousands, many (but not all of them) were permeated with the messianic fervor that had become the fashion: God himself had restored to the people of Israel the historic homeland he had promised them as well as holy Jerusalem which would never again be divided.

Morris discusses in detail the various peace negotiations under successive American presidents and Israeli prime ministers. Some of the peace talks were successful—the peace treaties with Egypt and Jordan which had not been brokered by outside factors. But there was no progress in the talks with the Palestinians except Oslo which did not last. Morris also deals with the two Intifadas and eventually the rise of Hamas and Hezbollah in Lebanon.

A radicalization took place in the Arab camp as manifested in the Hamas Covenant which rejects the existence of the State of Israel as a matter of fundamental principle. Morris believes that the Fatah slogan of a secular and democratic Palestine was not seriously meant but was propaganda for outside consumption meant to attract Western liberals.

He should perhaps have covered in greater detail the radicalization which took place, probably inevitably, among the Jews. Initially there had been suspicion of Arabs but no hatred; the only outspoken Jewish Arab hater I ever met in Palestine was a man whose family had been killed in the 1929 pogrom of the non Zionist Jewish community of Hebron. But there was a marked change in these attitudes following years of intifada, frequent attacks, large and small such as suicide bombings. And thus anti Arab feeling spread, most among the immigrants from Oriental countries, a result, above all, of the mistreatment they and their ancestors suffered in their countries of origin. There was a growing feeling that "Arabs are our sworn enemies," that "they will never accept us," that no compromises or good deeds on our part will make any difference, that force is the only language they understand. The mood of the country changed and this expressed itself in the elections which brought rightwing parties to power. True, a majority of Israelis opposed indiscriminate settlement on the West bank but no government dared to proceed against it.

What way out is there from the present impasse? Morris dismisses a binational state with political parity for the two communities as unrealistic. But a one state solution—a single Jewish state without an Arab minority—would involve the expulsion of 4-5 million Arabs (including those on the West Bank) whereas a single Arab state involving the expulsion of millions of Jews seems likewise impossible. But the prospects for a two state solution (more or less on the lines of the Clinton–Barak understanding) seem equally bleak, support for it among Arabs has been steadily declining.

And so Morris reaches the conclusion, without evident enthusiasm, that the idea of a confederation including Transjordan, mooted by the first British High Commissioner Viscount Samuel in 1920 seems to be the most realistic solution. While a Palestinian state consisting of West Bank and Gaza would not be economically viable, it might be a going concern in combination with Jordan. It could offer a solution for the redistribution of the overcrowded Gaza strip and the bulk of the stateless refugees in Lebanon. There is no certainty that such a scheme would work. But paraphrasing Sherlock Holmes, having ruled out all other possibilities which seem even more unlikely, only this concept remains.

The idea is not entirely new, Viscount Samuel apart it was also mooted by the late Yigal Alon and by Arik Sharon. And it has now reemerged in the writings of a historian more familiar with the past and the present state of the conflict than most politicians.

2

Some personal recollections: The concept of a single binational state seemed not always as outlandish as it now appears. There is no need to adduce the reasons why, given the smallness of the territory in dispute and the population involved. I believed in it prior to the establishment of the state of Israel. My belief was somewhat shaken when I became the victim of ethnic cleansing twice within a year—being expelled first from Issawiya, a village near Jerusalem, later, in December 1947, from the Jerusalem German Colony. But did not the inhabitants of Issawiya suffer subsequently much

30

more than I did, being expelled from their homes? Not quite, when I lived there the village had about a thousand inhabitants, now there are 14.000. I accompanied UNSCOP (the UN Special Committee on Palestine in 1947) and wherever we went there was total rejection on the Arab side of the idea of a binational state: It was their country, the Jews were the intruders and had no claim to be considered equal partners. Those few willing even to talk to the Jews such as Fakhri Nashashibi or Sami Taha, the Haifa union leader and even one of the Husseinis were assassinated. As a young journalist I had come to know these political figures. This tradition of killing Palestinian public figures willing to negotiate with the Zionists continued in later years. The victims included Said Hamami, the PLO representative in London, Issam Sartawi and others. In the circumstances support for bi nationalism among the Zionists, never very strong, collapsed—there was no partner to talk to. Furthermore, the experience of binational states in other parts of the globe has not been encouraging; it is difficult to think of more than one or two which have been a success.

All this now belongs to the distant past, perhaps there has been a change of mind in the years since among the Palestinian leadership, a greater willing-ness to collaborate as the result of the sad subsequent history of their people? They have tried all possible approaches—proto fascism, quasi-Marxist anti imperialism, Nasserist pan-Arabism and most recently Islamic fundamental-ism, all without notable success. But according to all the evidence there has been radicalization rather than greater willingness to compromise.

True, some Western well wishers of Hamas have argued that this move-ment would become more moderate if only the West would open a dialogue with them. This could be true—assuming that their demands concerning the elimination of the state of Israel were accepted.

The conflict was inevitable, given the fact that two peoples wanted the same country. A solution has been made more intractable as the result of Iranian intervention. The Iranian leadership rightly assumes that as long as global interest is focused on the Palestinian conflict, less attention will be paid to their attempts to gain hegemony in the Middle East. In any case, support for the Palestinian cause is popular among radical Sunnis as well as Shi'ites and will deflect, at least temporarily, attention from Iranian designs aiming at domination in the Middle East.

If there has been radicalization in the Palestinian camp so has there been in Israel and one wishes Mr. Morris had been dealing in greater detail with the unfortunate consequences of the war of 1967 and its aftermath on Israeli policy. 1967 was a great victory but, to quote Nietzsche, for human nature a great victory is more difficult to bear than a great defeat.

It generated in Israel a wave of mystical trance and messianic expectations, there were mass petitions not to give up a single inch of the territories that had been conquered. The national religious party which had been among the most moderate and peaceful political forces became one of the most fanatical. Its leader had declared immediately after the end of the war that one ought to get rid as quickly as possible of the non Jewish holy sites in Jerusalem for keeping them would only spell major trouble. But this was quickly forgotten and the Israeli parliament passed a law according to which Jerusalem should never again be divided, even if today's Jerusalem is de facto a divided city.

In an article published in August 1967 I wrote that most people in Israel were not aware of the enormity of the problems facing them: *The administration and policing of large areas populated by Arabs were bound to create nightmarish problems. It could be predicted with near certainty that there would be an increasing number of acts of sabotage and that the Israeli authorities would have to react sharply. And it was easy to imagine world reaction to such incidents. Israel now faces hard times—there is a massive propaganda onslaught about the new Hitlerites and their barbarous atrocities, already we have heard about Israeli gauleiters and Israeli extermination camps. And I ended: Pressure for revenge will be overwhelming. A military adventure is extremely probable not in ten or twenty years but well before.*

The prediction was accurate—the Yom Kippur war came a mere seven years later. Seen in today's perspective it was not an unmitigated disaster from the Israeli point of view—without this war there would have been no Sadat visit to Jerusalem and no peace with Egypt. Most Israelis including the political class did not pay attention at the time to the demographic implications of holding on to the occupied territories—that given the much higher Arab birth rate the number of Arabs in Greater Israel would be in the near future as large, or larger than the number of Jews.

True, the mystical mood quite apart there were rational arguments for holding on to the new borders. There was nothing sacrosanct about the Israeli borders of 1948 which made the country difficult to defend. And it is quite doubtful whether giving up the conquered territories would have affected in any way the rise of Muslim fundamentalism.

But there was at least a chance that giving up the territories would have had some effect whereas holding on to them was bound to lead to the disappearance of a state both Jewish and democratic. And since it should have been clear that sooner or later most of the occupied territories would have to be surrendered in any case, was it not more prudent to do so from a position of strength than weakness?

Which leads to the other cardinal weakness of Israeli policy in recent decades: This is the failure to accept that a small country with seven million inhabitants (of which about 20 percent were Arabs) had to behave according to its status in the world and its limited power.

I have tried elsewhere to imagine a different historical scenario (*Disraelia, a counterfactual history 1848–2008*). What if the state of Israel had come into existence some time during the middle of the nineteenth century and if it were now a state of, say, fifty million inhabitants, with a developed modern industry and technology, with substantial oilfields and other important natural resources? It would be a respected member of the United Nations, a pillar of world order, its humanity would be praised and admired and no one in his right mind would dare to attack it, physically or verbally, it would not be isolated but on the contrary admired and wooed, its neighbors may not love it but would not dream to antagonize it just as they do not dare to provoke the ire of Russia, or India or China even though there are many complaints about the state of Muslims in these countries.

But the state of Israel did come into existence only much later, millions of European Jews did not arrive, it has no major oilfields and the fact that it has a strong military deterrent does not prevent minor and major pinpricks on the part of hostile neighbors. In fact, the implications of Israeli power such as it is have not yet been fully realized by the more extreme of its enemies who do not accept that they can eradicate the state only at the price of self extinction. They believe that small attacks will wear it down, underrating the steadfastness of their hated adversaries, mistakenly believing that they have a monopoly on fanaticism.

There is a naïve belief in Israel, only slowly eroded, that on the international level there is one justice for all, that if (not only figuratively speaking) major powers can get away with murder, smaller ones can get too. In brief, many Israelis failed to understand what has been clear all throughout history even to minor mafiosi that facing a strong hostile coalition, the correct policy is to try to divide it. It needs all deterrents it can obtain but it also may have to take a low profile in order to survive. The benefits of such a strategy should have been clear given the many internal conflicts within the Arab world, but they were ignored for a long time.

3

The chances for a lasting peace between Israel and the Palestinians are virtually nil at the present time. True, no conflict lasts forever and circumstances will almost certainly change over time. The impetus of fanaticism does not last indefinitely, it is usually a matter of a generation or two. There could be far reaching changes in the international constellation and the global balance of power, one side in the conflict (or both sides) could be weakened to make a peaceful settlement more likely. There could be changes beyond our imagination such as global disasters as a result of which the urgency finding a solution to the Israeli–Palestinian conflict might be very much diminished as the world will face other, more urgent challenges. What are the chances of an imposed solution? It cannot be entirely ruled out—but only in conditions very different from those prevailing today. But who would impose it? Who would be willing to provide substantial military forces not just Blue helmets and UN observers?

The confederation plan outlined by Mr. Morris does not seem realistic; it is not clear why the Hashemites and their supporters ruling Jordan should abdicate. Nor does it seem likely that such a confederation could absorb the population of overpopulated Gaza and the Lebanese refugee camps. When I first visited Gaza soon after the end of World War II it was a sleepy little town of perhaps 25.000 inhabitants and Khan Yunis was even smaller. In a few years the population of the Gaza strip will be 2.5 million. True, the very high birth rate of Palestinian Arabs is declining but this will have little effect during the next few decades. Gaza is artificially kept alive by outside money, some 90 percent from Western countries. It would not be viable even if Israel did not exist, it will never be a second Singapore. Western humanitarian aid only prolongs the agony and makes the problem less tractable. It reminds one of a surgeon unwilling to undertake a necessary procedure because it would make the patient suffer. But the result of inaction will be much greater suffering at a later date. Emigration is the only realistic solution—to other parts of the Arab world such as the Gulf region, and to other parts of the globe.

The issue of the West Bank settlements is in some respects not dissimilar. There can be, of course, negotiations on border revisions and exchanges of territory but most of the settlements will have to go if Israel is to survive. That such a measure would not solve all problems goes without saying but it is a precondition—as is a compromise on Jerusalem. It is not certain that a removal of most settlements can be achieved peacefully; it could well lead to a small scale civil war. It will be a difficult decision for some—the choice between survival and holding on to Judea and Samaria as well as no compromise on Jerusalem. Some may well stick to their belief that democracy is not their highest value and that the existence of a state is not worth while unless it contains all parts of the Holy Land and that God will intervene to effect an outcome such as envisaged by the settlers. A majority does not share this view but all throughout history determined and fanatical minorities have been able to dictate their wishes to a hesitant majority believing that it may be possible to muddle through without taking painful decisions.

While the continuation of a "peace process" on past lines is very probably a waste of time and effort it will, of course, be continued. With a little luck it will result in armistices, periods of relative quiet, interrupted by fighting. No one can say with any certainty how long this process will continue.

Zionism Revisited

Theodor HerzI has entered political history as the author of two small books; one the *Judenstaat* (Jewish State), the other a piece of political science fiction entitled *Altneuland*. *Altneuland*, published in 1902, describes the visit of two European sympathizers with the cause of Zionism after an absence of many years to Palestine, now a Jewish state which they have never seen. They are awe struck by the enormous achievements that have been made over and above what even the most enthusiastic visitors could reasonably have expected. Had they postponed their visit a bit longer, their amazement would have been even greater.

Even those who knew Palestine in 1948, the year the Jewish state came into being, would not recognize it today. The number of Jews living in Palestine in 1948 was about half a million and it has increased tenfold since. It was a tiny community at the time, today it is more populous than half a dozen European countries including Norway and Finland. It absorbed during the first years of statehood a number of immigrants three times larger than those living in the country, a feat unique in the annals of mankind. Many hundreds of new settlements and suburbs came into being. While for years it depended on outside financial help, it gradually became economically viable. Its standard of living is comparable to that of many European countries, it has a vibrant cultural life with many universities, theatres, symphony orchestras and its scientific institutions are second to none (as indeed Herzl had envisaged). On many global statistics measuring progress Israel appears among the first ten or twenty countries. The quality of its domestic political life is far from ideal. There are too many political parties, and there has been corruption even on the highest level; minorities have not always been treated fairly. But elections are still free, the judiciary is still independent. the media enjoy total freedom. It is the only democracy in a part of the world in which democracies are conspicuously absent. Militarily, it does not depend on outside help but has armed forces capable in every respect to defend the country All this is true and yet the Jewish state finds itself in deep trouble during the sixth decade of its existence. Contemporary visitors to Altneuland having been

Preface to Walter Laqueur, *A History of Zionism* (2003 edition).

duly impressed by the fantastic achievements are bound to ask whether the society which came into being still corresponds in any significant way to the dreams of HerzI and the other early leaders of the Zionist movement.

Let us be realistic: *Altneuland* was, of course, a utopia, and utopias, need less to say, never come true. In the inevitable collision between dream and realties, realities always prove stronger. HerzI and his contemporaries did not really expect that the Jewish state would be somehow superior, more highly accomplished, more ethically motivated than other countries; they were primarily looking for a refuge for the persecuted Jewish people and were aware how difficult it would be to build a country like all others. If Israel has not lived up to expectations, it is certainly true that all the countries which came into being after World War II have been a disappointment to those who envisaged these countries and fought for them. Some of the basic reasons for such disappointments are rooted in history and it would be pointless to put the blame on human shortcomings. It was the historical tragedy of Zionism that it appeared very late on the international scene but it could not have appeared earlier on. The great majority of Jews did not want a state of their own before the twentieth century and when the storm clouds appeared on the horizon (and it is the historical merit of Zionism that it recognized this earlier than all others), when the necessity to find a shelter for the Jews of Europe became more and more urgent. The gates of Palestine were virtu ally closed. Nor was there a sufficient willingness on the part of European and American Jewry to make a major effort to invest energies and financial means in building a national home.

When the disaster came, a few hundred thousands had been saved but the millions of European Jewry perished. At the end of the war the great reservoir of European Jewry which the Zionists had hoped would build the Jewish state had disappeared. The Jews of Palestine wanted a state of their own because there was no realistic political alternative and to almost every one's surprise they resisted the onslaught of the Arab armies. But it was also clear that the demographic base for a viable state was far too small and hence the "ingathering of the exiles" became the commandment of the hour. This led to a profound social and cultural change in the composition of the population of the new country. Zionism had been a European move ment. Among the Jews in the Oriental countries there had been a messianic religious belief or a feeling of historical attachment towards Zion. But there was no overwhelming urge to move to Palestine. Zionist organizations were very small or non existent.

True, there was an increase in anti-Semitism in the Middle East and North Africa during the 1930s and World War II and a rise of rabid and xenophobic nationalism. Foreigners were expelled from Egypt and there were pogroms in Iraq, Libya and elsewhere. The majority of Jews in these countries would have had to leave and for a considerable part of them (but not the well to do and the intelligentsia) Israel was the obvious haven. But it is doubtful in retrospect whether the same is true with regard to Moroccan Jewry, the most numerous of these communities, they lived (as many of them later argued) more or less in peace with their neighbors. By urging these communities (not to mention more exotic ones like the Falasha) to move on to Israel the enthusiastic Zionist emissaries created problems of which, in all probability, they were not aware. There were complaints on the part of the North African immigrants about discrimination and exploitation.

This was certainly not true on the political level, presidents of Israel came from among their ranks as well as foreign and defense ministers, army chiefs of staff and so on. But a considerable part of them claimed not to be too happy in their new homeland, complaining about their inferior social status and the conditions in which they lived. They were not pioneers willing to accept hardship and sacrifice as the early settlers from Eastern and Central Europe had been and their expectations were high. They were unwilling to put up with conditions such as they prevailed in the development towns. They expected that the state would take care of them but the state was not rich enough to do so. And even if the state had done more, they would still have complained about paternalism and lack of respect for their culture and traditions. By and large their feelings of solidarity with their Ashkenazi coreligionists were strictly limited. Eventually they established a political party of their own in defense of their interests which while anti-Arab was not Zionist in character.

After the breakdown of the Soviet Union a million of Soviet Jews arrived in Israel. Few had expected this, I had certainly not believed that a Russian translation of the present book would appear in Moscow in my lifetime. The great majority of Jews who came after 1989 (in contrast to the Russian Jews who had arrived before) were not Zionists; a significant percentage was not Jewish. They came to have a better life for themselves and their children. But their absorption proceeded more smoothly than most had thought, mainly perhaps because their education had been on a higher level than that of the North African Jews and because they were showing greater initiative. The difficulties with them were on another level—culturally they kept apart and showed little interest to become part of Israel such as it was.

"We are a people. One people" Herzl had exclaimed in a famous speech in one of the early Zionist congresses to stormy acclaim. But was it still true? There certainly had been a Jewish people at one time but Zionism had probably come too late to reunite it. Its various branches had gone their own ways. They still shared some common features and traditions and felt a certain responsibility for each other at a time of crisis. But most of them felt no longer an urge for redemption and the building of a new kingdom of Israel. The Jewish community in Palestine in 1948 had been an elite and the influx of so many new immigrants, many of them not Zionist in the traditional sense led not only to normalization but to polarization. Once upon a time it had been one of the most egalitarian societies; if a family had three rooms and a car it was considered rich. Today next to the United States it is the country with the most pronounced disparities in income and property among developed nations. This trend was accompanied by ideological polarization. In every free country there is a left and a right wing, and also an extreme left and an extreme right. True, the old labels are frequently no longer fitting: The issue at stake is no longer capitalism vs socialism, for the rich suburbs vote overwhelmingly Labor whereas the development towns opt for the rightwing parties. As long as extremism is confined to relatively small groups it is politically irrelevant.

But if the extremes grow in influence and if the center which holds society together is shrinking, society faces a crisis. On the right over the past thirty years the belief has gained ground that the whole of historical Palestine is "ours by divine right" and this has resulted among other things in the mushrooming of settlements in the areas occupied in 1967, most of which do not make sense either economically or militarily, tying down a considerable part of Israel's defense forces. But they are a major obstacle on the road to some form—of peaceful coexistence with the Palestinians. This pseudo religious mysticism would have been wholly alien to earlier generations of Zionist thinkers who with all respect for traditional religion, were profoundly secular in outlook and would have regarded with abhorrence the intrusion of religion (or more often of superstition) into politics. If the indiscriminate "ingathering of the exiles" was a serious mistake, seen in retrospect, the failure of the state of Israel to adopt a constitution early on providing for a division between religion and state was another.

This new nationalism was not a product of the Enlightenment as Zionism had been, it was not connected with the struggle for political liberty and a free society. It feared alien influences, was antagonistic to strangers and individual freedom was not among its primary concerns. As one of the ideologues of this new creed put it "This Zionism does not seek to solve the problem of the Jews by setting up a Jewish state but it is an instrument in the hands of the Almighty which prepared the people of Israel for their Redemption." Earlier Zionism had not been based on religious zealotry and chauvinism. And even religious Zionism had stressed the international, universal message of the torah rather than national egotism. Jabotinsky was a nationalist in the liberal nineteenth century mould to whom the anti Western, isolationist character of the new Zionism would have been incomprehensible and repugnant.

What caused such regression in post-independence Zionism? Was it disappointment with the achievement of the state, or the enduring state of war with the Arabs? But the achievements of the state were not negligible. Probably it was the annus mirabilis of 1967 that caused so much ideological dizziness resulting in the loss of balance and a decline in the sense of reality. It might have had something to do with the rise of fundamentalism world wide and also a decline in the stature of leadership. Classical Zionism had attracted formidable intellects and leaders of considerable stature by any standards, even if they usually were generals without an army. In recent decades there has been a notable decline in this respect—the attraction of leadership and the feeling of mission and patriotic duty had lessened and those who could and should have been leaders were not drawn into politics but looked for political fulfillment in other fields of human endeavor. Such a decline in the quality of leadership took place in many other countries. But there was one important difference. A newly created and as yet embattled country, by no means as yet universally accepted, needed a farsighted leadership more than others.

As if this was not enough, Zionism was afflicted by yet two other plagues, essentially not new but appearing in a new guise. One was the ultra-orthodox camp which in Eastern Europe had rejected and fought Zionism tooth and nail since the very beginning. In Palestine too, there had always been a small anti-Zionist ultra-orthodox community in Mea Shearim and a few other places which had kept strictly apart from the organized Jewish community and its organizations. But since 1948 Mea Shearim has greatly expanded in view of the high fertility rate of the ultra-orthodox. The numbers of those attending yeshivot (religious seminaries) increased fifty fold or more between 1948 and the present day. All this would have little mattered if as in the olden days the haredim would have kept to themselves. But instead they have used their increased numbers to compel the state of Israel to support their institutions and to finance their way of life. (They refuse to serve in the army and most of them are not gainfully employed.) They began to impose their taboos on the rest of the population thus causing bitter conflicts and something akin to a *Kulturkampf* in places like Jerusalem.

Zionism had been opposed to the way of life of the East European ghetto and one of its main missions was to create a productive society in contrast to the parasitical life, the *Luftmenschentum,* so frequent in the shtetl. Yet the ghetto and its mentality proved to be resilient and it came to haunt Zionism in the country it had created. Given the fragmentation of Israeli political life the ultra-orthodox attained an influence in parliament and elsewhere out of proportion with their numbers and they also succeeded in extending their influence beyond the Ashkenazi ghetto influencing sections of the Oriental Jewish community even though they firmly believed that only they were the true bearers of the religious mission. They had the same feeling of superiority vis-à-vis the Oriental Jews the Arabs had with regard to non-Arab Muslims.

The other antagonist was also an old acquaintance in new clothes—Post-Zionism. Once upon a time the Communists, the Trotskyites and similar political groups had waged war against Zionism (including left wing

Zionism) because of its reactionary, imperialist character. Zionism as they saw it had been a colonialist movement. The Jews, they believed, had no right to have a state of their own, because this aim could be attained only as a result of expelling another people. The Zionists had been either lying or struck with blindness when they had argued that Palestine was a country without people. But the Zionists had not really argued this, for in *Altneuland* Arabs do appear. It is perfectly true that Palestine was not an empty country when Herzl convened the first Zionist Congress.

No country was totally empty, not even the Sahara desert. But what was the number of inhabitants of Palestine at the time? 400,000 perhaps and this included Bedouins, Christian Arabs, Greeks, Armenians and others who were not Muslims. Baedeker's Guide to Vienna published the year before the first Zionist Congress gives the number of the inhabitants of the city in which Herzl lived as 1,364,500; in other world the number of Palestinian Arabs was at most one third that of the Austrian capital. Perhaps Herzl might be forgiven after all for assuming that the presence of a few hundreds of thousands did not present an insurmountable obstacle to his plans. The next sentence in Baedeker's guide helps to explain why the idea of Zionism occurred to Herzl in the first place: It says: "including 118,000 Jews and 22,651 soldiers." There lived in Vienna at the time tens of thousands of Poles and Czechs, Croats, Hungarians, Italians, Slovenians, and many other nationalities. But only the Jews were listed in a separate category, perhaps they were thought to be transients like the soldiers.

Marxism went out of intellectual fashion in the last quarter of the twentieth century but the impulses underlying it did not, hence the appearance of new intellectual trends such as post-colonialism which provided the inspiration to the post-Zionist trend. (The term post-Zionism is, of course, value free, it appears on page one of the present book well before the Israeli post Zionists arrived on the scene.) They belonged to a young generation of Israeli academics who had never experienced anti-Semitism, for whom the holocaust was not a real historical experience, who did not have to face the danger of destruction and to flee Europe to save their lives. They were influenced mainly by the writings of Indian thinkers teaching at American universities but unknown in their homeland. Their rejection of Zionism (and frequently also of Israel) was psychologically understandable as a rebellion against the generation of the fathers and grandfathers.

The post Zionists deconstructing Zionist ideology made a number of discoveries which they thought were of great importance. They found that many of the stories taught in the school and based on the Old Testament were not rooted in fact but in mythology; it was not certain that the Israelites had ever lived in Egypt, crossed the Red Sea and Joshua's trumpet had in all probability not caused the crumbling of the walls of Jericho. King David's kingdom had not been a major empire but a small, local affair; they thought that there was doubt whether King David had ever lived. In their enthusiasm they tended to forget that the origins of every religion indeed of any nation from ancient Greece and Rome to the present time has not been in historical fact but shrouded in myth. Moving forward in history they doubted whether Trumpeldor the ex-Russian officer defending Tel Hai and being mortally wounded had ever said that it was good to die for one's country.

Sometimes their arguments were not quite consistent: on one hand they maintained that the Zionists should never have been in Palestine in the first place, but at the same time they accused them for not having done enough to save European Jewry during World War II. They had persuaded the displaced persons after World War II to move on to Palestine even though the DPs were reluctant to do so. In the war of independence they had not treated the Palestinian villagers with sufficient humanity but caused directly or indirectly the expulsion of hundreds of thousands of villagers and the destruction of their homes.

Those engaging in postcolonial (also called subaltern) studies were not many in number but exerted some influence as teachers and this eventually led to a situation in which Israeli school books included a picture of Gamal Abdul Nasser but not of Ben Gurion. The problem with post Zionism was not that it was all wrong but that what was correct was not new, and what was new was not correct. They seemed to be unaware of the fact (and here they deviated from Marxism which was far more realistic in this respect) that no state has ever been established by friendly persuasion or some legal contract. States were always born in violence, there have always been innocent victims and there was no reason to assume that the birth of an Israeli nation would be different in character. Seen in this perspective every state was immoral and had no right to exist, except, of course, that in many cases the crimes had been committed a long time ago which however from a strictly ethical point of view should not make any difference.

This is a history of Zionism, not of the state of Israel and even less of the Israeli-Arab conflict. But nor can the conflict be ignored for it affected to a massive degree Zionist ideology or what went for it after the foundation of the state. Palestinian Arabs had been wronged as the result of the establishment of the state but many Israelis found it difficult to understand their reactions—did they not live much better than before, was their lot not preferable to that of Arabs in the neighboring countries? It was a lack of imagination on the part of many Israelis, had they been born Palestinians would they not have reacted in a similar way? The Palestinian Arabs, on the other hand, failed to understand that the misfortune was at least in part of their own doing, since they had refused first the idea of a bi national state, later to accept their own state (in 1948) and rejected subsequently all other compromises.

It was the misfortune of Zionism and Israel that their country should be located in the middle of a very troubled part of the world which has shown in modern times particular ineptitude to establish civil (let alone civilized) societies, to make social and economic progress and to contribute to world culture. The travails, the frustrations, the resentments of the Muslim and Arab world are well known and need not be discussed in detail. The great majority of violent conflicts between countries and within countries in the contemporary world concern Arab or Muslim societies. In this situation there was the danger that the very existence of Israel was a provocation and should become the catalyst for much of the rage and frustration not just among Palestinians but the Arab and Muslim world in general.

It is more than doubtful that a conflict between Israelis and Palestinians could have been prevented given the fact that two peoples were claiming the same land. But far from trying to defuse the conflict and preventing its spread, Israeli policy has often added fuel to it, thus increasing the dangers confronting the state. Prior to 1967 there was nothing to discuss with the Arabs because they had not accepted the very existence of Israel. But after the Six Day War Israel was in a position to make concessions; it waited for Arab initiatives which never came. But why should it have surrendered the occupied territories if the Arabs were still unwilling to make peace? For the simple reason that it could not indefinitely impose its rule over so many people who did not want to live in a Jewish state and yet maintain the democratic character of the country. Establishing Jewish settlements in the middle of a hostile Arab population was not an answer, on the contrary it aggravated the problem. Sooner or later the settlements would have to be given up and the longer this was delayed, the more painful it was going to be. The second sin of omission concerned the Arab citizens of Israel. There is no certainty that they would have become Israeli patriots even if they had been given full rights, even if preferential treatment had been given to them. But only a half-hearted attempt was made to integrate them and there were too many promises which were not fulfilled.

The question of Jerusalem illustrates best the enormous difference between historical Zionism and the ideology which has replaced it. Jerusalem contains the holy places of three world religion and elementary prudence if not basic tolerance should have prevented declarations according to which Jerusalem was to remain forever undivided under Israeli rule. It was in any case an empty declaration, for in actual fact, Jerusalem was a divided city. When Herzl first visited Jerusalem he saw only the musty deposits of two thousand years of inhumanity, intolerance and impurity. He perceived superstition and fanaticism on all sides. Hence it did not come as a surprise that he suggested Haifa as the capital of the Jewish state. But it was not only Herzl, the assimilated Jew, who reacted in this unsentimental way, the reaction of the others was exactly the same. Weizman always feared to become involved in the Jerusalem imbroglio and the leaders of the second aliya such as Ben Gurion visited Jerusalem for the first time, two or three years after their arrival in the country because their emotional attachment was not overwhelming. For many years there was not a single Zionist leader who chose to live in Jerusalem. For Jerusalem symbolized the negative past of Jewish history, that part of the tradition from which they wanted to dissociate themselves. The idea that Jerusalem was the beginning and the end of Zionism, that Israel could not exist without having full sovereignty, emerged only after 1967 with the growth of a religious fanaticism and aggressive nationalism that had more in common with the ideology of the Muslim Brotherhood than the attitude of the founding fathers of Zionism.

Thus the holy sites became a nightmare and Jerusalem a dangerous flash-point. For Christian endtimers (basing themselves on the Book of Daniel as well as Revelations) as well as for some Jewish sectarians there was the temptation to attack religious sites in Jerusalem to precipitate Armageddon. Given the famous "Jerusalem syndrome," the madness of a few could transform a local conflict even further into a religious war with incalculable consequences.

International opposition to Zionism reached a new climax in June 1975 with Resolution 3379 in the United Nations which equated Zionism with racism and thus put it beyond the pale. This resolution was revoked after a decade but the attitude underlying it did not change as shown at the NGO world conference in Durban, South Africa in 2001 in which Zionism figured on the top of the agenda of the struggle for human rights. The issue at stake was of course not racialism but the existence of the Zionist entity (as the Arabs continue to call the state of Israel). There were more than twenty Arab and more than fifty Muslim states, rich in natural resources such as oil, a bigger market, more populous and generally speaking far more important in world affairs than Israel. The fact that Israel through its policy of occupation and settlement had given up the moral high ground did not help either. And thus "Zionism" became the Weltfeind (world enemy) number one, such as "Jewish Bolshevism" had been for Hitler, not only for the far left and the extreme right but also for some well meaning liberals and conservatives.

If anti-Semitism had gone out of fashion after World War II there still was a good deal of anti Jewish feeling and thus Zionism became a catch all concept—it was used against political enemies irrespective of their political, ethnic or religious origin—for some Lech Wałesa of Poland became a Zionist, for others Lenin, for others yet even the Afghan mujaheddin became Zionist agents. It was a grotesque spectacle and there was the temptation, especially inside Israel to put all the blame on the hostile outside world which "had always been against us." But this was not the whole truth, it omitted from view the mistakes committed, the lack of farsightedness, the failure to accept the fact that Israel was not a superpower but a small country and had to act accordingly to survive and if possible to prosper in a world which admittedly was not too friendly. The Jewish genius has manifested itself over the centuries in many fields, but wisdom in politics has not been among them, inevitable perhaps in a people without the experience and the responsibility of statehood, but vitally needed when Israel and the world at large faced a new period of unprecedented dangers.

The Terrible Secret

The research on this book was done in the late 1970s and it was published in 1980. It appeared in French (*Le terrifiant secret*) and other languages the year after. It dealt with the question of how the news about the murder of European Jewry had become known outside the places where the killing had been perpetrated even though the Nazis had made an attempt to keep it secret. It also dealt with the reaction of secret services, governments, international institutions and people in general who received this information—did they accept and believe it, did they fully understand what they were reading and hearing, were there attempts to suppress it?

It was clear to me that the issue was not of mere academic importance, because the reaction, be it inside Germany, in the allied and neutral countries and, of course, among the Jews, depended very much on the measure of knowledge available at the time. How many Germans knew about the murder, would Allied governments take measures to alert world public opinion and threaten the Nazis, would Jews in occupied Europe offer resistance or try to escape, if possible—these and many other issues were, of course, closely connected with the measure of knowledge available.

In the 1970s, not all the details were known that we know today. Even now there are major lacunae in our knowledge. I shall list further on some of the more important additions to our knowledge which were made in the last three decades. What we do not know even now refers above all to the former Soviet Union. The Soviet leadership must have known about events in the occupied territories from the GRU (military intelligence) and the NKVD (later the KGB). True, the facts about the murder did not have the highest priority in the agenda of Soviet Intelligence—but they still must have heard from a thousand informants. There has been no access to these Russian sources.

We do not know what information had been transmitted to the Vatican and when, and I am not at all sure whether in the depths of the archives of various governments and secret services or even in private hands some

Preface to Walter Laqueur, *The Terrible Secret*, New French Edition (Gallimard, 2010)

interesting information may not come to light in future. Whether it will greatly affect the general picture I doubt.

When I wrote this book most of the literature on the holocaust had not yet been published, most of the research institutes and specialized journals did not yet exist, let alone the detailed and very useful documentary movies. Researching and writing in the 1970s had however certain advantages. Some of the leading individuals figuring in this book were still alive. Dr. Gerhard Riegner for instance, of the World Jewish Congress, the young German Jewish lawyer then in Geneva, the author of the famous report in summer of 1942, probably the most important single source of information at the time, Jan Karski, a colleague of mine at the university in Washington—(his crucial role during the war had been all but forgotten and little did we think that he would figure one day in a novel), members of the Polish government in exile and their representatives inside occupied Poland, key persons in American and British intelligence, especially those working at Bletchley Park where the British decoded internal German wireless communications. A few of these witnesses refused to talk to me because they had once signed an undertaking never to reveal details about their wartime work—one of them was Walter Eitan, later head of the Israeli foreign ministry and still later ambassador to France. This both annoyed and amused me, for in the meantime some of Eitan's former bosses had published their recollections rightly feeling that whatever they knew was now of historical interest only. The German industrialist Eduard Schulte (the "man who broke the silence") and on whose evidence the Riegner report was mainly based was no longer alive, but I located his brother and his son, a German officer (who, it emerged, had been a classmate of mine at school) and this helped a great deal. (Schulte also figures in a recent novel.) I could talk at the time to many Jews, some of whom had been in leading positions in their communities during the war, others had lived underground in Germany and the Nazi occupied countries—what had they known and when? And how had they reacted?

In retrospect it seems to me that these direct contacts and conversations were invaluable. Hardly any of these witnesses is still alive and today's historians have to rely entirely on written evidence. I have no illusions inasmuch as the reliability of human memory is concerned. I came across well meaning people who had persuaded themselves many years later that they had been the first to alert the world about the holocaust; on closer enquiry it soon appeared that they had indeed reported some local outrages or, at best, events in one specific area, but that their information had not reached anyone in a position widely to disseminate it. But to have to rely entirely on archival sources involves even greater handicaps, quite apart from the fact that much of the source material seems to have been destroyed. The more sensitive a report and the more potentially incriminating, the greater the chances that it will be shredded or burned sooner or later.

I was not the first to ask questions about the spread of the information on the mass murder but no one before had tried to present a general picture. As such, my work was welcomed by serious students of this horrible chapter in the annals of mankind. It inspired others to follow up my work by focusing on specific countries and periods. Even some Holocaust deniers found it of limited use. For, as they argued, if all the facts about the mass murder had not become immediately known, did it not prove that it had never taken place?

Not everyone liked the conclusions of my work. The International Red Cross, for instance, or the Swedish government commissioned historians who were given much wider access to archives than I had, to present their own version. What emerged from these reports was, that the policy of the Red Cross and the Swedish government (and many other countries and institutions) in 1944 was quite different from what it had been two years earlier. Not a great surprise this—for in 1944 it was quite obvious that Germany had lost the war whereas in 1942 this was not clear at all.

My work had not been that of a prosecutor in court but a historian. My main concern was to understand: I did not blame the Jews in the occupied countries for not offering more resistance or for not trying to escape. I knew only too well the next to insurmountable difficulties facing a small, isolated minority consisting mainly of elderly people, women and the very young—if millions of captive Soviet soldiers perished without notable resistance, how to expect it from a defenseless group like the Jews?

I was quite aware of the fact that the Red Cross or the Swedish government felt endangered and under Nazi pressure in 1942. Swiss journalists, for instance, were threatened by Goebbels with deportation to Siberia. But the Nazis never reached Siberia, nor did the Swiss journalists. These considerations, to be sure, did not apply to the American and British governments and their inactivity well beyond the years 1941/2 when little could be done to stop the mass murder because the Nazi armies were still going strong. But in 1943/4 the railway lines leading to Auschwitz could have been bombed and even some of the death factories—and they were not. Reasons have been adduced why such operations would not have been very effective, but the reasons are not persuasive. It would have been possible to repeat these attacks—but they had no priority at all. Nor were the facts about the holocaust given sufficient publicity. For the Allied governments the fate of the Jews was a bothersome and not very important footnote to the war effort.

There was, to give but one example, the case of the Jews of the German occupied islands of Rhodes and Kos in the eastern Mediterranean. One would imagine that by July1944, when the whole world knew about the mass murder, these Jews could have been easily saved—the distance from these islands to Turkey was one kilometer or two, the mainland could be reached by rowing boat or a reasonable competent swimmer. The distance to Auschwitz was more than a thousand kilometers. And yet, the transport of 1,600 persons to Auschwitz by ship and rail proceeded without hindrance. A small British gunboat from Cyprus firing a few shots could have stopped this ghastly convoy, but nothing was done. It took the Jews from Rhodes three weeks to reach Auschwitz and they were about the last to be killed in the gas chambers.

The *Terrible Secret* provided a general survey about how the news of the holocaust reached various groups of people—and how they reacted. Since then there have been more specialized works broadening our knowledge and understanding. I should mention at least a few studies such as the books by Richard Breitman, David Bankier and Peter Longerich on Germany, by David Engel on the Polish government in exile, by Dan Michman on the Netherlands and Belgium, Jozef Lewandowski on Sweden, Dina Porat, Chawa Eshkoli, Dalia Ofer, Tuvia Friling and Yehiam Weitz on Palestine, Henry Feingold on the United States, Laurel Leff on the *New York Times* and the holocaust, Barbara Rogers on British intelligence, Michael Neufeld and Michael Berenbaum on the allied decision not to bomb Auschwitz. There have been several studies on Switzerland in wartime but I am not aware of any yet dealing with Vichy and occupied France—how the information about the fate of Jews who had been deported from Drancy and other such places reached the authorities and individuals in France—nor do I believe has the extent of knowledge among the Free French in London has been investigated.

The essential conclusions are the same as they were thirty years ago. Many issues concerning the Shoah continue to be discussed and disputed by some to this day, but the terrible secret is not among them. It is clear that the murder of millions of people could not be kept secret, too many people were involved in the execution of the crime, too many were aware that the Jews had disappeared never to return. True, the knowledge of most of these was limited to events in a specific place, very few except the statisticians of the SS had a general picture and knew the total figure of those that had been liquidated. Few knew about the technical details, how exactly those deported had been killed. But no great intellectual faculties were needed to put two and two together, if there had been mass shootings in one place, it stood to reason that the same had happened elsewhere—especially since Hitler in a famous speech before the war had predicted what would be the fate of the Jews.

Why was there nevertheless resistance among many Jews to understand what the Nazis had in store for them? I am dealing with this in the present book, these are frequent, indeed common psychological mechanisms of rejection and suppression facing people in mortal danger. Why did the neutrals and international organizations such as the Red Cross keep silent in 1942/3? Because they were afraid. Why did the Allies not do more to save Jews or at least to broadcast the facts about the holocaust? Because the Jews had no high priority on their agenda. It is true that little, perhaps nothing could have been done to save the millions killed in 1942. But of those murdered thereafter when the Third Reich was on the defensive, many thousands, perhaps tens of thousands, could have been saved.

Historians are notoriously reluctant to talk about lessons of history, because they know that each historical situation is essentially sui generis. But if history does not offer ready made advice what to do, it gives sometimes advice how not to behave. It used to be said at the end of World War II that the pessimists among the Jews (who hid, escaped or even offered resistance) had a far better chance to survive than the optimists. The same, *grosso modo*, could still be true today as mankind faces new dangers such as the weapons of mass destruction.

Bombing Auschwitz?

Military historians, more perhaps than others, have frequently chosen as their motto Leopold von Ranke's most famous dictum, that it is the task of the historian to find how it essentially was (*wie es eigentlich gewesen*). But as often as not, this has given rise to misunderstandings, for Ranke certainly did not mean that historians can be no more than chronologists, accounting on the basis of their sources what happened and when. They must be equally interested in the "how," and this leads them inevitably into questions about why a certain situation arose, why a certain decision was taken. In other words, they have to engage all along in a certain amount of counterfactual history. They have to ask whether alternatives existed, and what would have been the likely outcome if these alternatives had been adopted by the decision makers. True, they must also take into account the uncertainties, the "fog of war," and the benefits of hindsight. But in the final analysis, their judgment must be based not only on what happened but also on what might have happened. But for this, history becomes a chain of inevitabilities with one thing inexorably leading to another, and everything happens because it is predestined, as in a Greek tragedy or the *Song of the Nibelungen*.

To choose at random two examples: Various courses of action were open to Western governments at the time of the Great Depression, but to gain a fuller understanding of the alternatives open to them, one ought to go back well beyond Black Friday in 1929 by which time the disaster had already occurred. In a similar way, a consideration of the alternatives open to Britain and France at the time of the Munich crisis cannot possibly begin with Chamberlain's first meeting with Hitler in Bad Godesberg; it has to go back a year or two or perhaps even three, considering the state of affairs in France and Britain in the thirties and the policy of appeasement.

How far should one go back to discuss the question of whether Auschwitz should and could have been bombed in 1944? And is it legitimate (and even if it is legitimate, is it helpful) to discuss the bombing of Auschwitz in isolation from other actions that could have been taken to slow down the massacre of European Jewry? "Bombing Auschwitz," as I see it, does not pertain only to the question of the destruction of the gas chambers; it also concerns the destruction of the railway lines leading to Auschwitz, and this, by necessity, leads also to the question of bombing targets in the countries where the deportations originated.

It could be argued that only in the case of Auschwitz was the issue of bombing raised on the diplomatic level. But it was not only in Auschwitz that Jews were killed, and there were ways and means other than bombing to slow down the deportations that could have been tried. In the case of Auschwitz, there is fuller documentation concerning possibilities of rescue, but should historians be guided in their overall perspective only by the availability of archival material?

Thus, seen in a wider perspective, would it not be more helpful to regard the Auschwitz discussion as *pars pro toto,* in the wider framework of possible military and diplomatic efforts to stop or slow down the massacre, or at the very least to gain time? Analyzing the specific circumstances of the Auschwitz debate is still of interest, but so is the analysis of the number of bombers available at the time, the distances to be covered, intelligence available, probable weather conditions, accuracy of bombing, and so on. But it is less certain whether such an investigation should start on a certain day in May or June of 1944 when, as some historians have told us, it first became technically feasible to bomb Auschwitz in view of the Allied advance in Italy. The question of technical feasibility seems controversial to this day, but even if it were crystal clear, it is still a minor issue. For it leaves open the wider question of whether it might have become feasible earlier, if higher priority had been given to saving Jewish lives.

Against this, it might be argued that it is unrealistic to pose the question in these terms simply because no higher priority was given. But the question confronting us is not whether bombing Auschwitz was likely in the given circumstances, but whether it was at all possible. It is my contention that this argument cannot be accepted without some further investigation. How much political pressure would have been needed, and how extensive a diversion of resources from the general war effort?

Some historians argue that only in June 1944 was sufficient information available and only then could the Allied air forces based in Foggia in Italy reach targets in Eastern Europe. This argument leaves out of sight that Kiev had been in Russian hands since November 1943, that Chernovtsi (Czernowitz) had been reoccupied by the troops of the First Ukrainian Front by mid-March, and that Ternopol had been reoccupied by 14 April 1944. A look at the map shows that the distance from Auschwitz to Ternopol and Chernovtsi is less than three hundred miles, not as much as the distance from London to Hamburg or Cologne, which were bombed with devastating effect well before the summer of 1944. Auschwitz could have been bombed from these bases. But would the Soviets not have opposed this? They were less than enthusiastic, but they had accepted "shuttle bombing" on a few occasions. However, considering the strong position in which the western Allies were at the time vis-à-vis Moscow (the Lend-Lease Act was then in full swing), there is no doubt whatsoever that Stalin would have relented when faced with a determined Western demand.

But for London and Washington, these targets in Eastern Europe were of no particular importance, and following some routine requests and representations, they desisted. Perhaps they were afraid of putting additional strain on the alliance with the Soviet Union. But it can be said with certainty that the alliance would not have broken up if Roosevelt and Churchill had been more insistent and Stalin had accepted (probably for a price) the bombing of Auschwitz and the railways leading to it.

The story of the shuttle bombing reflects the general dilemma in a nutshell. It all depended on how much priority was given to a certain project. If it was thought to be of little or no importance (like the bombing of Auschwitz), even a small investment seemed too risky and unwarranted. If, on the other hand, it was deemed essential, no expense was spared, and the technical difficulties were overcome in no time.

Every military operation involves some risk. If the Germans had used poison gas on D-Day (a scenario for which the Allies were unprepared), the invasion of the continent might have ended in disaster. It would not have changed the outcome of the war, but the first nuclear bombs might have been used against Cologne and Berlin. Military leaders usually adduce technical reasons when asked to undertake missions that are not to their liking. If the decision had been left to the military, it is doubtful that the nuclear bomb would ever have been built; the Manhattan Project, after all, cost two billion dollars in 1945 (and the nuclear arms race from 1940 to 1995 cost four trillion). Could one not have produced a lot of hardware instead? There are difficulties and risks in war, as in peace. But there were few technical difficulties that could not be solved by a power that during the war produced 296,400 aircraft, 86,330 tanks, and 6,500 naval vessels.

Other arguments seem to me equally unconvincing, such as the alleged lack of knowledge about Auschwitz among the Allies. When I wrote about this subject in *The Terrible Secret,* I took a conservative line; as subsequent discoveries in the archives have shown, I erred on the side of excessive caution. The Allies did not need the Vrba-Wetzler report to learn about Auschwitz. If Professor Victor Klemperer, totally isolated in his *Judenhaus* in Dresden, without access to either radio or newspapers or useful contacts, had heard about Auschwitz in 1942, it stands to reason that the Allied intelligence services had also heard about it. But again, it was not a matter of crucial importance how many Jews were killed and where, and for this reason the people in intelligence no longer passed on these items to their masters. Unfortunately, it appears in retrospect that the question of sufficient information was not really relevant. Even if the most detailed facts about Auschwitz had been available in 1942 or 1943, even if the most accurate maps had been published in American and British newspapers, it would have made no difference as far as the strategic planners were concerned.

But what about the destruction of railway lines, bridges, and tunnels? Is it not true that such damage can be easily repaired? It is correct, by and large, with regard to railway lines, but it is much less true with regard to bridges and tunnels. The arguments against bombing rail lines also do not take into account that the whole purpose of a bomb attack would have been to slow down the deportation of Jews. And, as far as the deportation of Jews from Hungary is concerned, such bombing did succeed to a certain extent; thus, if the bombing had been more intensive, it would have had an even greater effect. It was certainly not beyond human ingenuity and the resources available to pick the right targets and to cause more delays.

It was a race against time; the millions of Jews who had been killed in 1941–43 could not be brought back to life. But there was a chance to save many of those who remained. What were the technical difficulties that could have delayed or prevented the deportation of the Jews of Rhodes and Kos—one of the most tragic and bizarre incidents in that summer of 1944? These two islands in the eastern Mediterranean are located a few miles off the shore of neutral Turkey, which can be seen with the naked eye and reached with a rowboat or, in the case of Kos, even by a good swimmer. There was a small, forgotten German garrison on the island, and following instructions, the commanding officer published an order that all Jews had to assemble within three days for deportation.

There was no secret at all about the operation, but no warnings were given over the Allied radio. As the deportation took place on 23 July 1944, Rome was in Allied hands, the Allied armies were in France, Germany was in disarray following the attempted assassination of Hitler, and the Allied bombing raids were in full swing. The Allies had full air and naval control in the eastern Mediterranean, and British intelligence knew all there was to know on the islands. Allied aircraft in Cyprus (less than two hundred miles away) and in Egypt were underemployed and could have taken off at a moment's notice. But neither sophisticated aircraft nor precision bombing would have been needed to intercept and divert the convoy of eighteen hundred Jews on three slow oil barges making their way, at a snail's pace, to Athens (it took them almost ten days). A motorboat or two, with twenty or thirty Allied soldiers equipped with a Bren gun or two, would have been sufficient to intercept the barges that, for all we know, did not even have a military convoy. There might not have been a fight, and if the British did not want to be burdened by yet another group of Jews, Turkey was gravitating toward the Allies by that time and would have given them temporary abode. (In fact, the only individual to do something to save Jews was the Turkish consul in Rhodes, who extended protection to a few dozen.)

It took this miserable convoy twenty-four days to make its way over the Mediterranean, through Greece and other Balkan countries and Hungary to Auschwitz, where it arrived on 20 August. Most of the new arrivals were killed within a day. Nor was it the only such case; on 31 July 1944, a transport of Jewish children left Paris and made its way slowly through war-torn Germany toward Auschwitz.

If the bombing of Auschwitz, the railways, the tunnels, and the bridges would have meant the diversion of some aircraft and bombs, how could it have been justified in strategic-military terms? This question takes us closer to the real dilemma: the Jews had no political influence at the time, much less than the Polish or Czechoslovak governments-in-exile. The official line was that everything had to be subordinated to defeating Hitler, and once this aim had been achieved, the Jews (or whatever remained of them) would be saved too.

There is no certainty that even from a purely military point of view such a distraction in Eastern Europe would have been a total waste. It is frequently argued that Allied bombing attacks suffered heavy losses against industrial and similar targets in west and north Germany precisely because German fighters and antiaircraft artillery were concentrated there. By increasing their air attacks in Eastern Europe, the Allies would have compelled the Germans to withdraw some of these forces and disperse them, which would have made Allied attacks in the West less risky.

The question of bombing Auschwitz boils down not to issues such as types of aircraft, accuracy of bombing, and the distance from Foggia. Stuart Erdheim shows convincingly, I believe, that bombing would have been feasible, even though no one can say with any confidence how many inmates would have been saved. The decisive question is, of course, what could have been achieved if greater priority had been given by everyone concerned to rescuing Jewish lives? World War II was not fought in order to save Jews from Hitler, even though the Nazis in their propaganda often suggested this and even though Allied officials were unduly apprehensive of the potential of anti-Semitic propaganda in their own camp. But what if, for argument's sake, one percent of the Allied war effort in 1944 had been devoted to this end? Or, to be more realistic, one-half of one percent? The war effort in 1944 accounted for about forty percent of the American GNP, rather more in Britain, and it is easy to translate this into dollars, pounds sterling, sorties flown by bomber aircraft, and the number of Allied broadcasts devoted to the massacres, naming names, warning, and threatening.

Deflecting one-half of one percent would not have fatally undermined the Allied war effort, but it would have made, in all probability, a difference with regard to the chances of saving people from certain death. We know with what minute sums the emissaries who engaged in rescue work in Switzerland and Turkey had to operate. What if millions had been at their disposal—say the budgets now allocated to the memory of the victims of the Shoah (to which one could add the production costs of the books now published arguing that nothing could have been done). Would more money and more bombing and more publicity have made no difference at all?

It is unlikely that the SS and Gestapo could have been bribed in 1942, but it is by no means impossible that they would have been more amenable in 1944. Hungarian and Rumanian officials almost certainly would have shown interest. Those engaged in rescue work firmly believed that more lives could have been saved if they had had at their disposal the sums that began to arrive from Jewish and non-Jewish sources after the war had ended. Perhaps they were overly optimistic, but to claim that there was no chance whatsoever in 1944 is unbelievable.

Most of the Jews of Poland, the Baltic countries, the Ukraine, and White Russia (to repeat once again) were dead by early 1944, but the inmates of the Lodz ghetto had not yet been deported to Auschwitz, Hungarian Jewry still survived, and so did tens of thousands of Jews in Slovakia and other parts of Europe, from France to Terezin (Theresienstadt) to the island of Kos.

Those claiming that nothing more could have been done to rescue Jews underrate the profound change that had taken place in Nazi-occupied Europe as the result of the German military setbacks and the retreat in the East. They also underrate the fall of Mussolini and the general dislocation caused by the bombing campaign in Germany. The fanatics still believed in the *Endsieg* (final victory), but a majority of people in Germany seemed to have doubted it. A great majority of people among Germany's satellites were convinced that the war was lost. Inside Germany, the Gestapo was losing control because so many offices issuing identification papers had been destroyed and because Germany was flooded by millions of foreign workers. Hiding and even escaping became far easier than before. If even Nazi officials inside Germany could be bribed to let Jews escape to Switzerland, the Nazis' helpers in countries such as Slovakia, Hungary, and elsewhere could have been made to work a little slower, to delay the deportations, to show less enthusiasm.

Once the deported Jews had reached Auschwitz, rescue attempts became exceedingly difficult. But what could have been done to prevent the transports from reaching Auschwitz? It is wrong to claim that such thoughts can only arise with the benefit of hindsight. On 21 December 1942, a four-page article entitled "The Massacre of the Jews" written by Varian Fry was published in the *New Republic.* It shows how much was known even outside government and the intelligence services by those who wanted to know. The article had been written in all probability in October 1942, more than a year and a half before the events discussed. It gave a fairly accurate description of the extermination centers, even though it did not mention names, and an equally accurate estimate of the number of people already killed. Toward the end of his account, Fry suggested a number of steps that should be taken to prevent total annihilation. Above all, President Roosevelt and Prime Minister Churchill "could and should speak out against these monstrous events." Even if this would not influence Hitler, it might have an effect on some other Germans. There should be a joint declaration in the most solemn terms by the Allied governments of the retribution to come: "Tribunals should be set up now to amass the facts." Diplomatic warnings should be conveyed through neutral channels to the governments of Hungary, Rumania, and Bulgaria, which might save at least the 700,000 to 900,000 Jews still in their borders. Pius XII should threaten with excommunication all Catholics participating in these frightful crimes; the Protestant leaders should do the same. The news about the crimes should be broadcast day and night to every European country. Fry decried the fact that the Office of War Information had allegedly banned mention of the massacres. The fact that the crimes were committed not in Western Europe but in the East, showed that the Nazis feared the effect on the local population of the news of the crimes. Why play into their hands? Fry made several other suggestions and also proposed that asylum should be offered to those succeeding in escaping. He quoted a correspondent from Marseilles who had written him that little Switzerland, by accepting nine thousand refugees since July 1942, "had done more for the cause of humanity that than the great and wealthy United States with its loud declarations about the rights of the people and the defense of liberty notwithstanding."

There were no military suggestions in Fry's article: this would hardly have been apposite in an article in the open press, nor might it have been practical at the time. It is known what happened—neither Roosevelt nor Churchill, let alone the Pope or the bishops, spoke out loudly and clearly; there were no threats; no resolutions; and radio broadcasts were kept to a minimum. No funds were allocated for rescue missions, and no military operations were planned. Two years passed, and next to nothing was done. The fatalists may still claim that nothing could have been done. All we know is that it was not even tried.

No Ease in Zion: Herzl and Lohengrin

Zionism, the movement that led to the establishment of the state of Israel is now called by some of the worst enemy of the Jewish people, as if the Jews did not have enough enemies. In fact, Zionism has not had a good press for a considerable time and it is not difficult to understand why. It appeared too late on the historical scene, but it could not have appeared any earlier. For Palestine was in the hands of the Ottoman Empire which had no wish to give up any part of its territory. By the time Balfour made his famous declaration (November 1917) most Jews saw no reason to move to a far away, primitive country of which they knew little. Zion for most of them had become an abstraction.

There was a great deal of opposition to Zionism from the very beginning both from outside the Jewish community and from within. The very religious were against it because to move to the holy country (except to die and be buried there) was sacrilegious prior to the coming of Messiah. Marxists were against it because it was a reactionary movement, a relapse into narrow nationalism at a time when the whole world was surmounting such narrow egotism, moving towards (proletarian) internationalism. Whatever the differences between Stalinists and Trotskyites, on Zionism there was full agreement between them. Most liberal and conservative Jews felt themselves culturally and socially deeply rooted in the countries in which they lived and regarded Zionism as unnecessary and even harmful. True, Zion appeared in their prayers, but as in other religions there was less and less praying.

All over Europe and America Zionism was a small minority up to the 1930s when it suddenly appeared that European Jews faced a mortal danger which had not been foreseen by Zionism's critics. The Zionists had been more aware than the others of the coming danger, but there was no independent

Review of Jacqueline Rose, *The Question of Zion* (London: Princeton University Press, 2005), Idit Zertal, *Israel's Holocaust and the Politics of Nationhood* (London: Cambridge University Press, 2005), Norman Finkelstein, *Beyond Chutzpah: On the Misuse of Anti-Semitism and the Abuse of History* (London: Verso Books, 2005).

Jewish state and in the end Jewish Palestine could accept only a few hundred thousands not the millions which eventually perished. And so by 1948 when Israel came into being it was a very small entity, little more than half a million Jews were living there.

True, during the decades that followed their number grew substantially but it still remained a small country. To engage for a moment in counterfactual history—what if the Ottoman Empire had collapsed not in 1918 but after the Crimean War, or preferably after the Russian–Turkish war of 1827/8? What if European Jews had moved there at the time and what, with a birth rate like that of the Gaza strip, their number would now be fifty or sixty million or more? What if in that Greater Palestine extending from the Nile to the Euphrates, substantial oilfields would have been discovered? True, there still might have been a war with its neighbors—such wars were customary at the time—but eventually the refugees (if any) would have been integrated or resettled, for one does not trifle with a major, powerful country; it would be an honored member of the United Nations and Israel's bitter critics would write songs of praise in honor of this miraculous rebirth of an old people in a spirit of humanism and freedom, a shining example for all mankind.

These are of course fantasies; unfortunately many Israelis have failed to understand that on the international level there is not one law for all and that small countries especially if they have powerful enemies, cannot afford to behave as if they were great powers. Why should they be judged by standards others than the rest of the world, why should they be singled out for misdeeds that in the case of others were forgiven or ignored? Hundreds of thousands have been murdered in Rwanda, in Sudan and Algeria and other places but the protest and revulsion (let alone the calls for intervention) had been strictly limited and condemnation by the United Nations infrequent. The fact that others had committed greater crimes could not be an excuse but how to explain that only Israel became the butt of constant attack, of isolation, of constant threats of near total isolation? The brief answer is that small might be beautiful in other respects but not in international affairs.

The main accusation against Israel was that it had been born in sin, that violence had been involved, that injustice had been done to Palestinians. This was quite true, but it was also true that it is difficult to think of any country (except perhaps some Pacific island) that has come into being as the result of a civil contract without violence and bloodshed.

However, was it not true that the early Zionists from Herzl onwards had been oblivious of the fact that Palestine was not empty and that they had ignored the local inhabitants, being totally preoccupied with the fate of the Jews? True enough, but the critics usually pass in silence over the number of those involved at the time. The year that Herzl wrote his Jewish State (1896) the number of non-Jews living in Palestine was about 400,000–450,000 (including non-Muslims and non-Arabs) which was about one quarter the population of Vienna where Herzl made his home. In these conditions the early Zionists should perhaps be forgiven if they thought that the problem of the indigenous population was not insoluble.

But was the establishment of a Jewish (and Palestinian Arab) state really a necessity, would a bi national state not have been preferable? Perhaps so, even though experience elsewhere from India and Sri Lanka to Cyprus and Yugoslavia has not been encouraging. There was among the Zionists a group consisting of some of the best minds and purest souls which tried hard and over many years to achieve such a solution. But it remained small and uninfluential because it could not find a partner among the Palestinians (and if they found one, he was likely to be killed within a few weeks or months). The Arabs saw no reason to give up full sovereignty and to give the Jews equal rights as far as running the country was concerned. If there was a Jewish problem in Europe, it was neither their fault nor their responsibility.

The absence of an agreement led inevitably to the UN partition resolution of 1948 providing for the establishment of a Jewish and an Arab state in Palestine. It was based on concessions on the part of both sides. The Zionists had to forgo Jerusalem, not only the Old City but also the Jewish part which was to become a *corpus separandum*. The Jews accepted it, but the Arabs did not, they went to war and they lost.

Seen in retrospect the years between 1948 and 1967 were relatively quiet, despite the Suez war and occasional attacks from across the border. True, the Arabs states did not accept the existence of a Jewish state and there was talk about throwing the Jews into the sea. But by and large uneasy coexistence prevailed.

This state of affairs could have lasted for a long time but Nasser, for reasons not entirely clear to this day asked the withdrawal of UN troops from Sinai and imposed an embargo on Israeli ships in the Red Sea which led to the Six Day War and the great Israeli victory. But the great victory (the occupation of Gaza, all of Jerusalem and West Bank) turned into a great calamity as some foresaw even at the time. Initially there had been no desire on the Israeli side to keep these territories indefinitely—it was expected that all or most of them except only Jerusalem would be returned within the framework of a peace treaty. But the heads of Arab governments in their wisdom decided not to negotiate let alone recognize Israel and the territories remained in Israeli hands. And thus the settlements were established and since the Palestinians resisted Israeli rule there was violence and counter-violence and the cycle of terrorism and repression came under way.

Israel should have gotten rid unilaterally if need be of the territories as quickly as possible to preserve the democratic character of the country. Instead, the longer the occupation lasted the more deeply ingrained among sections of the Israelis became the belief not to give up territories since the other side was not willing to make peace anyway. The events of 1967 must have been a commandment from heaven. Thus the great victory turned into a political defeat and the image of the ugly Israeli emerged, murderers of women and children guilty of unspeakable crimes, a nightmare of cruel oppression, worse than anything in living memory.

The situation created after 1967 cost Israel many sympathies and generated a hostile literature which often argued that not only the occupation policy was to blame but that Zionism was somehow blemished from the outset. One of the more interesting such recent works is Jacqueline Rose's *The Question of Zion.* The author is a professor of English literature at Queen Mary College with an interest in psychoanalysis. She has studied certain strands in modern Jewish intellectual history and reached some firm conclusions and even suggestions how to solve the conflict. Her conclusion is that messianism has been the bane of Zionism, coloring it (including secular Zionism) at every turn. Seen in this light Theodor Herzl, the founder of modern Zionism, was no more than a second Sabbetai Zvi, the seventeenth-century pseudo messiah who promised to lead the Jews back to Palestine (and ended up a convert to Islam).

Indeed, there were for centuries messianic hopes among Jews mainly in Eastern Europe even though they became weaker and weaker as time went by. It is not too difficult to find invocations of these hopes in the works of a variety of writers and even some public figures. But how important were these sentiments and hopes politically, that is to say in the real world rather than in the world of ideas? The brief answer is "very little." The early Zionists emphatically dissociated themselves from the old religious messianic variety, disavowing all mysticism and no longer identifying with messianism (the words are Max Nordau's, another founder of modern Zionism).

Professor Rose does not deny this but being a psychoanalyst she does not believe them and looks hard for subconscious messianic motives. This, to stress once again, is not too difficult for the revived secular Hebrew language especially of the early years of the twentieth century was replete with concepts such as "redemption" which the author believes were explosive and potentially catastrophic. But Professor Rose mistakes symbolism for reality, the Zionist movement contained a religious element from the very beginning—not the ultra orthodox who rejected it *tout court*—but the religious Zionists were relatively uninfluential, they were not messianic and above all, they were the most moderate politically, averse to all political adventures.

As for the "explosive language" which the author finds so meaningful, it had become even by the 1940s a butt of jokes ("Zionut"), not always in good taste for many of the young generation in Palestine/Israel, these were empty and pompous phrases used in speeches on festive occasions but not taken very seriously. The 2005 Israeli Dictionary of Slang by Rubik Rosenthal defines Zionism as "preaching moralism." In any case Zionism was not, as Professor

Rose writes, one of the "most potent collective movements of the twentieth century." There was no sudden messianic revival; it became of political importance only because of Hitler and the growing persecution of Jews in Europe. Zion was seen not as the fulfillment of messianic hopes but as a place where Jews could hope to escape at a time when virtually all other gates were closed.

It was not by accident that Zion (meaning the city of Jerusalem) attracted very few of the newcomers to Palestine, and later to Israel—and of the Zionist leaders no one settled there. For Jerusalem (Zion) was everything they resented in the diaspora. They wanted a new modern society and Zion, paradoxically, was not Zionist. Palestine to be sure, was not regarded as a mere temporary asylum for refugees such as Shanghai but a place where Jews could live freely—masters of their own destiny (to the extent that small peoples can ever be truly independent.)

While there are occasional references in this book to such issues as the water supply in contemporary Israel, it is essentially an essay in the history of ideas, or to be precise, some undercurrents at the exclusion of others. And for this reason, however emphatic her political opinions, the author seldom descends to the level of political realities. She thinks that Zionism should not have become a national(ist) movement aiming at the establishment of a state. But she does not discuss alternatives.

Martin Buber was an important religious thinker and being an opponent of statehood he is one of the heroes of this book. What should he have done in 1938? Should he have followed the personal advice of Mahatma Gandhi who told him and the rest of the Jews to stay in Germany and practice satyagraha (passive resistance)? He did not do so even though by moving to Jerusalem he may have contributed to the aggravation of the Jewish–Arab conflict. What was the alternative to statehood facing the Jews of Palestine in 1946/7—since the other side rejected a bi-national solution? Hannah Arendt, another heroine of this book, advised them to look closely (and to emulate) Soviet nationalities policy which she thought was a success story—in retrospect this does not appear such a wonderful idea either.

The author recalls time and again the warnings of the late Gershom Scholem, the great student of Jewish mysticism against infusing messianism into politics but side by side with such well made points there appear in this book strange asides such as the alleged impact of the *Lohengrin* performance in Paris in 1895 on Herzl and Hitler. According to her narrative, the very same performance of Wagner's opera which inspired Herzl to write the *Jewish State* inspired Hitler to write *Mein Kampf.* But Hitler never was in Paris except for a few hours in 1940. He would have been aged six or seven at the time. A student of Lacan (Professor Rose being one) should have remembered what the master wrote about the paranoiac element in all knowledge.

Instead of looking for the disastrous impact of messianism where it did not exist, it might have been more rewarding to analyze the collective Jerusalem syndrome of 1967 ("Temple Mount is in our hands") which had indeed very negative political consequences, turning a political and territorial dispute into a religious conflict. Messianism was involved but other explanations are also possible. The Jews of Palestine and Israel had been admonished for a long time to shed their Western traditions and mentality and to become integrated ideologically as well as politically and socially in the East. And so (partly as the result of the immigration of Jews from Eastern countries, partly as the result of a worldwide fundamentalist trend) Israel did become more Oriental in outlook and its reactions more like those of its neighbors. This did not cause great joy among those who had suggested de-Westernization earlier on but it is a development that could have been foreseen.

Ms. Rose's knowledge of recent Jewish and Israeli history is less than perfect—localities are misplaced, a well-known female literary critic undergoes a sex change, and her general asides are also sometimes doubtful; Herzl and Vaclav Havel are not (as the author believes) the only political figures who also wrote plays. From Beaumarchais to Jean Giraudoux one could think of a dozen in French literature alone. But these are minor details, the real weakness of this book is more basic: What could psychoanalysis contribute to resolving a political conflict? Freud and his main disciples steered clear of giving advice except in the most general way. Professor Rose plays the role of the analyst in the therapeutic encounter but she faces a problem which may well be insurmountable. The analyst should be detached (blind himself in Freud's words or in Bion's who also appears in this book). What if the analyst has a hopeless aversion against the patient which he (or she) cannot possibly overcome? Such a situation is said to occur not that rarely and it may be no one's fault. But would it not be preferable in such cases to refer the patient to a colleague less emotionally involved?

On the other hand, psychoanalysis might be of help shedding light on why some Jews write Zionist books and others anti Zionist. As for the latter, Jewish self-hatred is frequently invoked which is not always justified. The late Professor Y. Leibowitz of Jerusalem, an orthodox Jew and one of the sharpest critics of the new Israel was certainly anything but a self-hating Jew. But if anti-Zionism is the only known Jewish activity of an individual, the charge deserves to be further explored. Self-hatred is neither a rare nor a specific Jewish quality (Pascal's *Le moi est haissable*) and the issue deserves to be studied without undue emotion whether it regards Jansenists, Jews, lapsed Jews or others.

Ms. Idit Zertal, unlike the two other authors, is a native-born Israeli, she knows the language, literature, and history of modern Israel and can hardly be faulted on matters of detail and accuracy—except when her temperament gets the better of her judgment such as when she claims that the preparation of the Eichmann trial was Ben Gurion's "finest hour" (which is not meant as a compliment). Her book is dedicated to the memory of Hannah Arendt who also plays a central role in Professor Rose's book; it would be interesting to know why Hannah Arendt as a political commentator has so many more admirers among women than among men.

Ms. Zertal successfully deconstructs a number of myths in recent Israeli history beginning with the case of Josef Trumpeldor, a Jewish officer in the Tsarist army who was killed in the defense of Tel Hai in Galilee against Arab marauders in 1919. Trumpeldor's last words allegedly were that it was good to die for one's country, which entered the schoolbooks but it is not certain whether he really said it (and if he said it, whether it was in Russian or Hebrew) . . . She then proceeds to analyze the attitude of the Zionist leadership to the resistance fighters in Poland during World War II. As the author sees it Zionist leaders overemphasize the role of Zionist inspiration in triggering off anti-Nazi resistance in Poland, and they belittle the role of Communists and Bundist socialists. But if the Zionists were selective, so is Ms. Zertal who forgets to mention the role of the right-wing Zionist youth organizations which also played a certain role in the resistance.

All this is quite interesting but it is not entirely clear what the author intended to accomplish other than writing an essay in the history of ideas. There are such myths in the history of every nation, some ancient, some modern; there are few scientific certainties concerning the origins of nations but merely heroic sagas and tales, usually exaggerated, sometimes freely invented. Take Switzerland—it is not at all certain whether Wilhelm Tell ever lived (or Romulus and Remus) and the true story of Jeanne d'Arc or the *Chanson de Roland* was almost certainly different from what some schoolbooks relate.

This tradition of nationalist hero worship continued among the nations which gained independence only relatively recently; even a Czech patriot forged some ancient manuscripts. It can be found in America and Russia as well as Japan not to mention the Arab world with its martyrs and there is no reason to assume that Israel would have been an exception. It is fasinating to be reminded that a poem by Nathan Alterman in the nineteen fifties about the heroes of the Jewish resistance in Europe generated a storm. But it was a very little storm, it did not enter the collective memory of the national religious in Israel nor the ultra-orthodox, neither the Moroccan nor the Russian Jews. In brief, to put it inelegantly, it was a storm in a teacup and the young generation in Israel today will not have heard of many of the myths deconstructed with so much admirable gusto in this book.

With Mr. Finkelstein we move from the realm of academic post-modernism and post-colonialism of Lyotard and "hegemonistic Zionism" to something more earthy and very shrill in style and content. Finkelstein's book is a useful collection of anti-Zionist and anti-Israeli quotations. It is a polemic against a book by Harvard law professor Alan Dershowitz who wrote *The Case for Israel* a few years ago.

Its focus is rather narrow for it boils down not so much to issues of substance but to the question whether Dershowitz plagiarized (as Finkelstein argues) a book by Joan Peters entitled *Since Time Immemorial* (1984). Mrs. Peters, provoked apparently by Arab writings claiming that Jews had no historical connection with Palestine at all, argued in her book that the number of Palestinians prior to the twentieth century was quite small (especially in the coastal plain) and that Arab immigration was in fact larger than Jewish. There may well have been some truth in this but Mrs. Peters, neither historian nor professional demographer, used also some doubtful sources, a fact which was pointed out by Israeli historians soon after her book was first published. Her book would by now be forgotten but for the relentless efforts of Mr. Finkelstein to refute it, beginning with his doctoral dissertation more than twenty years ago. But his field of specialization is not historical demography either and being wholly dependent on secondary sources the exchanges that ensued were anything but dispassionate and shed little if any new light on an interesting issue. In brief, those familiar with Mr. Finkelstein's earlier work will find little that is new in this book; he has not become a believer in the Zionist cause and his arguments are the old ones.

The authors of these passionate attacks against Zionism seem to believe that it is still a potent ideological and political force. But is it really-or did the Zionist age in Jewish history come to an end many decades ago with the establishment of the state? The Russian immigrants who came were not Zionists in their overwhelming majority, nor were those from North Africa. The orthodox Jews are not Zionists and even the national religious visionaries of 1967, the radical settlers, are not Zionists in any meaningful sense. Their doctrine has as much to do with historical Zionism as Hugo Chavez and Carlos the Jackal with Karl Marx. Contemporary Jerusalem has a non- or anti-Zionist majority and its last mayor was not a Zionist either.

Zionism was a latecomer in the liberal-humanist tradition of 1848, of Mazzini, Kossuth, and Masaryk. It believed with Mazzini that without a country of their own the Jews were bound to remain the bastards of humanity. This kind of national movement was bound to be a disappointment; only political movements whose histories do not extend beyond the utopian phase retain their pristine virtue, all others cannot possibly live up to expectations.

The history since 1948 is that of the state of Israel. The ideology of this state in its post-Zionist phase (if it has an all embracing ideology in the first place) consists of a great many strands. The attacks against Zionism at this late stage are anachronistic (unless one uses Zionist as a code word, as some do, meaning something quite different). It is not particularly courageous as some of the writers of blurbs for these books tend to think; there are no Victoria Crosses to be gained for flogging a non-existent horse.

The Jewish Century?

To come across a daring, original work of history of great sweep based on great erudition in this age of ever-growing narrow specialization is not just a welcome event. It is almost a sensation. Professor Yuri Slezkine who teaches Russian history at Berkeley has reached the conclusion on the basis of his studies that the twentieth century is the Jewish Century; modernization is about everyone becoming Jewish. The Jews were the most creative entrepreneurs in the socioeconomic as well as the cultural field. Marxism was Jewish so was psychoanalysis and even nationalism; one could have added the theory of relativity and much of modern medicine but the author, wisely perhaps, refrains from mentioning it. For all one knows anti-Semitism too should be added to this list.

1. In the beginning the author shows how the Jews came to play this role; he moves easily from Greek mythology to the Hwach'ok chaein in medieval Korea, from Proust to the Burakumin and the Kooroko of Wasulu (a tribe in Africa) as well as the Kanjar in Pakistan, he quotes in Chinese, Malay, Tuareg, various Gypsy and Ladino dialects, a mind boggling performance of which Toynbee and Spengler might have been envious. He proves that traveling ethnic groups ("Mercurians") have been doing consistently better adjusting to modern times than peasants and other primary producers (whom he calls Apollonians). He also shows that the Chinese and Indian diaspora but also Syrians and Lebanese, Parsi and Armenians have been doing very well outside their homeland.

   To call Mr. Slezkine a widely read man would be an understatement; this is an awe inspiring, virtuoso performance. But what about his central arguments? They remind one vaguely of two German sociologists of a hundred years ago—Georg Simmel (who wrote about the role of the Jew as a stranger) and Werner Sombart; Sombart well before World War I argued that America owes entirely what it is to the Jews—its American nature. Slezkine goes much further asserting the Judaization of Europe ("the painful transformation of Europeans into Jews") and the whole world.

Review of Yuri Slezkine, *The Jewish Century* (Princeton, NJ: Princeton University Press, 2004)

All this information about the Hwachok and the Burakumin and other nomadic tribes is fascinating but how reliable a guide is Mr. Slezkine for the history of the Jews? In the very first sentence he claims that "there was nothing particularly unusual about the social and economic position of the Jews in medieval and early modern Europe." But there was a slight difference, for they lived in a ghetto whereas the others did not. There is a problem with the author's generalizations from the very beginning; he rightly notes in considerable detail that some Jewish entrepreneurs did very well during the last decades of Tsarist Russia. But it is equally true that the great majority in Poland and Russia lived in dire poverty and that this was one of the main reason for their emigration.

He deals rather briefly with the social and cultural rise of the Jews in Germany, Austria-Hungary as well as France and it is of course true that once the walls of the ghetto came down there was a tremendous release of creative energy. Jews streamed into trade and banking, and the professions and they took a notable part in the cultural life of these countries.

But there never was a Jewish century and it is misleading even as a metaphor, there was at most a decade or two of Jewish cultural prominence in Europe (and this is what the book is mainly about) prior to World War II; politically, socially and economically there was not even this. It is difficult to think of a predominant Jewish cultural influence in postwar Britain or Germany or Italy or indeed any other European country in the second half of the twentieth century.

The major part of the book deals with the role of the Jews in the Russian revolutionary movement and the Soviet Union. Mr. Slezkine interprets "Jew" in a somewhat sweeping way, including a few non-Jews, more than a few half Jews, converted Jews, anti-Jewish Jews and husbands of Jewish women. However, by and large he is right, their part was very big, but this has been known for a long time and when the Nazis launched their massive campaign about Judeo-Bolshevism and Stalin being a puppet of the Jewish puppet masters, a new class had already emerged and the Jews had been squeezed out and quite often disappeared altogether—into the Gulag or a better world. Jewish prominence in Soviet cultural life lasted perhaps a decade longer or two, but there was no Jewish century, only perhaps a Jewish moment in Russian history. True again, after the breakdown of the Soviet Union some non-Jewish Jews, the so called oligarchs established big conglomerates; a few years have passed and Messrs Berezovski and Guzovski are in exile, Mr. Khodorkovski is in prison and the prospects of Mr. Abramovitch, the owner of Chelsea football club in London, are not that rosy.

This then is a strange book with astute observations on a variety of topics such as Russian nineteenth- and twentieth-century history, Joyce's Leopold

Bloom, the family names of the early Jewish settlers in Palestine or the Frankfurt school of "critical theory." But it is also replete with far fetched, abstruse analogies and generalizations—often side by side in the same paragraph. The history of the rise of the Jews in the Western world in the last two centuries remains to be written but it will have to include the misfortunes and disasters and it will be altogether a more modest and less sensational story.

Abuse of History

Ms. Margaret Macmillan is a Canadian-British historian, author of an excellent and much-praised study of the Versailles peace treaty of 1919, warden of an Oxford college. Her recent book *Dangerous Games: Tthe Uses and Abuses of History* is timely; there has been an inflation of unhelpful and downright misleading historical analogies and comparison. Gestapo and Gulag are too often adduced when they do not belong and even "appeasement" may not always be fatal. Kipling's Danegeld

If once you have paid him Danegeld
You never get rid of the Dane.

But the Dane has not been seen for a long time.

The *New York Times* reviewer called her book a "provocative indictment of the myriad ways in which history is too often distorted" and the *Washington Post* reviewer wrote that the book should be "read by anyone concerned with making the public dialogue as open and honest as possible."

In brief, a praiseworthy, noble enterprise. But it has its pitfalls as we shall see in a moment, for what individuals regard as the abuses of history could be a little subjective. It is a small book and the author cannot possibly cover all the major distortions committed; there is a heavy emphasis on writers such as Norman Podhoretz and David Frum, on Shabtai Tevet and Ilan Pappe, on Golda Meir, David Ben Gurion, Ariel Sharon, Elazar ben Yair and Masada, Ben Zion Dinur and Benny Morris, on the illegal occupation by Israel of Palestinian territories, on Dan Bar-On and the misdeeds of Israeli archeology. This heavy preoccupation by some British academics with a small country in the Middle East has become quite common in recent years. A visitor from outer space might well reach the conclusion that such intense focusing must be an indication for an impending mass conversion to Judaism and perhaps even the decision of many of these British academics to emigrate to Israel, but this would probably be the wrong explanation.

If not—what could be the reasons? If Ms. Macmillan argues that Israel's holding on to the territories occupied in 1967 is illegal she could be right.

Review of Margaret Macmillan, *Dangerous Games: The Uses and Abuses of History* (New York: Modern Library, 2008)

But such claims open a Pandora's box: There are no Neanderthal men and *homo heidelbergensis* left, there have been constant migrations all over the world since time immemorial, countries have been occupied and reoccupied, populations shifted. In what country has there been no change in the composition of the population except perhaps some South Sea islands? What is legality in these conditions?

Ms. Macmillan is a native of Toronto, in the state of Ontario in Canada; but the very names Toronto, Ontario and Canada are not, I believe, Anglo-Saxon or Scottish but Huron or Iroquois, pointing to the fact that they were founded by other nations. Subsequently, foreigners settled there including the parents or grandparents of Ms. Macmillan and the original residents may regard them as colonialists (as I believe the remnants of the Six or Seven Nations still do). It could be argued that if such population movements happened two hundred or three hundred years ago they are by now legal but if they happened only one hundred years ago and if the original settlers were not squeezed out or killed they are illegal. I do not know the answer, it is a problem that ought to be left to moral philosophers.

But there are other fascinating questions. I happen not to agree with most of the views of Messrs. Podhoretz and Frum, but why focus on them? Does she consider them the leading politicians or historians of our time or the worst abusers of history? Ms. Macmillan's expertise is European diplomatic history in the first half of the twentieth century and specifically the aftermath of World War I. One of the leading figures in that period was David Lloyd George, former prime minister of Great Britain—and, incidentally, the great grandfather of the author. He also engaged in historical analogies which are of considerable interest.

Lloyd George visited Adolf Hitler in Berchtesgaden in September 1936. What were his impressions as described in a longish article in the *Daily Express*? What he reported was not unexpected; in an earlier speech (September 1933) he had said that if Hitler were overthrown Communism would come to Germany—and there were more such utterances. Hitler, he wrote, has achieved a marvelous transformation in the spirit of the people, in their attitude towards each other. His movement has made a new Germany. The country had been broken, dejected and bowed down with a sense of apprehension. It is now full of hope and confidence and a renewed sense of determination to lead its own life. There is for the first time since the war a general sense of security. The people are more cheerful. There is greater sense of general gaiety of spirit throughout the land. It is a happier Germany—Lloyd George saw it everywhere. One man had accomplished it, a magnetic, dynamic personality with a single-minded purpose, a resolute will and a dauntless heart. As to his popularity especially among the youth of Germany there can be no manner of doubt. The old trust him, the young idolize him. It is not the admiration accorded to a popular leader. It is a worship of a national hero who has saved his country. He is immune of criticism as a king in a monarchy. He is something more: "He is the George Washington of Germany."

And so on: The idea of Germany intimidating Europe with a threat that its irresistible army will march across frontiers form no part of the new vision. They have no longer the desire to invade any other land. The establishment of German hegemony in Europe which was the aim and dream of the old pre-war militarism is not even on the horizon of Nazism.

Adolf Hitler, the miracle maker, the George Washington of the new Germany—an interesting topic for reflections on the uses and abuses of history. It is a truly monumental statement which, I believe, dwarfs anything uttered by Messrs. David Frum and Norman Podhoretz; it might be of greater personal interest to Professor Macmillan than all the writings of Benzion Dinur.

Part 2

Whither Russia

Russia: The Years to Come

The year 2010 witnessed considerable changes in U.S.–Russian relations, or at least the desire and promise for change—the "reset" of the Obama administration and the Russian comments about "seismic change" following the unofficial publication of an official document in May of that year. The prospects for Russian–American relations cannot be discussed in isolation from wider questions: In what direction is Russia moving? What will Russia be like in ten or twenty years from now? Russian commentators maintain that Russian policy vis-à-vis the United States has always been reactive. I believe that American policy vis-à-vis Russia has been even more reactive.

The belief in a manifest destiny is part of Russian history, the idea of Moscow as a "Third Rome," the mission of world revolution (or the building of socialism in one country), and the contemporary doctrines of a "Russian Idea" and neo-Eurasianism. It dominated Russian literature; no such cogitation has ever been complete without reference to the famous last passage in Gogol's *Dead Souls* about the troika "whither are you speeding to? Answer me. But no answer . . ." Was Gogol right? The Russian troika is not speeding at the present time, and other nations are not gazing askance (as Gogol wrote) and stepping aside to give her the right of way.

Speculations on the future of nations rest not only on some near certainties but also on imponderabilia, which cannot possibly be measured let alone predicted. Demography provides some near certainties. Given the fact that over 20,000 villages and little towns have ceased to exist over the last two decades, that the exodus from Russia in Asia continues, and that the Russian birthrate, even if it has slightly risen off late from 1.2 to 1.5, is not near the reproduction rate (2.1), a radical reversal seems quite unlikely. There will be fewer Russians in the future Russia; it will also be less Russian as far as its ethnic composition is concerned. Will it be able to hold on to the Russian Far East and all territories of Russia beyond the Urals? No one can say.

As for the imponderabilia: If it had not been for Gorbachev and Yeltsin, the Soviet system, while doomed, might have been able to hang on to power for another decade or two. In this time the price of oil has gone up from $2 a barrel in 1972 to almost $150 in 2007. In other words, the enormous windfall would not have been ascribed to Putin's wise and energetic leadership but to Leninism and the farsighted successors of Andropov.

Russia's future political prospects still depend to a large extent on the price of oil. Experts predict an economic growth rate of 4–5 percent in the years to come. Such estimates seem quite realistic; there are no signs that a concerted Western energy strategy will emerge to lessen its dependence from the import of oil and gas, in particular from Russia and the Middle East. The long-term economic prospects depending on efficient modernization as envisaged by Putin and (more so) by Medvedev may be less than brilliant. But if the predictions of global warmers are correct, the Russia of the future will have access to great quantities of rare and important raw materials that cannot at present be extracted because of permafrost. Thus, even if modernization fails, there would be no dramatic economic deterioration, and the political stability would not greatly suffer.

If as a result of a war in the Middle East Persian Gulf oil output would be much reduced, Russia would greatly benefit, at least temporarily.(But the ensuing world economic downturn would substantially reduce demand.) One could think of other exercises in counterfactual history—or futurology. Perhaps Gogol's great question marks were justified after all.

There have been optimists and pessimists among those pondering Russia's future, but the optimists too had their hours of despair—and *vice versa*. In 1854, Alexander Herzen met in London a visitor from the United States, James Buchanan, soon to become president. Buchanan, who had been minister to St. Petersburg and no doubt wanted to be polite, told Herzen that "your country has a great future." Herzen did not reply.

He had written that if the tyranny in Russia lasted too long, there was the possibility, indeed the probability, that the backbone of the people would be broken and irreparable damage be done. But he also said on another occasion that "our lungs are stronger," meaning that the Russian people would be able to survive repression and dictatorship better than others.

As for anti-Americanism—in a little known long essay (John Tanner) Pushkin was scathing about American democracy—and democracy in general. His anti-Americanism was disinterred under Stalin and is remembered even today when "democrats" and "democracy" have become a term of opprobrium among wide sections of Russian society—not just the far right. But there is an important difference in motivation; Pushkin despised the egalitarianism that was part of American democracy, whereas present-day antidemocratic feeling in Russia was largely generated by the amassing of great riches by a few strategically well-placed individuals during Yeltsin's age of democratization. Democracy in these circumstances became a near synonym for kleptocracy and oligarchs. The fact that much of their wealth is now offshore has not contributed to their popularity.

Historically, the Russian far left and the extreme right were anti-American. But it should always be recalled that Russia's preoccupation virtually up to the World War II was with Europe, not America. The West, hated or beloved, was Europe; America was a faraway country about which little was known despite the tremendous popularity of Fennimore Cooper and Tocqueville. The publication of Tocqueville's classic study in Russian was hold up for twenty-five years by the Russian censors, but in the end every educated Russian had read it.

2

It took Germany fifteen years after the defeat in World War I to reappear as a major power; it took Russia even less time. The oil and gas windfall greatly improved the economic situation and strengthened it politically. This process reached its climax in 2006/7 with a series of Putin speeches. In Luzhniki, the great Moscow sports arena, in November 2007 he called his opponents jackals funded by the West who, like their sponsors, wanted a weak, chaotic Russia. In Munich the same year, Putin commented on the decisive changes in the global balance of power, the emergence of BRIC as the wave of future, and the decline of America and Europe. This was the time when Putin defended Stalin against his detractors; now, under "reset," he does not shy away from using the "T" word (totalitarianism) much to the horror of some Western academics who believed that only incorrigible Cold Warriors would use such a loaded, propagandistic term.

On another occasion, Putin predicted that in 2020 Russia would not only be among the richest and most powerful states with the fifth largest economy in the world but also the most progressive and exciting. (At present the Russian GNP equals that of France—$2.15 trillion.) His advisers (or interpreters) declared that the whole world would be grateful to Russia for having been a counterweight to the American superpower and counteracted its policies. In the three years that followed, this mood changed to a certain extent, largely as a result of the global depression that affected Russia as much, if not more, than the United States and Europe.

There seems to have been some rethinking off late in the field of foreign policy. In most Russian documents on future strategy and military doctrine up to 2009, NATO remained the main threat. This also applies to the official new "military doctrine" of 2009, even though first deputy prime minister Ivanov declared in June 2010 that NATO was no longer a threat, only a danger. Second thoughts did occur: Perhaps one had overrated the prospects of BRIC. China and India, to give but one example, did not have that many interests in common. One had certainly underrated the internal social and political stresses facing these rapidly developing countries in the years to come. In what way would the rise of China and the diminished status of America and Europe benefit Russia? Could the drawbacks perhaps outweigh the gains, for America is far and China very close, especially to the Russian Far East and Siberia? What of Afghanistan after the American and NATO exodus? The Central Asian republics would be immediately threatened by the Islamists even if Taliban at present argues that they have no such intentions. These regions are certainly considered part of the Russian "privileged zone of interest" (and thus part of a zone of responsibility), not to mention the great and growing drug problem originating largely in Afghanistan, which, according to Russian spokesmen, is an even graver danger to the country than terrorism.

It seems gradually to have dawned on at least some Russian strategic thinkers that NATO in its present state does not really present a major threat—to Russia and perhaps to anyone. The idea of including Ukraine and Georgia has been shelved. At the same time Washington, following the European example, has tuned down its criticism of Russian violations of human rights and its support of what are regarded as separatist or hostile aspirations of some of Russia's neighbors.

While protests against human rights violations are still made on occasion, their character has become largely ritual. If the West needs Russian support in various fields, it has to take account of Russian sensibilities. The impression has gained ground in Moscow, not without reason, that the Russian claim for a zone of privileged interest has been accepted by the West. Fears of Russian pressure by some of its neighbors may be justified, but there is little Western countries can do to help.

In brief, Russia and America (and Europe) have certain common interests, and a policy of rapprochement has much to recommend itself precisely because America's and Europe's weight in world affairs is declining—as is Russia's.

These considerations seem to have influenced the decision in Moscow to move toward a rapprochement with the United States and Europe. They were seldom voiced in official statements; in the famous May 2010 seventy-two-page position paper prepared by the Russian foreign ministry and published by the Russian edition of *Newsweek*, the emphasis is almost entirely on "modernization." The document has the unwieldy title: "Program for the Effective Exploitation on a Systemic Basis of Foreign Policy Factors for the Purposes of Long-Term Development of the Russian Federation." A shorter title would have been Detente for Modernization. It goes into considerable detail envisaging steps to be taken in relation to over sixty countries from Brunei to Mongolia; the United Kingdom is not mentioned; and Moscow still seems to be angry about the fuss made by Britain over the murder (by thalium) in London of Alexander Litvinenko, the KGB defector.

The document (and the new policy) seems to be based on a compromise between various elements in the Russian leadership; the differences between them may not be enormous, but they still are significant. Even the ultranationalists and the so-called left (the Communists) are not in principle against modernization because they stand for a stronger Russia: The moderate conservatives such as Putin, his deputy chief of staff Surkov, and his foreign policy adviser Yuri Ushakov understand that the dependence of their country on gas and oil has to be reduced and that modernization involves a political price, they are fearful that this process may go too far and that the price could be too high.

The Medvedev faction, which seems to have instructed the foreign ministry to produce this statement, is willing to take some more risks; it could also be that the "modernization" argument, while essentially true and of vital importance, has been used by them as a selling point at home for a *détente* policy.

The new *détente* has shown itself in a variety of events and gestures: Russia voting for the Iranian sanctions, Russia showing remorse about Katyn, an agreement reducing nuclear weapons, NATO soldiers being invited to march on Red Square on Victory Day, France selling warships to Russia, Russian proposals for joint Russian–EU crisis management, and some others.

But there are difficulties ahead; they will not be easily overcome and they may even derail *détente* just as the *détente* of 1970s came to a halt and floundered.

3

Contemporary Russia is a conservative country and fearful of change. The Russian people have witnessed too much negative change during the last hundred years of its history. Putin, it is said, is a liberal compared with much of public opinion. According to the polls, a majority of Russians is satisfied not only with their leadership but also with their present conditions. (It is also true that such approval could rapidly and radically change.) This has been Putin's strength and explains his backing by a people that prefers stability over democracy. There is discontent especially among the better educated sections of the population. But the support Putin and Medvedev enjoy has been higher than that of virtually all Western leaders and would be probably as high if Russia had wholly free elections, free media, all political freedoms, and an independent judiciary. Therefore, there is much reason to assume that not only the tandem (Putin and Medvedev) or some of the same orientation will lead Russia after the elections of 2012 but also there will be tandemocracy for a decade to come. Some astute and highly knowledgeable Russian observers maintain that the regime is much weaker than it appears and may collapse; they may well be right in the longer run, but most of those outside Russia are not persuaded that these predictions may come true in the near future.

What modernization is wanted, and what reform is likely to succeed? The subject has been discussed in Russia since the days of Peter the Great. In recent years, there have been countless conferences, speeches, blueprints, and position papers discussing various ways to achieve it. Everyone is in favor, but there are a great many different interpretations of what is wanted and how to proceed. Why modernization? There is not much dissent—the infrastructure of the Russian economy (and of city life) is very poor and the dependence on the export of oil, gas, and other raw materials is undesirable and, in the long run, dangerous. It will make it more and more difficult to compete on the world markets to maintain its status as a great political and military power, let alone to strengthen its position on the global scene.

The differences occur once the ways to achieve it are discussed—on the one hand there are the advocates of top-down modernization with a minimum of political change, step by step, with the state as the main agent, authoritarian modernization "vertical state intervention" in the language of the Putinists. Their case is briefly as follows: Russia's traditions are not those of the West; in its present labile state, more democracy would be harmful, possibly fatal.

Even in many Western countries (except the Anglo-Saxon), the state played a central role in modernization. (This is an argument recently mentioned by Surkov, Putin's deputy.) They have nothing against technology transfer from the West; indeed they strongly advocate it. As Putin put it when negotiating with the French about the purchase of warships, "Russia would not be interested unless the deal involved technology transfer." New technologies should preferably be introduced first in the army that is said to be better prepared to absorb them than the private or semiprivate sector. (But other experts report that corruption, mainly in the form of major kickbacks in the military industrial complex, is at least as frequent as that in the civilian sector and that in recent years most of the investment aiming at modernizing the army—as distinct from the air force—has been wasted.) As for Western investment in the Russian economy, they believe that this will happen anyway, given the precarious state of Western economies and the search for profitable ventures. In any case, Western investors want above all political stability in Russia, and this is better granted by an authoritarian regime than by democratic chaos.

There are a number of other considerations seldom if ever mentioned but very much in the mind of the proponents of this school. Russia after all acquired nuclear technology, to give an obvious example, without democratization. Had Andropov, Brezhnev's successor as leader of the Soviet party and state and head of the KGB, lived longer, his modernization plans might have succeeded. A Western commentator recently argued that nanotechnology cannot be developed in a Byzantine empire. But Mr. Putin's historical advisers might tell him that Byzantine technology was quite developed. Next to the emperor's elevator throne there were two pneumatic roaring lions; the Byzantines invented both "Greek fire" and siphons.

Furthermore, modernization, however essential, should proceed slowly. Its benefits will not be immediately obvious; it is bound to come up against opposition by the victims of modernization of which there will be many—the bureaucracy, the general inertia, the inefficient enterprises and the many who thrive on them, the numerous monopolies in the Russian economy, and the instinctive resistance against innovation on the part of many. Last but not least—the personal interest of many members of the Russian political elite in maintaining the *status quo*. The situation would be different if Russia were a country poor in raw materials and had no oil and gas to export, but since a steady income seems assured for years to come also without experimenting with modernization, there appears to be no particular urgency.

Most of those favoring deep modernization do not envisage political democratization on the lines of the European model. But they want some steps in this general direction: they argue that modernization as tried in recent years in Russia has not worked, partly because it was limited to certain projects or branches of the economy and the absence of competition. State-of-the-art technology can be bought or borrowed (or stolen), but experience has shown that more often than not Russian industries for a variety of reasons have been unable to absorb them and make them work. The state bureaucracy is not capable to take the initiative and be the arbiter in the field of innovation, nor has Russian capital shown much interest to invest in this field. Putin may tell the Russian Academy of Science (June 2010) to do more for the modernization of Russia, but this will not be easy at a time when the Academy budget is cut and when many scientists have protested against dismal working conditions.

However, massive foreign investment will not come until it feels reasonably confident and comfortable, protected by the law. This involves, for instance, the independence of Russian courts that at present does not exist and doing away with what has been called "the embrace of businesses by the secret services and the police." The Andropov model may have had its uses combating hooliganism in the street, but it will do nothing to promote the creative thinking needed in a modern information society. Skolkovo, a small campus some twelve miles west of Moscow, the prototype of Silicon Valley, has been opened; a U.S. Nobel Prize winner and some companies such as Nokia expressed willingness to cooperate, but to so far it has all been a state project. A comfortable business climate also involves the absence of major tensions between Russia and the outside world, in other words a *détente* of sorts.

These, in briefest outline, are the positions of the two camps with as always a number of views in between. Most outside observers believe that while modernization in Russia may be inescapable in the long term, the prospects for the near future are poor. Not a mere change of policy is needed but of mentality—among both rulers and ruled. Such changes are possible, but they occur usually as a result of immediate need, clear and the present danger—which does not exist in Russia now, hence the seemingly

81

overwhelming temptation to muddle through attempting economic modernization with a minimum of political liberalization.

4

When does a mentality, a mood, a mind-set change? One can think of such changes, but they are not very frequent. They have occurred as a result of a major military defeat, or with the emergence of a new generation eager to break with tradition, and they have also happened for unfathomable reasons. Through its history, Russia like other countries has been subject to a variety of mind-sets, quite often to different ones at the same time. This is particularly true with regard to its attitude toward the West—is it part of the West, and if not what is it? At present the belief in a specific Russian way seems to be far stronger than a feeling of solidarity or friendship with the West. At one time Panslavism was fashionable, but this is no longer so. Later on Russian thinkers (not only their poets) tended to believe that they were Scyths or Panmongols, a strange doctrine that had a revival in some circles in recent years. It is of course quite true that Russian history followed its own path (but this is also true of other countries), and there has been resentment that its role for centuries as a bulwark against invasions from the East has not been sufficiently appreciated.

With all this most Russians are aware that despite their misgivings and reservations about Europe and America, they are not really Scyths. If so, how to explain the negative attitude toward the West going back to the nineteenth century if not further, first concerning Europe, later on particularly *vis-à-vis* the United States? This refers to the belief, even a hundred years before NATO was founded, that the West would do everything it could to harm Russia. Religious and nationalist beliefs played a role in the nineteenth century; during Communist rule, official ideology said that aggressive capitalist robbers were about to invade the worker's paradise.

Add to this the specific Russian propensity to believe in conspiracy theories, the more absurd, the more popular. Such theories have their believers in every country including the United States, but in Russia (and some Mediterranean and Near Eastern countries), the percentage of believers seems to be higher than elsewhere. An organization such as the KGB in which Mr. Putin and other leading figures in contemporary Russia received their training tends by its very nature to believe in worst case scenarios as far as the outside world is concerned and it is also convinced that, but for its presence and activities, the ever-present internal enemy would cause Russia irreparable harm.

There is also the genuine belief that the collapse of the Soviet Union was the greatest catastrophe of the twentieth century and that Russia has not and cannot have any true friends and allies except its own infantry and artillery (Putin said it and before him tsar Alexander III). There might have been some mellowing in recent years as a result of exposure to the realities of the outside world. It is difficult to argue at one and the same time that the West is rapidly declining and that it is the most powerful threat. But 'it is still an essential clue toward understanding early twenty-first-century Russia.

On the Russian far right, there has been a frantic search for alternatives to closer cooperation with the West. There is admiration for China and its achievements, but there is also fear because China is so much nearer Russia than the United States. Japan does not appear in these calculations nor does India figure highly for the time being except inasmuch as trade relations are concerned. There remains the unquiet Muslim world with all its internal conflicts. Some Russian political thinkers are closely advocating an alliance with some Muslim countries, above all former enemies such as Turkey. They argue that the two sides not only have a common enemy (the West) but also cultural and even religious affinities, Islam being closer to the Orthodox Church than Western Christianity. Other experts on the contrary warn of the "Islamization of Russia" given the presence of a substantial Muslim minority in Russia, not to mention Russia's Caucasian problems.

In short, geopolitical games of this kind are not leading to realistic alternatives. Eurasia is a fantasy; normal relations with these countries are desirable, and higher expectations lead nowhere—at best.

Deeply rooted political convictions apart, a few more arguments remain against closer cooperation with the West. This refers, for instance, to the predictions of the total collapse of America (falling apart and divided into half a dozen units) and even more of Europe. Not to be affected by the coming economic disasters, Russia is advised to follow a policy of autarky—easily said, impossible to achieve.

5

How far will *Reset/Détente* go? According to present indications, the course seems to be toward stability, meaning more of the present. Greater Sovietization seems unlikely, so does democratization. There may be discontent in Russia but not to the extent to turn into a significant political factor in the near future. In its foreign policy, the Kremlin wants to strengthen its sphere of influence, meaning the parts of the former Soviet Union that seceded in the 1990s and to normalize at the very least, relations with the former popular democracies. Physical reconquest seems very improbable.

It seems to have been realized in Moscow that there are certain common interests with the West. Moscow prefers to deal with countries (Germany, France, and Italy) individually rather than the European Community. At the same time, Russia wants at the very least normal relations with the rest of the world and prevents a deterioration in relation to newly found friends such as Hugo Chavez and Ahmedinejad. Combining these various aims will not be easy.

Despite Russia's return as a great power and the oil and gas windfall, it remains a weak country; by and large, to use an English cricket metaphor, it is batting on a sticky wicket. But Putin has shown all along supreme confidence on the assumption that in present world conditions Russia has little to fear what with Europe in decline and America weakened by the financial crisis, preoccupied with domestic problems and, as they see it, under a weak leadership. As far as the threats facing Russia, Putin (like the Russian right) is still preoccupied with NATO, largely oblivious to the lengthening shadow of China and aggressive Islamism. Perhaps we are facing a change of mind, but if so it has only just come under way and will take a long time. But it is, to repeat once again, precisely the weakness of the West that makes a *détente* with America and Europe more realistic and attractive. Russia needs Western capital and Western technological know-how.

But there is the danger that these hopes will at best be fulfilled only in part. This is not a good time to attract a massive infusion of capital from Europe; there is not that much available, and Europe is already providing 80 percent of foreign investment in Russia. Individual venture capitalists or corporations (such as Siemens) may show interest assuming that if things go wrong, their governments would bail them out. There certainly is a European (and Western interest) that the Russian economy should function. A poor Russia could be more dangerous than a relatively wealthy one; the political consequences of a bankrupt Russia, what with its thousands of nuclear devices, can easily be imagined. But such a danger hardly exists now given the certainty that massive oil and gas exports will continue. What will Europe and America gain from helping Russia to modernize? The Russian foreign minister Serge Lavrov said that the quid pro quo questions are not the right ones to ask, but they will be asked. A lessening of international tensions is desirable. But international relations are based on reciprocity: Russia would become stronger, but what would be Western benefits? The price of oil and gas will certainly not be reduced.

It does not therefore come as a surprise that there have been voices coming out of Europe to the effect that while Europe should take an active part in the modernization of Russia, the lead role ought to be played by America, which is in a better position to do so. Washington should certainly welcome outstretched hands in the interest of world peace. If it does not do so, it will be blamed by critics for decades to come for having missed unique opportunities. It remains to be explored what these opportunities are.

What is the Russian agenda concerning *Reset/Détente* other than the concerns already mentioned? Immediate demands are Russia joining the WTO and the abolition of visas with Europe; Europeans have suggested joint security committees to deal with crisis situations. But past experience with such commissions (with NATO) has not been encouraging. A variety of other small steps have been taken, not only to be belittled but also not to be exaggerated. There is a change in the political climate: Fewer anti-Western speeches, articles, books, movies; but since most Americans and Europeans were not even aware of these manifestations of anti-Westernism, they may not appreciate it sufficiently.

Far-reaching political democratization on the Russian home front is not on in the cards; perhaps it is an impossible desideratum at the present time given Russian history. Perhaps one should not even press for it, given the fact that the majority of the Russian leadership and the Russian people seem not now to favor it. But will it be possible, to give but one example, to have fair trials and legal protection for foreign enterprises only—something like the foreign concessions in China a hundred years ago? Russian leaders believing in authoritarian modernization might be disappointed when they realize that without true competition the new schemes will not work, foreign capital alone will not help. The new *détente* depends, last not least, on the support the West (and above all the United States) will receive from Russian foreign policy, which wants to keep all its options open. To what extent will it be able to count on Russia confronting threats in the years to come?

Russia's present situation reminds one in some ways of the dilemma of Akaki Akakievich, the hero of another Gogol story (*Shinel*—the Overcoat). This is one of the milestones in Russian literature, as Dostoevsky said "we all came out of Gogol's Shinel." Akaki Akakievich is the owner of an old and shabby mantle that makes him the butt of many jokes and general derision. He decides to buy a new one though he can hardly afford it. But almost immediately thereafter he is robbed of the coat that leads to countless misfortunes and the owner's early death. Russia needs the new overcoat, but there is no saying what the consequences will be for Russia and the rest of the world.

Russia's Muslim Strategy

1

A few years ago Aleksei Malashenko, one of Russia's leading (and most reliable) experts on Islam predicted that Islam was "Russia's fate." This may be an exaggeration but not perhaps by very much. Demography is also Russia's fate; if the situation and the prospects would be less critical, Islam would be less of a threat. With equal justice it could be said that Russia's historical misfortune (and fate) is its obsession with non existing dangers and ignoring the real ones facing it. Stalin, it will be recalled, trusted no one, especially not old Bolsheviks, but he was certain that Hitler would not attack the Soviet Union. It is a fascinating syndrome and one that has become again of crucial importance with the reemergence of Russia as an important player in world politics.

It took Germany after the defeat in World War I a mere fifteen years to reappear as a major power on the global scene. It took Russia about the same time to reemerge after the breakdown of the Soviet Union. The reasons for this second coming are known and need not be listed in detail, it was above all the boom in the price of raw materials such as oil and gas (to mention only the most important by far) which Russia has abundantly and made its reemergence possible. With all the violent ups and downs in the world economy the demand for these raw materials will continue to be a source of strength for Russia.

At the same time the new Russia confronts major domestic and external challenges that did not exist (or did not exist to the same extent) before. Russia's future depends from how it will cope with them. One of the main challenges facing it is indeed its relationship with Islam, both on the internal front and in its foreign policy. It would certainly be too much to say that the Russian leadership and public opinion has failed to recognize this, but the full importance of the issue has not been accepted so far, just as the problem of Russia in Asia and its relationship with China has not been fully understood in its whole magnitude. The reasons are not shrouded in secrecy, it is the deeply rooted belief that America, and the West in general, constitute the main peril facing Russia in the past, present and the foreseeable future.

87

The Russian encounter with Islam dates back many centuries, in parts of Russia Islam appeared on the scene before Christianity. If Europe was for years under pressure from the Ottoman Empire, Russia was threatened by Muslim powers from both the East and South. If this danger no longer existed after the defeat of the Turks at Vienna in 1689 the decisive date for Moscow was 1552 when Ivan IV (the Terrible) occupied Kazan and soon later the whole middle Volga region. But there still was a powerful Crimean Khanate which raided South Russia for many years after and in 1571 occupied and burned Moscow.

However, once the wars with Turkey had lost their importance and the Tsarist empire had established itself firmly from the Prussian border to Vladivostok, neither the relations with the Muslim minorities inside Russia nor its relations with neighboring Muslim countries figured very prominently in the Russian conscience. The Russian conquest of the Caucasus inspired two generations of Russian writers from Pushkin and Lermontov to Tolstoy, but it seemed to be just another colonial war comparable to similar wars fought by other imperial powers. It was the attraction of a strange and exotic world that inspired them comparable perhaps in some ways to Kipling's fascination with India. There was the occasional hostile or contemptuous remark—such as Lermontov's famous lullaby about the evil Chechen with his *kinzhal* (big dagger) crawling about the house, obviously up to no good. The fact that Lermontov had called one of his fellow officers a *gorets* (highlander) led to the duel in which he lost his life. But by and large, these were the exceptions. Griboedov, one of the greatest Russian writers of his day (and a diplomat) was killed by a fanatical mob in the Teheran Russian embassy. But this, though sadly received did by no means generate Islamophobia but was considered more or less normal behavior in less civilized countries.

Islam as a religion and a spiritual influence hardly preoccupied the Russian Orthodox Church. Russian philosophical and religious thinkers of the nineteenth century such as Chaadayev, and the Slavophils, Khomyakov and Soloviev occasionally mentioned Islam in their works but one had to dig deep to find anything of relevance on the subject; they were not very well informed about the subject and most of it was speculation. Ismail Gasprinski predicted towards the end of the nineteenth century that Russia would soon be a major Islamic power. But he was of Muslim origin (a Crimean Tatar) and a pan-Islamist and his views were not shared by many. The Moscow man in the street hardly encountered Islam except perhaps when meeting his janitor; among whom Tatars were strongly represented.

Resistance against Russian domination continued on a local scale but it was suppressed by the central authorities without much difficulty (for instance the Central Asia rebellion in 1916 when about one third of the Kyrgyz people fled to China or the Basmatchi campaign once the Bolsheviks had taken over which lasted almost seven years. These were considered events of limited local importance, tensions inevitable in the relationship between colonial powers and their subjects.

According to widespread belief among Western observers in the 1930s and even after World War II, the Soviet Union whatever its other shortcomings had succeeded in solving the national question. This was the consensus emerging from the books of experts such as Hans Kohn and Walter Kolarz and Hannah Arendt shared their view. Up to a point the impression was not mistaken. Soviet power had managed to win over sections of the native political elite and to educate a new intelligentsia which accepted the official Communist ideology. This local intelligentsia had been integrated given leading positions in their republics and some had even been accepted in the center of power just as the Caucasian aristocracy had been socially and politically accepted in tsarist St. Petersburg and Moscow.

But the general inertia and stagnation (*zastoi*) of the 1970s and 1980s also had strong repercussion in the Muslim regions and Brezhnev, a leader trying to evade conflict whenever possible, upbraided on more than one occasion the Central Asians for not pulling their weight, depending on economic and other assistance from the center which could ill afford it, and became more and more of a burden.

2

The situation quickly aggravated with the breakdown of the Soviet Union when it appeared that the often invoked friendship of the people (*druzhba narodov*) was not, to put it mildly, deeply rooted. Many millions of ethnic Russians left the Central Asian Republics feeling unsafe and unwanted.

The major Muslim republics became politically independent but in many other respects their dependence from Moscow continued or became even stronger, the quality of the new leadership was bad, and the ideology that had faded was partly replaced by Islam and Islamism spearheaded by emissaries from Saudi Arabia and other Arab and Muslim countries. Hundreds of new mosques were built, various religious-nationalist organizations launched and the *hadj*, the pilgrimage to Mecca organized albeit on a modest level (about 20,000 pilgrims a year).

The Moscow central authorities tolerated this influx of foreign money and ideas, partly because their main preoccupations were elsewhere in those years, partly because they felt powerless to intervene. The KGB seems to have been concerned about the spread of "Wahhabi" influence particularly in the Northern Caucasus and also the appearance of other radical Muslim sects and movements such as Hizb al Tahrir. According to some reports the KGB (now FSB) established some Islamist groupings of their own in order to be better informed about the activities of these circles.

The religious-political reawakening of Islam (and often of radical Islam) coincided with the growth of a radical nationalist mood among the Russian population. This had partly to do with the influx of Muslims in the major Russian cities. Greater Moscow is reportedly now the home of close to three million Muslims (many of them illegal residents); it is certainly the European city with the most numerous Muslim population. Following individual attacks against Muslims in these cities there were in the 1990s complaints among Muslim leaders about the "demonization of Islam" and, like in Western Europe, growing "Islamophobia." In truth, the attacks were more often than not turf wars in or around local markets, but there is no denying that the very presence of so many alien newcomers generated hostility and xenophobia.

If the Russian security services worried mainly about the subversive–separatist character of the influx of radical Islam, the Russian foreign ministry on the contrary was preoccupied with the foreign political impact of anti-Muslim sentiments in the neighboring Muslim countries. Following the initiative of the then foreign minister Evgeni Primakov, the Russian ministry of foreign affairs arranged a high level conference in 1998 devoted to damage limitation. (Primakov had started his career as an orientalist and later one rose to the highest positions in the state apparatus and the KGB.) The reputation of Russia in the Muslim world had suffered in any case as the result of the Afghan war and the first Chechen war (1994–96). To repair some of the damage the Foreign Ministry argued that if Islamophobia was to grow in Russia this would be a fatal blow to the Russian tradition of tolerance and integrity. In truth, they were more concerned with the danger of Russian isolation and possibly missing certain political chances in the Muslim world—about this more below.

However, anti-Russian sentiments as the result of these two wars were by no means universal in the Muslim world. The Organization of Islamic States (to give but one example) refused on more than one occasion to accept as a member the political organization (Ichkeria) of the Chechen rebels. Once Russia withdrew from Afghanistan it ceased to be a target of both outside Muslim propaganda and military (terrorist) action. There were individual cases of anti Russian propaganda and even some sporadic, half hearted preparations for terrorist action (for instance against Russian diplomats in Iraq) but a great deal of solidarity with Russian Muslims and their political demands could not be detected. On the other hand Russian Muslim interest in the affairs of their coreligionists in other countries was also strictly limited. An appeal to contribute money to the victims of the Gaza campaign in 2009 resulted in the collection of 100,000 rubles, not an impressive sum considering the presence of more than 20 million Muslims in Russia.

During the 1990s and the years after something akin to a Russian strategy vis-à-vis Islam developed. Old illusions with regard to a close alliance with the "progressive" Arab countries such as had prevailed in earlier decades had vanished; it was well remembered that massive arms deliveries to Arab countries had seldom if ever been paid for and certainly did not generate political support. But the idea that Russia could play the role of a mediator between the West (above all America) and the Muslim world began to take root. Moscow did not approve of the first, let alone the second Iraq war, it tried to mediate in the Tadjik civil war (which would have petered out anyway after more than 100,000 people had been killed), it made certain suggestions in the context of the Iranian nuclear program (which led to nothing) and in 2006 it invited the Hamas leadership to Moscow. Neither Hamas nor Hezbollah are now included in the list of terrorist organizations of the Russian intelligence services.

It did not take long for the Russian leadership to realize that such attempt of mediation failed to produce tangible results, they certainly did not generate any benefit to Russia. Nevertheless, low level contacts continued without, admittedly, great expectations. Mainly perhaps to demonstrate that Russia was still interested in the Middle East and had to be taken into account as a major player. Moscow continued to argue that Iran could be persuaded not to use its nuclear installations for military purposes even though there was little factual evidence to this effect. In 2006 (and again in 2007) the Hamas foreign minister Mahmud Zahar paid another visit to Moscow without any tangible results. This cooling off in relations with the Palestinians had begun even earlier. When Arafat visited Moscow in Gorbachev's days, he and the other members of the delegation reached the conclusion (as one of them put it) that "this man is not our friend." He was not an enemy either, but he had many other, more urgent worries. The only benefit accruing to Russia as the result of its activities as mediator was that Muslim countries refrained from giving open support to fellow Muslims inside Russia, somewhat to the disappointment of the Islamists inside Russia.

In brief, Moscow followed a strategy of mediation without attaching great hopes to it. It stressed on many occasions its respect for Islam, the Muslim countries and their leaders as well as the need to promote reconciliation between different cultures and civilizations. At the same time there was among the Russian ruling circles distrust and the deep seated conviction that any rapprochement with the Muslim world could only be of a tactical character. Quite obviously the Muslim countries would not have launched a campaign against Russia (just as they refrained to do so in the case of China and India) even if Russia had not attempted to play the "honest broker" simply because they were fully preoccupied with confronting the West and Israel. Russia was a major nuclear power, so were China and India and these considerations were decisive.

3

Russia's internal Muslim problems are no doubt of greater political importance than the relations with the foreign Muslim countries. Russian attitudes towards its Muslim minorities are full of contradictions, probably inevitably so. Moscow insists on absolute loyalty on the part of its Muslim citizens but does not want (and cannot) fulfill many of the demands of even the more moderate elements among the Muslims. This refers above all to the Muslim republics on the middle Volga such as Tatarstan and Bashkorstan. They have a measure of autonomy but want much more. The present rulers and political elite date back to the Soviet period; Murtaza Rakhomov and Mintimer Shaimiev (both were replaced in 2010), the political bosses of the two republics, both in their seventies, began their career in the Communist era, gained the order of Lenin and similar distinctions and have been in command since 1991 and 1993 respectively. If anything, they belonged to the orthodox wing of the Communist Party which was opposed to the Gorbachev reforms.

There has been an infiltration from abroad of Islamist cadres and ideas, some of the mosques and schools came under their influence but they were apparently successfully repulsed. The economic situation in these two highly industrialized regions has been better than in most other parts of the Russian federation, largely in view of the oil industry and its various branches. Nevertheless (or because of it) there have been growing demands from Moscow in both the political and the economic field. The idea that the first deputy prime minister (or president) of the Russian Federation should be a Muslim seems to have originated in the Volga region.

Political separatism has not good prospects in this region unless there should be a sudden dramatic weakening of central state power. This for a variety of reason: Tatarstan and Bashkorstan are cut off from the other Muslim regions. The Russian ethnic element is strong in both republics (almost half in Tatarstan—more in the major cities such as Kazan and Ufa) and there have been many mixed marriages. The Bashkirs are a minority in their own republic, the Muslims amount to a majority only if the Tatar sector is added. However, the relations between the two ethnic groups have not always been smooth. The influence of modernist Islam (jadidism) remains strong, there has been, and continues to be criticism and even contempt of fundamental Islam. ("We do not want to return to the middle ages.") Opposition to Moscow is based more on nationalist than on religious grounds.

The second major concentration of Russian Muslims is Moscow. Estimates of their number vary greatly—between 1.2 and 3.0 million, but walking the Moscow street their massive presence is unmistakable; whole quarters of the Capital have been taken over by them such as Butovo in the far south, but also regions in the north west Degunino, Saburovo even Izmailovo as well as near the big official and unofficial markets. There are new mosques, among them four or five truly big ones, one near the Olympic village another close to the international airport. Muslim cultural clubs have been opened, hospitals, schools, kindergarten, food shops and even halal supermarkets such as Appelsina claiming to be on the European level. It is announced that more will be opened soon. There are no major bookshops as yet and no Muslim Russian newspapers but a great deal of activity on the Internet. However, the works of Sayed Qutb, Mawdudi, and other radical Muslim thinkers have been translated and can be obtained without difficulty.

The authorities have been trying to expel the illegals of whom there are a great many, closing down some of the major markets. (This was directed not only against Muslims but also against Chinese other Asians and "people of Caucasian background" in general.)

On the other hand, Luzhkov, the former influential Moscow mayor has gone out of his way to gain popularity among the Muslim residents, allocating funds for some of their religious and cultural institutions (which remain firmly under the observation of the KGB), and, perhaps more important, Putin and Medvedev have done the same, sending greetings to the Muslim community on the occasion of their holidays and even visiting one or the other major mosque. Such practices, aimed at the domestication of Islam would have been unthinkable ten or even five years ago and it reflects the growing importance of the Muslim presence in the capital.

Northern Caucasus is the third and most dangerous Muslim concentration. The basic facts are well known and need not be reiterated in detail, above all the first and second Chechen war. Some 160,000 soldiers and civilians are believed to have perished in the two wars. Eventually, Russia succeeded imposing, for the time being, a solution and relative calm is prevailing; Grozny, the heavily destroyed capital, is being rebuilt. Chechnya has become a partly autonomous Muslim region in which the sharia is the law of the land. The local authorities have been pressing for the legalization of polygamy. To what extent the new Chechen leadership believes indeed in fundamentalist Islam is by no means clear; more likely they feel the need for an official ideology that could serve as a uniting force and at the same time counteract the accusations of the rebels, that the members of the ruling pro-Putin clique are apostates, hostile to Islam. The rebels which suffered heavy blows not only hate the Russian occupiers but also bitterly attack America which (they claim) supports Russian oppression and denounce the Jews, the source of all global evil. However, not all the declarations attributed to the Chechen opposition on the Internet can be taken at face value; Russian black propaganda also seems to be at work.

Nevertheless, the Russian policy of appointing more or less trustworthy satraps such as the younger Kadyrov offers no guarantee as far as the future is concerned. Moscow is quite aware that their local representatives will press for more and more independence (and money), are difficult to control and in the final analysis cannot be trusted.

However, the end of the Chechen war brought by no means peace to Northern Caucasus. On the contrary, attacks by terrorist gangs against the authorities in Daghestan, Ingushetia and other republics and regions increased in 2009, resulting in the killing of police chiefs and other leading officials; in June 2009 Yunusbek Yevkurov, president of Ingushetia narrowly escaped death in an attack but was injured. The situation was deemed sufficiently serious for Medvedev to visit (for the second time in one year) Daghestan and Ingushetia, which, it is thought, no Russian president has ever done before. Asked for the identity of these and subsequent attackers Yevkurov said that he could not image that any Arab country was behind these outrages and if so it must be America, Britain, and Israel. But Yevkurov's enemies also attacked him as a Zionist collaborator. Thus, Zionists were fighting Zionists in the Northern Caucasus, as if they had not sufficient other problems. An interesting, if not very plausible explanation. Kadyrov has voiced similar views about the West being to blame for the Islamist attacks against his regime and the Chechen supreme Mufti demanded (in September 2009) that ex- president Bush should be brought to court in connection with the Islamist terrorist attacks in the northern Caucasus.

No solution seems to be in sight for stabilizing the situation in Northern Caucasus, partly because of the continuing attacks of the jihadists, but also because there seems to be an inherent, traditional inclination towards long wars in the region. However, Shamil, the legendary head of Caucasian resistance who fought the Russians for about twenty five years in the nineteenth century was not only a talented military commander but also a political leader. There is no political leader in the present day Caucasus. If there is no outside enemy, Caucasians seem to enjoy to fight each other. Seen in this perspective, the Russian-Georgian conflict was an unwelcome distraction. In Daghestan alone some forty nationalities and thirty languages are counted and the situation in other parts of the region is not very different. During the Soviet era the conflicts were suppressed, and the Islamists may believe that if they succeed in defeating the Russian militarily and expelling the Russian civilians they would also impose a pax Islamica.

4

The Middle Volga region and the Caucasus apart, Russia confronts radical Islam in the Muslim republics of the Soviet Union which seceded with the breakdown of the Soviet Union—the Central Asian republics and to a lesser degree Azerbaidjan.

The infiltration of radical Muslim influences and the invasion of guerrilla and terrorist forces sponsoring them have been covered in detail elsewhere and there is no need to go over the same ground once again. (Such as the studies by Ahmed Rashid, Martha Brill Olcott and Adeeb Khalid to name but a few.) Russia keeps a close interest in Central Asia. If radical Islam were to take over political power in these republics or even only one or two of them, this would be a major disaster for Russia which considers this vast region an integral part of its "privileged zone of influence." Radical Islam has attempted to gain a strong foothold in a variety of ways. The high tide of the activities of IMU (the Islamic Movement of Uzbekistan) which joined forces with the Taliban was between 1999 and 2004, Hizb al Tahrir began to send its emissaries even earlier. (It was banned in Russia in 2003 and is banned now in most other republics but probably maintains small underground cells.) Their campaigns were defeated by repression, often brutal and off late there have been relatively few terrorist attacks. However, there is reason to assume that radical Islam has gained roots in at least some regions and the governments remain unpopular. It is difficult if not impossible for outsiders to know how deep these roots are and what forces the jihadists could mobilize.

If NATO and the U.S. were to leave Afghanistan (and it is unlikely that they will ever be given sufficient manpower and a free hand to deal with the situation) it would almost automatically become a problem for Russia as well as China and India. China may try a non-aggression pact with Kabul on the assumption that it would recognize the Taliban regime if there will be no intervention in Chinese affairs from bases in Afghanistan. But it is not certain whether such an arrangement will work; it will certainly not work with regard to Russia and India and the Central Asian republics.

In addition to the extremist opposition to the Central Asian governments there are more moderate forces, also opposed to the authorities and it would be wrong not to differentiate between these two forces as the local governments tend to do.

These governments are authoritarian (only in Tadjikistan is the opposition represented in parliament), corrupt and fairly inefficient. It could be argued that Central Asia has never in its history been exposed to good, efficient and incorrupt rule, and that, as in many other countries, nothing will work in these places without at least a modicum of corruption. However, there are degrees of corruption and at time of acute economic crisis these republics will be vulnerable facing an onslaught of Islamist movements pretending to combine the orthodox practice of the true faith with honesty and greater efficiency.

5

If Russia has an overall strategy vis-à-vis Islam and the Muslim world it is replete with contradictions, and can be understood only within the framework of the general picture—how Russians see their place in the world now and in the years to come. There is the constant contradiction between a feeling of worthlessness and the sentiment of superiority, of having a mission to fulfill. Worthlessness found its classical formulation in Chaadayev's *Philosophical Letters* (1836)—we had neither a Renaissance nor an Enlightenment, we have contributed nothing to world culture, we have not added a single idea, but we disfigured everything we touched. We belong neither to West nor to East. Chaadayev was declared a madman by the Tsar who sent him his doctor several times a week. But Chaadayev's diagnosis has influenced

Russian thinking to this day and is frequently quoted. On the other hand, there is the feeling of superiority, Russian being the Third Rome and having a unique mission to fulfill in the world.

These ideas about a feeling of mission were not prominently voiced during the late Soviet period or the decade after but with the economic recovery they became not just respectable but achieved almost the status of an official ideology.

Similar contradictions exist in relations with the Muslim world—on one hand the conviction that Russia ought to strive for an alliance with the Islamic countries or at least some of them (above all Turkey and Iran, the Arab countries usually figure last and Pakistan does not figure at all). On the other hand a deep distrust prevails—Putin's "Russia has only two reliable allies, its infantry and its artillery"—the saying was borrowed from Tsar Alexander.

A new Russian doctrine was needed as Marxism–Leninism faded and was discredited. Marx is hardly ever quoted these days and Lenin only seldom. Stalin had a major comeback but as a Russian patriot not as a Marxist. The new Russian doctrine has many facets and it ranges from the relatively sober to the obscure, farfetched and bizarre (which suddenly became respectable) to the clinically mad. To begin with the last mentioned: Yuri Petukhov, recently deceased, was a widely read science fiction writer. Shortly before his demise he formulated his political views and prophecies in *Novy mirovoi poryadok* (The Russian World Order). According to him all foreigners are Neanderthalers and degenerates (the term appears about a thousand times in his book), Europe and America were created by Russians and should be repossessed, all Russian leaders including Lenin and Khrushchev (a weakling who did not dare to go to war over Cuba) were traitors, excepting only the great Stalin, so was Solzhenitsyn, Hitler was a romantic, the first and World War II were unleashed by the treacherous Americans and the British. Pearl Harbor was a magnificent operation and so on. The third world war was started by America which caused the Chernobyl nuclear explosion of 1991. The American degenerates in collaboration with the European jackals want to destroy Russia which will however prevail in this epic struggle. There are many more fascinating observations and suggestions in this book such as the abolition of the totally useless English language which cannot all be mentioned here.

Petukhov expressed the thoughts and feeling of not a few simpleminded compatriots. On a somewhat more sophisticated level Alexander Dugin and Igor Panarin are among the leading figures. Ten or fifteen years ago few took them seriously but more recently they have become respectable and even influential with contacts (reportedly through Vladislav Surkov, Putin's political mastermind) and support in the Kremlin. Dugin began his ideological odyssey in the ranks of Pamyat, the ultra rightwing anti-Semitic group in the last days of Soviet rule but soon realized that such primitive outdated views had no political future and established his own school. (The writings of Andreas Umland are the best and most detailed source on Dugin and Duginism.) Panarin, on the other hand originally belonged to the liberal dissidents but later worked his way to the other end of the political spectrum. He became known in the West following his predictions that America would not last beyond 2010. There would be a civil war and the country would be divided into six separate states.

Dugin seems to enjoy considerable respect among the military, the media and even in academic circles whereas Panarin's influence is mainly felt in the academe and the foreign ministry academy. Dugin tried for many years to present a synthetic new ideology, a mixture of some of the more disreputable Western elements (Italian neo fascists such as Evola, Alan de Benoist and the new right in France and neo-Nazi geopolitics). He later realized that some specific Russian elements were needed and adopted a new updated version of Eurasianism, an ideology first developed in the 1920s among Russian émigrés. He was not deterred by the difficulties facing him—how were the Asians to be persuaded to cooperate with this new Russia? Japan was ruled out, China, economic ties apart, was generally regarded a rival rather than an ally, India was far away and little interested.

The neo-Eurasianism of Dugin and others encountered sympathies among some Russian Muslims. At a conference in September 2009 Gainutdin the chairman of the Russian Muftis roof organization declared in a speed that Russia owned not only its statehood but its greatness to the Golden Horde. These Mongol invaders, most of whom converted at a later stage to Islam subjugated much of Russia for about three centuries. But this historical construct had not great chances to be accepted by Russian historians who had always believed that Russian statehood have been achieved not owing to the Golden Horde but on the contrary in the struggle against it.

Furthermore, given Russia's demographic weakness, the probability that within several decades even Iran and Turkey would be more populous countries than Russia, wasn't there a danger that in such an alliance Russia would be the junior rather than the senior partner, something which was clearly not intended by Dugin and his comrades? Nevertheless, such ideas in one form or another widely spread among Russian political elite. One example should suffice. *Put Voinov Allah. Islam i Politika Rossii* (The Road of Allah's warriors: Islam and Russian politics) seems to be a basic text in both the

---

(1)   A personal note of recollection: I visited Northern Caucasus four times between 1957 and 1966, one of the first foreigners to be admitted to this region. The strongest impression gained during these visits (apart from the magnificent landscape—Switzerland without the tourists) was the tension between the nationalities even if this did only seldom find open expression.

Russian Military Academy and the university of the security services. The book was authored by Zhuravlyov, Melkov and General Shershnev, all three teachers at these institutions. It regards Islamist separatism a major threat to the survival of Russia and has no sympathy for countries which have adopted the sharia and sponsor jihadism.

But when it comes to strategies how to confront these dangers, the following picture emerges: The world is facing a deadly crisis (this "according to the well known American sociologist and economist Lyndon La Rouche"). There is no chance for a recovery and—ex oriente lux—the world has to turn as soon as possible to the East rather than the West for inspiration and leadership to find a way out of this deadly crisis towards salvation.

Since Russia alone is not strong enough to achieve this aim thus counteracting American and European influence the creation of RIKI, an alliance of Russian, China, India and Iran is envisaged. (The authors, otherwise not distinguished by a sense of humor, mention that they are aware of Riki-Tiki-Tavi, the heroic mongoose in Kipling's *Jungle Book*). These countries behaved very well in the past not exploiting the decade of Russian weakness after the breakdown of the Soviet Union. Furthermore, there are many spiritual values in common between them even now and cooperation between them has to be intensified since America has already launched the fourth world war for world domination against Russia and the other RIKI countries. The RIKI countries are also religiously close to each other—Russian ethics are close to Asian ethic and have nothing in common with the capitalist and usurious Protestant ethic as described by Max Weber and Benjamin Franklin .The authors also note that Catholicism is a far greater danger for Russia than the largely mythical Islamic threat, which contradicts the statement noted earlier on that Islam was a major menace. Seen in this light RIKI would become not only the leading political and military global factor but also the moral leader of the world. These are ambitious plans especially considering that they emanate from countries who have in fact very little in common but deeply distrust each other—Russia and China, China and India, Iran and the rest of the world, show no great eagerness to collaborate too closely and are among the most corrupt in the world. It ought to be noted in passing that Europe does not fare any better than America in the view of these thinkers—all throughout its history Europe has shown black ingratitude towards Russia, never accepted it as an equal belonging to Europe. And to this day Europe does its utmost to steal from, humiliate and destroy Russia. This then is the world view conveyed to the trainees of the military forces and the state security services.

It is widely shared by sections of the Russian extreme right who do not follow the lead given by Dugin in such as influential weekly *Zavtra* edited by Alexander Prokhanov. Or to give another example Alexander Vavilov, a professional Russian orientalist in a book published in 2009 argued that while Osama and his ilk were "utopians," other Islamist militant groups such

as Hamas and Hezbollah should be considered allies by Russian policymak-
ers (*Politika S. Sch. A. v musulmanskom mire*—U.S. policy in the Muslim
world).

6

The nationalist right wingers, both moderate and extremist, agree that the
United States and its European allies are Russia's most dangerous enemies
by far. While such views of Europe prevailed in some circles of the Russian
intelligentsia for a long time, America hardly figured prominently on the
Russian political horizon prior to World War II. It was only with America's
emergence as a superpower that it generated such strong feelings among the
Russian political establishment. The fact that the Soviet Union lost out in
the Cold War and eventually collapsed seemed to confirm Russian fears and
this has shaped Russian strategy to the present day and probably will do so
in the foreseeable future. Even if the more extreme fantasies about American
intrigues and crimes (some of which were mentioned above) may not be
shared by the mainstream Russian establishment, the preoccupation with
America has blinded large sections of the Russian elite with regard to other
threats facing their country. While the demographic decline, the shrinking
of Russia, has been realized with some delay, the political repercussions of
this disaster are far from fully clear among those shaping Russian policy.
Malashenko who was mentioned earlier on, believes that neither in the short
range nor by 2050 will there be any reason to speak of the Islamization of
Russia. Other observers take a less sanguine view; they draw attention, for
instance to the ethnic background of the recruits to the Russian army which
is increasingly of Muslim origin. In any case it is not just a matter of statistics.
Much depends from the measure of integration of national and religious
minorities in Russia; will they be loyal to regime or will the separatist trends
become stronger?

If the Russian political establishment agrees on the overwhelming danger
presented by America, there is disagreement with regard to policies to be
followed vis-à-vis the Muslim minority at home and Islam in Russian foreign
policy. The Russian authorities have every reason to prevent the spread of
the Caucasian unrest to the other Muslim concentrations. The jihadists are
facing in many ways an uphill struggle: They are preaching a version of Islam
which disregards local traditions and customs. They draw their inspiration
not so much from Wahhabism (which is a misnomer, deliberately used by
the authorities to discredit all opposition) but from the more radical sections
of the Muslim Brotherhood and similar groups believing in terrorist action
who indoctrinated the leaders and activists of the Russian jihadists and above
all the preachers trained in the Arab countries. This radical version of Islam
may appeal to the thirst for action among the younger Russian Muslims (in
opposition to the old, established leadership), but many others prefer to

stick to the old Sufi (and folk religion) traditions still deeply rooted in their communities. The brutal exploits of the Caucasian rebels such as (to mention but a few) the mass murder of women in Buinaksk in Daghestan in August 2009 do little to generate sympathy for their cause. The Russian authorities, needless to mention, support the traditional leadership.

As for the Muslims in the big cities and the middle Volga region, they have been exposed for too long to the temptation of modernism and modern life—in contrast to the Caucasian highlanders, and most of them will not easily accept the teachings of the jihadists. The central Asian republics remain more vulnerable; their future very much depends from the general political situation and the balance of power in this region in the years to come.

While strictly observing developments inside the Muslim communities (and intervening if need be) the Russian authorities are trying to keep their Muslims happy and to prevent national strife ("Islamophobia"). But they face the growing xenophobia promoted by the Russian right—and popular opinion in general ("Russia for the Russians"). The Russian Orthodox Church follows with grave misgivings what they regard a policy of appeasement of Islam on the part of the authorities. They want to preserve their old/new status as the state religion, and while the Kremlin is vitally interested in good relations with the Orthodox Church it finds it increasingly difficult to pursue a balancing act between the Orthodox and Islam. Appeals for a dialogue between the religions are mere eyewash, there is no such readiness to talk on either side.

The Caucasus remains Russia's soft underbelly and no solution is in sight. Most of the action has shifted from Chechnya to Daghestan, Ingushetia and some of the other regions. Daghestan is very poor and an independent Daghestan without constant help from Russia could hardly exist. But such economic considerations will not stop the fighting; the rebels can always argue that they aim at a united Northern Caucasus. This may be no more than wishful thinking but useful as a powerful myth while the fighting continues. Russian policy will continue as before, brutal repression of separatism on one hand and the imposition of a leadership considered trustworthy by Moscow (and collaborationist by the jihadists). At one stage the Kremlin envisaged a unification of Muslim religious institutions establishing one central authority, but this was given up for a variety of reasons. Such attempts have failed in other European countries and they would probably not succeed in Russia.

Russian foreign policy vis-à-vis Islam and Islamism has been undecided, trying to keep all options open. With America still looming as the great threat, Islamist anti American activities should have been welcomed without reservation (and often were) but there seem to have been doubts off late about the wisdom of such a policy. The Kremlin may follow with schadenfreude, the misfortunes of the West in Afghanistan but if the U.S. and NATO were to withdraw from Afghanistan, it would again become a Russian problem as a base for jihadist activities in Central Asia. If Iran will have nuclear weapons, it would try to establish itself as a leading force in the Middle East—which would not necessarily be in the Russian interest.

Some Russian rightwing Eurasian ideologues have suggested (as mentioned earlier on) closer relations with Iran but these fantasies seem to have evaporated. Dugin and his followers, on the other hand have suggested an alliance with Turkey; on his forays to Turkey he allegedly became involved with criminal elements (*Ergenekon* which is said to have both mafia and terrorist connections). But such embarrassment has not prevented an improvement of Russian—Turkish relations under the Erdogan government and even dreams of a close alliance. Earlier on the Turkish authorities seem to have extended some political and military help to the Caucasian rebels by way of the Cypriote Turkish authorities which generated Russian ire. Russian relations with the Arab world have been distinguished by considerable caution, they wish not to be left out but not to get too deeply involved either for the time being.

By and large Soviet strategy is still dominated by the American shadow, the conviction that what helps the United States must be bad for Russia. This appears strange if, as initially mentioned, Islam should indeed be "Russia's fate." The belief in American and Western malevolence sometimes bordering on an obsession is likely to change but it may be a long learning process.

The Cold War: Two Histories, Two Narratives

The Cold War—is it finally over? World history during the second half of the last century was shaped by the Cold War and its consequences are felt even now, especially in Europe and in U.S.–Russian relations, more than twenty years after it ended. For decades the causes of the Cold War have been discussed and disputed, how did it start, whose (to put it somewhat crudely) fault was it, could it have been prevented, were opportunities missed in the decades after Stalin's end, and when and how and why did it end? As long as Soviet rule existed Russian historians and commentators were not in doubt with regard to the answers to these questions. A "Cold Warrior" was a Western (mostly American) hardliner, distrustful of Soviet peaceful intention, probably with a vested interest in the maintenance of tensions and conflict, a hopelessly prejudiced individual, an obstacle to world peace and quite likely a warmonger. In some Western circles there was agreement with this Soviet image of the "Cold Warrior."

Since the end of the Cold War an enormous amount of hitherto inaccessible source material (but by no means all) has come to light, mainly from Soviet archives and has been carefully studied. As a result some of the more extreme theories have all but disappeared—for instance that Washington provoked the outbreak of the Korean war. But there still is a wide discrepancy of interpretations and the great divide today is perhaps not so much between Western and Russian commentators but inside the two camps. This expresses itself even in the very language used. Many Western historians are most reluctant to use the term "totalitarian" with regard to Stalin's Russia, which, they believe is a loaded, even propagandistic term, not to be used by serious, dispassionate analysts. Many Russian historians and commentators have no such compunction; even the president of Russia has not shied away from using these terms on occasion. Medvedev in an interview with *Izvestia* May 6, 2010: "If we speak honestly, the regime that was built in the Soviet Union cannot be called anything other than totalitarian."

A comparison of two recent works is illuminating—the three volume *Cambridge History of the Cold War* (no mentioning of totalitarianism there) and the equally massive two volume Russian history covering the last century; the enormous second volume largely devoted to the Cold War period. These books are the work of many hands (more than fifty contributors each). The cooperation of so many experts added no doubt to the quality of these works but it makes it difficult to generalize because their contributions are by necessity not only of varying quality, the authors also expressed—within certain limits—different viewpoints. But if there is no "party line" there still is much common ground in each of the two series.

Where to look for the origins of the Cold War? The Russian study (Professor Andrei Zubov acting as the editor in chief) has few doubts. Chapter 3 of the second volume reads "Russia and Stalin's preparations for a third world war—which did not take place" Dimitrov, last head of the Communist International, is quoted to the effect that as early as January 1945 Stalin declared at a reception in his dacha outside Moscow that while Russia was fighting now with one capitalist faction against another, it would fight in future against its present allies. Stalin believed that as a result of a post war capitalist economic crisis and conflicts between the Western allies, America will be compelled to withdraw its forces from Europe which would enable Russia not just to dominate Eastern Europe but to extend its influence to all of Germany as well as France and Italy. Stalin brought pressure on Turkey and Iran to gain control of the straits and Azerbaijan but as the Russian study notes with evident disbelief and perhaps even amusement Western politicians continued to put their trust in the peaceful intentions of "Uncle Joe" and "simply did not want to believe in Soviet expansionism" (p. 215). According to the same source a more sober approach began to prevail in the West only following Churchill's Fulton speech which is rendered in full—extending over five pages. Further stages in unleashing the Cold War were the Berlin blockade (provoked by Stalin), the Prague take over (February 1948) and the rapid Sovietization of Eastern Europe. The chapter heading reads "The preparation of Soviet society for a new war" (p. 238). Soviet military doctrine in the early 1950s was (according to Marshal Akhromeyev) based on a powerful trust carried out by tank divisions reaching the Atlantic and occupying Western Europe. As for the outbreak of the Korean war, the initiative came from Kim il-Sung, the North Korean leader, but Stalin gave him the green light in February 1950, provided enormous quantities of arms and other military equipment and " fully consciously (*soznatelno*) attempted to draw America in a new conflict which could eventually lead to a third world war." In brief, Stalin was a monster and eventually a disaster for Russia even more than the rest of the world.

Nothing so crude and outspoken will be found once we move from the Russian version to the cautious and balanced approach of the Cambridge history. It consists of essays by leading students of international affairs, covering every aspect of the Cold War, admittedly sometimes a little remote. Twenty years earlier, still under the impact of America's involvement in Vietnam and a heavy distrust among Western intellectuals of American motives in general such a mainstream Western academic history would probably have been "revisionist" to a smaller or larger extent. It would have been based on the assumption that in most international conflicts responsibility is divided. Was it not true that Washington did not accommodate sufficiently legitimate Soviet security interests, that many opportunities to prevent a conflict or to bring an existing conflict to a speedy end had been missed, that Western leaders grossly exaggerated Soviet political ambitions engaging in one sided condemnations?

Following glasnost and the breakdown of the Soviet Union western academic and the access to Soviet archives Western academic consensus has moved away from revisionism, sometimes not that far but still significantly. The story of the origins of Korean War as told in the Cambridge History is not that different from the Russian version. The former mentions the Gulag a few times (though not as often as McCarthyism), even Tom Lehrer appears (albeit less frequently than Boris Pasternak) and contributors to the *Cambridge History* do not hesitate on occasion to brand Stalin as a dictator.

Both histories have their strengths and weaknesses. The Cambridge history in contrast to most earlier works in this field deals not only with diplomatic history and its scope is much wider than Europe—admittedly the main battlefield in the Cold War, which is, of course all to the good. One of the great weaknesses of the revisionist school was that it was mainly written by Americanists focusing on American policy which resulted in an incomplete and sometimes distorted picture. The Cambridge History includes not only Russian authors but also American students of Russian history and politics providing a much fuller picture. And yet the emphasis even now is more on America and the West. There is, to give but one example, a chapter on American grand strategy but no such essay on Russian strategy. This would perhaps make sense if the West had been the more active party in the Cold War taking the initiative most of the time with the Kremlin merely reacting. But this cannot be seriously maintained for containment was the Western strategy. There is a chapter on culture and the Cold War in Europe from which the reader learns that American cultural propagandists were innocents abroad who lost the battle against native European anti-Americanism whereas the Russians won the argument that high culture flourished in the East. But a few references to East Germany apart the reader does not learn about Soviet cultural propaganda during the Cold War—how successful it was in Poland or Hungary or the countries of Western Europe? The chapter should have been entitled American cultural propaganda—but it was not. The Cambridge history is an encyclopedic work but, as an earlier reviewer (Sir Lawrence Freedman) noted, it does not make it quite clear what the Cold War was all about—was it just a conflict between two superpowers, each with its own legitimate interests, or was there perhaps a certain asymmetry between these powers?

The Russian history is written from a certain political point of view which will not be shared by everyone, not even in Russia, and makes few bones about it. It deals, for instance in considerable detail with Russia abroad—meaning the Russian emigration and the Russian church inside the Soviet Union—as well as other religious denominations. These are legitimate, often neglected, topics, but they were not very important as far as the history of postwar Russia is concerned. The activities of the Pravoslav (Orthodox) were kept under strict control by the Soviet leadership and the church was heavily infiltrated by the KGB. The political importance of the emigration was very small; the dissident movement inside Russia (about which we read less) had a greater impact. Solzhenitsyn appears quite frequently, but his impact was much greater outside the Soviet Union than inside.

Stalin's successors, above all Khrushchev, wanted to reduce military expenditure and détente with the West. But at the same time he stood for "revolutionary diplomacy similar to that followed by the Communist International in the 1920s (Zubok, p. 357). When Kennedy tried to solve peacefully the German problem and other bones of contention of the Cold War, Khrushchev interpreted this as the weakness of the young president (p. 373) and began to exert pressure on Kennedy—hence the Cuban and the second Berlin crisis. The Cambridge history sees this differently and speaks of Kennedy's "reckless policy of aggression." If the rules of détente were violated in Angola, "the principal culprit was the United States" (II, 346).

Following various other crises we reach the age of détente. Where did the main impulse for détente come from? "Research and documents show that the main impulse came from the West" according to the Zubov volume (p. 432). It was based both on leftwing trends in Western Europe, "illusions to the effect that the USSR had become a normal country" and Nixon and Kissinger's concern to get out of the Vietnam War. The Cambridge history feels less sanguine about the merits of Western détente initiative and while praising Nixon and Kissinger it blames them because their secrecy undermined popular support for it. By and large there is a good deal of agreement between our two Cold War histories as to détente and the Brezhnev doctrine; both sides wanted to stabilize great power relations; true, the Soviet leaders had reached the conclusion that the overall balance of power had shifted in their direction and would continue to do so but nor did they want to bring about dangerous confrontations. The Russian history quotes Brezhnev to the effect that he was genuinely against an arms race but does not quite believe him be it only because he was under constant pressure on the part of the military leadership and Communist party grandees to achieve strategic superiority (p. 440/1).

The reasons for the breakdown of détente are well known, above all conflicts in the third world and there are no basic differences between the two histories of the Cold War, even though the language of the Zubov volume is certainly more emphatic; it refers to "Soviet adventures in Africa and Central America, the scattering of Soviet resources, the crisis of the Soviet global empire" (p. 442).

There are certain fascinating omissions: While the *Cambridge History* has a chapter on intelligence in the Cold War and "active measures," the Zubov volume mentions KGB helping to finance Western peace movements whereas the Cambridge history does not.

The Russian Cold War history makes the Bulgarian and Russian secret services responsible for the attempt to kill Pope John Paul II (p. 472), the Cambridge history does not mention the affair at all.

The Russian Cold War history reports that the Soviet leadership did not at first take the Reagan rhetoric too seriously and thought that he would eventually "sober up" (p. 503) but subsequently became very alarmed and even believed in the possibility (if not likelihood) of an American nuclear attack.

The Cambridge history devotes a whole volume to the circumstances and the causes of the end of the Cold War and the disintegration of the Soviet system, the Russian history in contrast hardly deals with it at all. Partly perhaps because it thinks the causes self evident in the light of Soviet history—the house built by Stalin could not last. It could also be that the issue is still considered too controversial for detailed discussion; did not Putin argue that the collapse of the Soviet Union was the greatest disaster in twentieth-century history?

Studying these two histories leads the reader to a number of fascinating questions to which there may be no easy answer. With all the common ground between the two there are marked differences: How to explain that by and large the Cambridge history takes a more benign view of Soviet policy during the Cold War than the Russian history? Is it merely Western academic convention not to use extreme language even when dealing with extreme situations? Or should one look for deeper reasons?

The Russian history which has been quoted here is the most ambitious and massive such enterprise so far. But it is certainly not the new official version of Soviet history, On the contrary, when Vladimir Putin convened a history teachers conference in June 2007 to provide guidelines for the patriotic education of the young generation the suggested doctrine consisted of elements of Tsarist and Soviet historiography with an admixture of Solzhenitsyn ("live not by lies")—admittedly not an easy combination.

But why attribute much political importance to the interpretation of Soviet history—or the Cold War? There is at least one good reason—the state and the future of American–Russian relations.

While the Cold War lasted America (and NATO) considered the Soviet Union its main enemy and vice versa. This was however decades ago and in the twenty first century the common interests outweigh the disputes between the two countries. But the improvement in relations has been modest. President Obama has gone out of his way in favor of "resetting" U.S.–Soviet relations but this went not much beyond certain arms cuts agreement. Contemporary America faces many problems and threats but Russia does not figure high among them. On the other hand, according to all public opinion polls a majority of Russians sees in the United States not just the main culprit of the downfall of the Soviet Union but the greatest enemy of Russia at the present time and the foreseeable future. This doctrine is preached day in day out in many Russian media not just by a few retired generals, neo Stalinists, neo Eurasians and spokesmen of extremist fringe groups. It reaches far into the centrist Russian political establishment. Edward Lucas, former East Europe correspondent of the *Economist* calls his new book *The New Cold War*, Alexander Prokhanov perhaps the best known ideologue of the Russian right entitles his new book *Forebodings of a New Cold War*. True, there is some support for improving relations with Washington in the country and also among the Russian leadership but they seem to be in a minority. There was talk in May 2010 about a new decisive Russian willingness to improve relations with the West and above all the United States, but it remained unclear whether this was meant to go very far beyond enlisting American economic and technological help for the modernization of the Russian economy.

A blatant case of false consciousness, misjudging the real dangers facing present day Russia both domestically and beyond its borders, how to explain it? One could go back to the nineteenth-century Slavophils, to Dostoevsky and Danilevsky who regarded the West (at that time Europe rather than America which hardly figured in Russian thinking) as Russia's eternal enemy. There was the firm conviction that Western Russophobia was deep and immutable and that the West was out to harm Russia always and in every possible way. But the Slavophils were educated people and with all their fear and loathing of the West, the threat was more of a cultural–spiritual character for them than political–military in character.

The tradition of anti-Westernism is deeply rooted but Danilevski is no longer that widely read in Russia—his best-known work, an anti-Western manifesto entitled "Russia and the West" first published in 1869 was reissued though in 1991. Which takes us back to the not-so-distant days of anti-American Cold War propaganda. It is a heritage which despite some promising beginnings still remains to be to overcome. It certainly deserves further study.

References

Melvyn P. Leffler and Odd Arne Westad, eds., *The Cambridge History of the Cold War*, vols 1–3 (Cambridge: Cambridge University Press, 2010), pp. 1999.
A. B. Zubov, ed., *Istoria Rossii*, vol. 2 XX vek 1939–2007 (Moscow: Astrel, 2009), pp. 847.

Part 3

Europe, Our Great Hope

Better Fifty Years of Europe?

Predictions on Europe's future range from impending suicide to its emergence as the leading economic and political superpower. Off late predictions and visions, especially those coming out of Europe, have been rather skeptical, and it is refreshing to come across a book (by Steven Hill, *Europe's Promise*, University of California Press, 2010), which reaches the conclusion that the European model is not only superior to the American in almost every possible way but also the best hope in an insecure age. Everything in Europe is better; with its smart power, it will even solve the problem of the Iranian bomb.

But what is the European model? There is no easy answer—some point out that there is no European model, only a variety of models, and that the United States is closer to certain of these models than they are to each other. The Europessimists say that there is no European social model, only a social disaster. But let us assume for arguments' sake that those who use this term really refer to the European welfare state.

What of these models should America take for guidance? Probably not Spain with almost 20 percent of unemployment nor Italy under Berlusconi. Not the Balkans or Eastern Europe or Greece, which went bankrupt. Not England, which does not belong to the EU, not even France and Germany—they would not recommend their own present model but want far-reaching reforms. There remains Scandinavia, but Sweden, the biggest northern country, has fallen back substantially on the prosperity index. Norway has been doing well; *per capita* average income is now $53,000, and it has the lowest murder rate in the world. In brief, a more accurate title for Mr. Hill's book would be *Why the Norwegian Way Is the Best Hope in a Secure Age*—rather than *Why the European Way Is the Best Hope in an Insecure Age*. But there are problems with the Norwegian model too. It is a country of 4.8 million inhabitants, and what works in a country of this size is not necessarily applicable in a country of three hundred millions. Norway, which was the poorest northern country, has been doing well economically—almost exclusively owing to North Sea oil. And lastly, Norway is not even a member of the European Union.

It is easy, too easy, to ridicule at this time the Eurooptimists whose writings resemble prospectuses of travel agencies recommending luxury resorts at cut-rate prices rather than serious political description and analysis. And

111

yet, while the European model may be in grave trouble, its motivation and experience deserves serious consideration. It aimed at a more democratic society, reducing the extremes of wealth and poverty, and providing essential social services. For several decades, it nearly achieved these aims and had every reason to be proud of it. The reaction in some circles in the United States, the fear of "socialism," bordered on the hysterical; Bismarck, the spiritual godfather of a rudimentary welfare state, was not after all an extreme socialist. I, for one, never understood why the United States could not afford (as the saying went) the extravaganzas of the European welfare state because it involved unacceptably high taxation. Nor could I understand why a nation that is spending almost 17.3 percent of its GNP on its health services could not deliver a service that was as comprehensive and equal in quality as France's, which spent on it only half that percentage—like most other European countries. That the present time of economic crisis is not the ideal moment for reform is yet another story.

True, during the last decade, the European welfare state has been under growing pressure, services had to be cut, and there have been growing worries about its future, as expenditure continued to rise and budgets were shrinking. The political economy of the welfare state was based on the assumption that there would be substantial economic growth, but what if growth dwindled or ceased altogether? These issues are now widely discussed in Europe. But there is no reason to dismiss the European experience even if the European model has been grossly and foolishly oversold.

There is however another, even more important, reason why Europe's decline will be harmful to American interests. America passes through a crisis; the recovery may take years. As Lawrence Summers asked: "How long can the world's biggest borrower be the world's strongest power?" It is precisely in this situation that a strong European Union sharing democratic values with the United States would be needed on the international scene. According to the Eurooptimists (and some of the declarations coming out of Brussels), they are prepared to accept this assignment.

The more realistic voices argue that Europe will not be a world power, but it will play a mediating, pacifying role in world politics. It is quite true that (according to the polls) many more countries believe that Europe will play a more positive role in world affairs than the United States. One suspects, however, that such European popularity rests precisely on the assumption that Europe is powerless and in no position to interfere in other nations' affairs, exerting pressure, complaining about violations of human rights and other such issues. Europe and the European Union have not exactly been treated off late with the respect due to a world power. It was sidelined at the recent Copenhagen conference. President Obama has absented himself from meetings with European leaders; China and Russia have not been very respectful either.

The United Nations are perhaps the most relevant yardstick for the measure of European influence and standing. Europe is the most important donor as far as needy countries are concerned (about 60 billion Euros out of a total of 80). America and the European Union cover more than half of the budget of the United Nations. One would expect that such massive soft power translates itself into influence, but this, to put it cautiously, has not been the case. European influence has been hemorrhaging in the words of the British *Guardian* (not a stalwart supporter of the West, not a bitter enemy of the UN). Whether the issue at stake was Zimbabwe, Sudan, or Burma or some other place where blatant violations of human rights or aggression took place, the West has been invariably outvoted.

This trend has been clearest in the Human Rights Council where, according to European representatives, they have been marginalized and are mired in despair and a pervasive sense of futility. This should not have come as a great surprise because the council's majority consists of countries that are not great believers in human rights but, on the contrary, regard the council as a means to present a common front to avert arrogant and irrelevant Western complaints about subjects such as genocide.

How to explain this striking decline in European influence on the global scene? There is a variety of reasons. It reflects the changing global balance of power. Europe's strength was its economy, but this is no longer the case. Europe will recover to a certain extent, but its former leading position it will not regain. One major reason of Europe's weakness is its dependence from oil and gas supplies from Russia and the Middle East. This dependence certainly influences its foreign policy. Europe suffers from serious demographic weaknesses that have been discussed in detail. The number of native Europeans is declining, and the number of immigrants and their offspring is rising. Immigration may be inevitable in order to keep the economy going and the welfare state financed. But it causes political tensions. The decisive issue is not even whether European cities will have a Muslim majority in ten or thirty years from now, but whether the immigrants will be integrated, and whether they will make a contribution to the welfare of their adopted countries, its culture, its competitiveness, its general strength—as other waves of earlier immigrations did. In seems likely that such an integration will take place in the long run, but probably not within the next generation or two. What will be the character, the foreign policy of such a new Europe? Certainly not the one of "old Europe."

If Europe were serious about keeping its old status in the world, it would get its act together and have a common foreign, defense, and energy policy. But if it proved to be difficult to have a common agricultural policy, to gain coordination let alone agreement in these political fields has seemed to be impossible. According to the Lisbon treaty (2009), the national interests and national sovereignty will be subordinated to the resolutions of the institutions of the European Union. If this were to pass, it would be an enormous step toward European unity, Europe speaking with one voice and acting together. But this resolution is not worth the paper on which it is written. It is unthinkable that France (or indeed any other European country) will subordinate its own national interest to those of the EU. The European governments do not want it, and the European voters want it even less.

Europe seems not even to create the impression that it has a common European foreign and defense policy. For that purpose, some well-known politicians of international renown would have been chosen to give the new setup the appearance of some importance. Instead, two unknown politician were picked, lacking experience and reputation—the British Baroness Lady Cathy Ashton (who began her political career in the antinuclear movement of the 1970s, which led to embarrassing questions about the financial aid given to this group by the Soviets) and Herman van Rompuy, a former Belgian prime minister. Their welcome has not been enthusiastic (plastic garden dwarfs; it would be churlish to add to such insults). The appointments reflect pretty accurately the importance attributed to a common foreign policy by its own members.

What progress has been made concerning European energy supplies and defense? "Energy is what makes Europe tick" and "The time is ripe"; these are the official slogans. A sustainable energy week was scheduled for March 2010, and a nuclear energy academy is set up. But the dependence from Russia and the Middle East persists, which is in effect growing as the North Sea oil reserves are shrinking . . . The slogan of European defense is "A secure Europe in a better world," and some small forces have indeed been stationed in Eastern Chad (this should have been an assignment for the United Nations and the Organization of African States). But the small rapid reaction force, which had been in the making for twenty years or more, still needs sixty days for its deployment. In any case, none of these groups has ever been deployed, and there is the suspicion that they exist only on paper. In a recent article on "The unraveling of the EU," Charles Grant, head of the Center on European Reform, writes: "On many of the world's security problems, the EU is close to irrelevant. Talk to Russian, Chinese Indian policy makers about the EU and they are often withering. They view it as a trade bloc that had pretensions to power but has failed to realize them . . ."

Twenty years ago, even then the outlook was less grim. True, there had been ups and downs almost from the beginning in the complicated road toward European unity. The 1970s had been a decade of Europessimism; in the 1990s, there had been exchanges as to whether Europe was in good shape or not. But there had been some progress after all such as the introduction of a common currency. The apex of optimism was reached in the Lisbon conference of 2000 when it envisaged a "quantum shift" facing "the best macro economic outlook for a generation." Its strategic goal for the next decade was "to become the most competitive and dynamic knowledge-based economy in the world"; in brief, the leading global force because only these issues counted any longer. Military power was outmoded; power in general was measured in economic terms.

It was against this background that a new literature and a new ideology appeared—the twenty-first century was to be the century of Europe, which was to serve as a model for the rest of the world; the values of Europe would become the values of the world—exemplary democracy, an unqualified respect for human rights, sustainable economic growth, stability-orientated monetary policy, and social justice. Europe had enormous transformative power; it would run the twenty-first century.

Disillusionment sat in well before the economic crisis of 2007/8. It had to do with a variety of factors. European growth was less than had been expected; Chinese and India developed far more rapidly. But it is doubtful whether economic factors were the decisive ones in the change of the mood. The European Union had always tended to overemphasize the economy; it was perhaps no accident that Jean Monnet, the father of the Union, at the end of his long life conceded that if he were to start all over again, he would not take the economy as the base for the unification of Europe.

The basic problem seems to have been the fact that there was no real wish to build a political union that would have involved far-reaching concessions concerning national sovereignty. There seemed to have been no real need for such sacrifices in a world in which power politics played no longer a significant role.

Was this belief in harmony and a better, more peaceful world based on naïveté, or was it a rationalization of weakness? For it cannot have escaped European leaders and ideologues that in view of its demographic weakness Europe faced serious internal problems. Given these weaknesses, it is not certain that even if Europe were to speak with one voice and do more for its defense, it would be a leading force in the world. But its prospects would certainly be better.

On top of all this, there had been subacute abulia (a psychological term first used in the nineteenth century) connoting listlessness and apathy. No one has as yet provided a satisfactory explanation for this condition either regarding individuals or collectives. It was also connected, of course, with a decline in Europe's self-confidence, a weakening of the belief in the values it stood for. But why this had happened is again a matter of speculation; perhaps there are no obvious answers. The history of mankind is after all the story of confident rising powers and of tired, declining ones. The feeling of a great mission, of preaching the virtues of a better world, certainly vanished. The European model became closer to that of Latin America. These countries, after all, also lived in peace with each other.

What will Europe be like in ten and twenty years from now? With a little luck it will gradually recover from the present economic difficulties, but it will find it difficult to compete because it will have to pay dearly for energy and raw materials. Again, with a little luck the domestic transformation resulting from the changes in its ethnic composition will be gradual and relatively peaceful.

Will it be a political and cultural center? The prospects are not great. It will have to lower its voice as a champion of human rights as befitting its reduced standing in the world.

It is not that there is no need for a world power as envisaged in the fantasies of the Eurooptimists. The assertions of Kishone Mahbubani and like-minded thinkers about the loss of Western moral authority and the ascendancy of Eastern moral values seem a little premature. Asia might be more efficient than old Europe, but as for the moral values Alfred Lord Tennyson's feelings expressed some 150 years ago still seems closer to reality.

Better fifty years of Europe than a cycle of Cathay

What could Europe galvanize Europe out of its lethargy—a major crisis? There have been such beneficial shocks in history. But shocks could also have the opposite effect. By 2020, a little more will be known whether to trust Mahbubani or Tennyson.

Europe's Long Road to the Mosque

Justin Vaisse is not yet a household name but this young man may go far. Of North African background, he has taught at Sciences Po in Paris and been a speech-writer for the French Minister of Defense. Currently at Washington's Brookings Institution, he is the leading French expert on—and the nemesis of—the neoconservatives. The fact that he is spending time in America may not necessarily affect his political prospects. After all, Georges Clemenceau did the same. Of late, he has discovered and given publicity to what he calls a new genre in American literature: Eurabia. Among the chief protagonists in this new genre he mentions above all Bernard Lewis, the greatest Orientalist of our time, and Bat Ye'or, who popularised the term "Eurabia" to warn against the Islamicization of Europe. In view of the Homeric struggle between the two sides—Lewis has been accused of appeasement if not worse by the other side—it seems somewhat far-fetched to find a common denominator for them, but Vaisse is a resourceful man.

Among the European protagonists of the Eurabian thesis, Vaisse mentions Ayaan Hirsi Ali, who was born in Somalia and now lives in the U.S. Yours truly is also named, although it helps him very little that in *Last Days of Europe* (Thomas Dunne, 2007) I devoted several pages to my unhappiness with the very term "Eurabia" which, for a variety of reasons, I have never used and thought misleading. The great majority of Muslims in Britain are not Arab but Pakistani or Bangladeshi in origin. In Germany, the Turks greatly outnumber all other Muslims. In France, the majority is North and West African. In Belgium, Turkish and Moroccan, and so on. These are not minor, pedantic issues because traditions, culture, language and even the forms of Islam practiced differ considerably in Europe. While the Arabs have tried to attain positions of leadership in the European Muslim communities, this has merely given additional impetus to tensions (and among the Arabs there is a bitter struggle between Shias and Sunnis). Arabs traditionally believe that only they are the true sons of the Prophet, giving them a feeling of superiority over other Muslims.

Vaisse has not been alone in his campaign against the prophets of Eurabia. He found several sober, level-headed and well informed experts such as

Jocelyne Cesari at Harvard or Jytta Clausen, a Danish scholar at Brandeis. Dr. Cesari argues that there has been in the Muslim communities a strong trend towards conservatism, but that this is not tantamount to support for terrorism. This is true and some in the West have paid insufficient attention to it. But even here a word of caution is necessary. Most of our knowledge on the mood and the political orientation of Muslim communities all over the world rests on public opinion polls, most prominently of the PEW. How reliable, though, are these polls? To give an example: a figure of 13 percent is usually given for those in Britain sympathizing with al-Qaeda. But can it be taken for granted that those asked will reveal to strangers (who, for all they know, may be agents of the police or other security forces) the innermost secrets of their hearts and minds? The answer seems obvious.

To return to Vaisse's fellow experts: Professor Clausen is a happy soul. The author of *Islamic Challenge* (Oxford University Press, 2005), she reached the conclusion that there was no such challenge. She had interviewed some 300 professional Muslim men and women in various European countries, all middle- or upper-class businessmen, professors, lawyers and physicians, all of them reasonably content with their life and circumstances, identifying with their new countries and eager to collaborate in their social, political and economic life. There are indeed such people: the emerging Muslim elite. But the fact that these contented people are only so far a happy few seems not to have occurred to Professor Clausen. What influence do they have in their respective communities? Do the young people listen to them or to the imams? To what extent do they still identify with their erstwhile community? In Europe, most of them have moved out of Muslim ghettoes. This is not the case in India, where the Muslim middle- and upper-class prefers to live with their co-religionists.

Professor Clausen attained fame a year later as the result of the Danish cartoon affair, having written a book about the subject. Yale University Press, the publishers, decided to delete the controversial cartoons rather than use them to illustrate the text. This, in turn, generated some protests, but Yale did not budge, and the impression was created that Professor Clausen in her book was breaking a lance for freedom of expression. Her intention, however, was to criticize the Danish government and even its society, which she thought intolerant. This was based on the belief that if integration did not work, this must have been the fault of the state, the authorities and the ethnic majority, not the religious or national minority, for it was the former that had to make the concessions.

Vaisse's and Dr. Cesari's points of view were shaped largely by the French riots of 2005. The view can be summarized briefly but not unfairly as: "It's Marx, not Muhammed, stupid." In other words, the deeper causes of the unrest in the *banlieues* (housing estates) were social and economic, not religious fanaticism. This point of view is not entirely wrong, for if the people in the *banlieues* were as prosperous as Professor Clausen's happy few, it would indeed be less likely that they would engage in burning cars or in suicide missions. This generalization should not, however, be pressed too far. Osama bin Laden and many of his intimates never went to bed hungry and did not come from poor backgrounds. For the deeper reasons, we do not find an answer in *Das Kapital*. How do we explain the fact that Muslim immigrants in Europe have not been doing remotely as well as newcomers from other countries? How to account for the fact that pupils in European schools from other cultures, for example China and India, have often been doing better than their classmates born in Europe—and that Muslim students have been doing much less well and that the drop out rate among them has been so high?

Optimism with regard to the prospects of multiculturalism (or more recently of integration) usually went hand-in-hand with optimism concerning the future of Europe and its standing in the world and it is easy to see why. In the *Last Days of Europe*, I tried to point to the important social and cultural changes taking place in Europe and to the other grave dangers facing it. These arguments were neither sensational nor very original. Leo Tindemans, the former Belgian Prime Minister, had written in a position paper in the 1970s on the future of Europe that a house half finished would not last and that economic unity without a greater measure of political union would not work. Chancellor Helmut Kohl, the father of the Euro, had expressed similar concerns. But the views I had expressed were not popular. They were criticized in the *Economist* and the *Financial Times*. It was not the message one wanted to hear. Only a few years have passed and one does not now see many new books or articles predicting that Europe will be the world's leading superpower and that the whole world would try to emulate the European model. The prophets of the European superpower have turned to other subjects whereas the critics of the Eurabian model have not given up so easily.

Before taking our discussion of Eurabia any further, there's need for a brief historical reminder. Those indignant about the use of the concept seem to be unaware that its origins are by no means Western and were not concocted in the cabals of the neoconservatives. It is a Muslim, or rather specifically Arab, concept. Among Middle Eastern public figures and writers, the idea that Muslims would be a majority in Europe goes back a long time. One early well known example is the speech made in the United Nations General Assembly in 1974 by Houari Boumediène, the then President of Algeria, in which he argued that in view of the high birth rate of Muslim women (and the low and declining birth rate in Europe) such a development was more or less inescapable. He was referring specifically to the "wombs of our women." Boumediène was not among the leading demographers of his generation (nor was Libya's Colonel Gaddafi, who made a similar statement in 2006) but no special training was or is needed to observe the changes taking place in Europe's cities.

The idea he voiced has been repeated on countless occasions in speeches and on placards displayed in demonstrations in many European countries. The changing European situation has been described in great detail in books and articles in the Arab media. One recent example should suffice: an article written in May in English by Ajaz Saka Syed (by no means an extremist) in the Saudi *Arab News*, observed in Brussels that "the capital of the new Europe increasingly looks like Beirut, Istanbul or any other great city in the Middle East." He is pleasantly surprised by the impact of the growing Arab and Muslim population on life in Europe, adding: "This is not just Brussels, scenes like these can be found in London and Paris, in Berlin, Copenhagen and Amsterdam." He reports that European media have been buzzing with talk that "the Muslims are coming" and about the demographic time bomb. He advises his European colleagues not to get overexcited and to wish the immigrants away but to accept the facts. Those who are invading Europe will transform its profile forever. But they are needed to rejuvenate an old and exhausted continent: "Like them or hate them, Europe has to learn to live with its Muslims."

Recent years have witnessed a flood of demographic literature, professional and less professional, about the number of Muslims already living in Europe and also projections far into the future. According to the UN, by the year 2300 Europe will be a black continent. There have been endless debates about whether to include in these statistics only new immigrants or also the second- and third-generation and those who acquired the citizenship of their countries of adoption. Those warning against alarmism have pointed out that the high birthrate among Muslim communities is declining and in all probability will continue to decline. This seems to be true, and it is also doubtful whether Muslims will continue to come in droves, but it is also true that the considerably lower European birthrate will probably not recover to any significant degree. It has nowhere reached reproduction rate (2.1 per family). In countries such as France, which is close to reproduction rate, the figures are probably misleading because they include births in the immigrant community. In any case, for the achievement of major political, cultural and social influence, 51 percent is not the magical figure.

How significant are these demographic discussions? With all the differences of opinion there is some common ground. Everyone agrees that the present number of Muslim immigrants in Europe is relatively small—between five and ten per cent. But it is also true that their number among the younger age cohort is two or three times larger, which means that within one generation their percentage in the general population will be considerably higher. Five percentage points is a low figure, but if the five percent consume 40 percent of the social service budgets at a time of severe cutbacks and provide a similar proportion of young inmates of the prisons, this is bound to generate political problems. There are certain concentrations of Muslim immigrants where the percentage of immigrants is at least one third: in Brussels, Roubaix in northern France, Malmö in Sweden, Duisburg and its vicinity in Germany, Bradford and in the Eastern Midlands, to name but a few.

However, the demographic aspect is only part of the story, and less important than the cultural one. The history of Europe (and of other continents) is the history of migrations. Given its low birthrate, Europe can preserve its standard of living only with new immigrants—young, strong, intelligent, law-abiding, eager to work (to follow the definition of our Saudi visitor to Brussels). But neither Pakistan nor the Middle East has produced such people in abundance. Moreover, women in many Muslim communities are not permitted to work outside their home. The second and third generations of immigrants tend to be more radical than their parents. This radicalism by no means stems from deep, fundamentalist religiosity: the most radical are not the most pious believers who pray five times daily and scrupulously fulfill the other religious commandments. This is a generation of resentment, because unlike other groups they did not make it. Why did they not make it? Not because they were school dropouts, they believe, but because the dominant society discriminated against them in every way. They see themselves as the victims par excellence and their frustration turns into aggression. Their ideology is a mixture of religious and nationalist elements, combined with an enormous number of conspiracy theories, the more absurd the more popular. There is a distinct danger that out of these victims (as they perceive themselves) a new underclass is developing in some ways similar to what French nineteenth-century historians called *classes dangereuses.*

True, some of them did make it, sometimes against heavy odds. Some of these successful Muslims are showing greater toughness and realism vis-à-vis their communities than their non-Muslim counterparts. Ahmed Abu Taleb, the mayor of Rotterdam, holds both Dutch and Moroccan nationality. This has not prevented him from advising those of his coreligionists who did not like it in the Netherlands to go back to their country of origin. Job Cohen, the mayor of Amsterdam, would hardly have dared to make such a statement, not in any case, before he resigned as mayor to become head of the Dutch Labour Party. Since then, he has been considerably more outspoken. Nyamka Sabuni, an African Muslim and the Swedish minister for gender equality, suggested a medical investigation of Swedish schoolgirls to find out the extent of genital mutilation. Nothing became of her initiative but it is unlikely that any of her Swedish-born colleagues would have dared even to mention a subject like this.

The decisive issue is not the numbers but the integration of the new immigrants. About half of the newcomers—more in some countries, fewer elsewhere—have expressed their wish to adopt the values and customs of their new homes, but half are rejecting them as incompatible with Islam. The authorities in some countries (notably France and the Netherlands) claim that Muslim integration has been more successful than generally believed. No major terrorist attacks have succeeded in Europe in the last five years since the London and Madrid bombings and the murder of Theo van Gogh. However, these claims cannot always be taken at face value. In Germany, the optimism is based on an investigation of all immigrants, including the many who came from Russia. In England, glowing accounts have been published about certain state-supported Muslim schools. But on closer investigation, it appeared that they were preaching that most things British were sinful, including Shakespeare and cricket. Many dozens of young Muslims from Germany, Denmark and the UK have gone to fight the infidels (or their own brothers) in Afghanistan, Pakistan, Somalia, Yemen and elsewhere. But the issue is not terrorism, important as it is, but integration or the "rejuvenation" of Europe.

What then of the second and third generation? A well-known Berlin imam has said that "the road to the mosque is long and the temptations are many." It is not clear what temptations he had in mind: probably not Western political philosophy but those of the flesh such as the less savory aspects of contemporary Western civilization—drugs, drinking, pornography. While the second and third generation of Muslim immigrants is generally more radical, this may well change over time. But it is unlikely to change soon. It may take several more generations. Islam once had a great civilization and there could be a revival after centuries of stagnation and decline. But what kind of "rejuvenation" can Europe expect in the years and decades to come?

It will probably be impossible to keep Muslim communities residing in the West in isolation from the outside world however intense the internal pressures and ideological indoctrination. The most obvious example is gender equality. Orthodox Muslim society is opposed to it and to more sexual freedom in general, which is considered corrupt and deeply sinful. Undermining this fundamental attitude would mean undermining male domination in society and there will be tremendous resistance against it. Not ethical purity and moral superiority is at stake, but domination. Why some women should participate in the process of keeping their status in society inferior by wearing the *niqab* and in other ways is a fascinating psychological problem that certainly deserves further study. The same is true with regard to secularism in general: concessions to secularism undermine not just deeply rooted and cherished beliefs, but the rule of the mullahs who will not easily surrender.

How far will European societies go in accommodating a fast growing minority that not only faces great difficulties with social and cultural integration but is to a considerable extent basically opposed to it? Positive discrimination helped in some societies but not in others. A German minister recently stated that a Muslim prime minister was no longer unthinkable, and a Dutch minister has expressed the belief that sharia may become the law of the land. But what kind of prime minister and what version of sharia? European banking systems have adjusted their financial procedures to conform with sharia principles. But it is doubtful that even the most liberal archbishop will justify honor killings, genital mutilation and similar practices in the foreseeable future.

Meanwhile, there has been growing resistance to the most striking manifestations of Muslim "otherness" in various European countries such as Belgium and France. This refers to mosques and minarets in Switzerland and *niqabs, hijabs,* and *burqas* in France. The ban on wearing these in public was supported by not a few Muslims but attacked by others as a restriction of the freedom of religious practice. Wearing them is not stipulated by sharia but is a sectarian invention and political in motivation, designed to make it clear that the wearer wants nothing to do with the culture and way of life of the others. It is a form of protest against integration.

European societies have indeed to learn to live with their Muslims as the cities of Europe begin to look like those of the Middle East. This process increasingly affects not only outward appearances but the general quality of life as well as competitiveness and most other aspects of culture and the economy. And it is also clear that this process has an impact on the foreign policy of European governments. The discussions as to whether such changes are taking place should cease: in Arab vernacular, they are *kalam fadi* ("empty talk"). Debates should now focus on the future. The problem is not a "takeover" but gradual and probably irreversible changes. How far will they go? In any event "rejuvenation" is hardly the most fitting term for this process. There is bound to be a backlash but to maintain political and social peace accommodation might still be inescapable.

One major country is usually ignored in the discussions on Europe's future, the one with the greatest number of Muslim citizens. Russia. Books with such titles as *The Islamisation of Russia* appeared in Moscow well before Western Europe. The number of Muslim citizens in Russia is estimated at 25–30 million. Some, especially in the Middle Volga region, are highly assimilated, unlike in Europe there has been a fair amount of intermarriage. Moscow is believed to have between 1.5 and two million legal and illegal Muslim inhabitants, the majority of whom have made it clear that they have no wish "to return to the Middle Ages." Others as in the Northern Caucasus are engaging in terrorism and guerrilla warfare against Russia, just as their ancestors did in the nineteenth century. The Russian government has tried to accommodate Muslims but this policy collided with the growing xenophobia not just among the Russian Right and the Orthodox Church but with wide sections of the general population demanding "Russia to the Russians." The demands of the moderate Muslim communities, while not extreme, have been growing and are increasingly influencing Russian foreign policy; Russia is now a member of the Organization of Islamic Conference (OIC). It has asked that the deputy head of the Russian state should by law be an ethnic

Muslim. Since their birthrate is much higher than the Russian average, their importance in Russian life is increasing. In a decade from now, it is estimated that one in three recruits to the Russian army will be of Muslim origin. These and other tensions are unmistakable. They might be contained, except perhaps in the Caucasus. But the real test is bound to come after the retreat of NATO from Afghanistan, when the Taliban and other such groups will be free to devote their energies to the former Soviet central Asian republics, considered by Moscow part of its "privileged zone of influence." At present, many Russians, including some in high places, believe that they are doing the West a great favor by permitting supplies to reach coalition contingents there. There could be a rude awakening.

Islamic Fascism, Islamophobia, Antisemitism

The use of the term Islamic fascism and Islamofascism by both politicians (including the president of the United States) and publicists in various countries has created a minor storm and led to a search for the origins of the term. I have been among those mentioned in this context in some Arab media and the Wikipedia; this is less than half correct but it is probably true that I was among the first to explore the origins of the term clerical fascism and its meaning. In *Fascism: Past Present Future* (Oxford University Press, 1996) I noted that the term "fundamentalism" was imperfect for a variety of reasons, but in the present context it had come to represent a radical, militant fanatical movement trying to impose its beliefs on others by means of force. I also wrote,

> Fundamentalism, is not of course, an Islamic monopoly as it can be found in Christianity and Judaism as well as in other religions. In extreme forms it is manifested in political terrorism (such as the antiabortionist murders in the United States, in Kahanism in Israel, in Hindu attacks against Muslims in India). Fundamentalists have exerted political pressure on secular governments in America, Europe and Asia. But only in the Muslim world have radicals acquired positions of influence and power and are likely to have further successes, from Algeria to Afghanistan, Bangladesh and even beyond.

I see no need to add or subtract to these lines looking at them at perspective of a dozen years.

The term clerical fascism is very old. I found it first mentioned in 1922 even before Mussolini's march on Rome. It referred to a group of Catholic believers in Northern Italy who advocated a synthesis of Catholicism and fascism. A multi volume German language Encyclopedia of Religions published in the 1920s contained an essay entitled "Faszism (sic) and Fundamentalism in the USA" and it argued that political fanaticism fueled religious intolerance, how extreme nationalism and populism went hand in hand with radical religion and how the Ku Klux Klan cooperated with the fundamentalists. Both were based on the same social strata, the poorly educated and discontented looking for primitive and violent solutions.

In later years it was often argued that there could be no lasting under-standing between fascism and religion simply because both were holistic weltanschauungen staking claims to the whole human being in all respects. Furthermore, a fascist-religious synthesis was said to be impossible because all varieties of fascism were deeply nationalistic; modern secular nationalism was irrelevant, if not anathema—especially to Islam. However, if Hizb al Tahrir and some other radical Islamic groups rejected nationalism and advocated Khalifat, a Muslim world state, many other militant Islamic groups found it not particularly difficult to combine a fanatical religious belief with militant nationalism (and this is true also for some East European countries). The same is true with regard to the present leaders of Iran who with all their religious fanaticism aim at the domination of the Persian Gulf region (and beyond) not by Islam but by the Persian state—and never made a secret of it.

A German Catholic emigré writer Edgar Alexander (Edgar Alexander Emmerich) published an interesting work in 1937 in Switzerland entitled *The Hitler Mythos* (which was translated into English and reprinted after World War II) in which he compared National Socialism with "Moham-medanism" and found similarities between them. Alexander was no Islamic expert, in his book he stressed all along the central importance of hatred and fanaticism in the Nazi movement, the brutality of its repressive policy, its strong appeal to social and national resentments. He referred frequently to Hitler's "Mohammedanism" but made it clear that this referred only to external organizational forms (whatever this meant), to mass psychologi-cal effects and militant fanaticism. Alexander believed that Mohammed's religion was based on sincere religious fanaticism (combined with political impulses) whereas Hitler's (political) religion and its fanaticism had different sources. Alexander also quoted in this context Hitler's *Mein Kampf* to the effect that ideology however truthful and vital was insignificant as long as it was not represented by a fighting movement. In other words—the sword as the means of the propagation of the new religion.

So much about religious and quasi religious impulses. Fascism made cer-tain inroads in the 1930s among secular elements in Egypt, Syria and Iraq. It should be recalled that Haj Amin al Husseini the Mufti of Jerusalem spent the war years as Hitler's guest in Berlin. But in retrospect there are doubts with regard to the depth of Haj Amin's religiosity. He requested for instance the bombing of Jerusalem by the German air force. It is unlikely that a truly pious Muslim would have acted this way.

Some general observations about fascism: How much did the various European parties and governments of the 1930 and 1940s which we now call "fascist" have in common? A great deal, they were anti democratic, anti liberal, nationalistic, populist militarist, aggressive, they believed in violence, there was one party and a leader; when in power, propaganda and terror (from above) played a decisive role. But there were also considerable differences between them—Hitler, no doubt, would have emphatically rejected the fascist label—Nazism, as he saw it, was a specifically German phenomenon and despite certain ideological communalities and common interests was quite different from Italian fascism. Later day political scientists have frequently invoked a "fascist minimum" such as the specific features mentioned earlier on. Unless a certain movement shared this minimum of features it would be misleading to call them "fascist." The debate as to which features are crucial continues to this day.

Thus the Austrian catholic regime in power from 1934 to the Anschluss in 1938 was often called clerical fascist by its enemies, but it was certainly far more Christian than fascist in inspiration. The same is true, for instance to the Slovak regime headed by Monsignor Tiso during World War II which was authoritarian rather than totalitarian. In Franco's Spain there was a fascist party but it was one among several political forces and by no means the decisive one. The country was far more similar to an old fashioned military dictatorship than a modern fascist regime. Argentine under Peron was regarded by some political scientists as an ideal-type fascist regime but this assessment never gained wide currency because Peron was far more in the tradition of Latin American caudillos, military dictators of the populist variety than in the tradition of European fascism.

On the other hand it is not difficult to find strong religious influences among certain Europe fascist movements, not at all in consonance with the pagan influences in Nazism or the anticlericalism of Italian fascism. Romania is a good example, priests took a prominent part in the activities of the Legion of Archangel Michael (later the Iron Guard) the same is true with regard to the Ustasha regime in Croatia. The fascist Rexists in Belgium were originally the leading Catholic youth movement in that country. Sir Oswald Mosley, the leader of the British fascist leader wrote after the war that his movement would have been far more successful if it had been more religious and one could also refer in this context to Father Coughlin in the United States (or the Reverend Gerald Smith) who believed in the coexistence of a Christian spiritual revolution and fascism.

In brief, fascism was less monolithic than Communism, there were significant differences in theory and practice from country to country and coexistence with militant religion was by no means ruled out in principle or in practice.

In their search for the origins of the term Islamofascism investigators have relied, not surprisingly on computer search engines which have pointed to two leading students of Islam in this context—the distinguished French Orientalist Maxime Rodinson and the British writer Malise Ruthven. In 1978 in a polemic against some of his leftwing friends such as Foucault who welcomed the revolution in Tehran as a great progressive achievement. Rodinson wrote in *Le Monde* that far from being left wing in any meaningful sense, movements such as the one headed by Khomeini and the Muslim Brother-hood were predominantly fascist, or to be precise constituted a form of "ar-chaic fascism." This comparison was picked up on later occasions by several other students of Iran sympathizing with the Iranian opposition, but the Iranian president Khatami also warned of the danger of fascism in his country in a speech in 2001 even though he did not use the term Islamic fascism.

Malise Ruthven, the godson of the famous traveler and Orientalist Freya Stark wrote in an article in the London daily *Independent* in 1990 that unlike other non Western religions Islam has found it impossible to institutionalize political divergences: "authoritarian government, not to say Islamic fascism, is the rule rather than the exception from Morocco to Palestine."

The use of the term "fascism" by both Rodinson and Ruthven is open to criticism. "Archaic fascism" is a contradiction in term, because fascism was a modern form of dictatorship quite distinct from older authoritarian regimes. Ruthven too seemed to be unaware of the difference between authoritarian-ism and totalitarianism (and the debates on these lines). Ruthven followed up his comments in a number of books on Islamic fundamentalism in later years. Neither Rodinson nor Ruthven could be possibly charged with lack of sympathy for Islam and the Arab world to which they had devoted their life's work. Both were outspoken anti Zionists and critics of Israeli politics. Rodinson, the son of Jewish immigrants from Russia was a Marxist and for many years a member of the Communist party; his autobiography (*Souvenirs d'un marginal*, Fayard, 2005) conveys an interesting account of his younger years in radical Paris circles.

But computer search engines do not go back very far in time and it is the merit of Martin Kramer to have disinterred a leading textbook of the 1960s *Politics of Social Change in the Middle East and North Africa* (1963, Princ-eton University Press) by the late Princeton professor Manfred Halpern in which he wrote that the neo Islamic totalitarian movements are essentially fascist movements. They concentrated on mobilizing passion and violence to enlarge the power of their charismatic leader and the solidarity of the movement. I knew Halpern, albeit not very well, and have to confess that I did not pay much attention to his argument at the time; it seemed to me misplaced. To what movements could he refer in 1963 when Gamal Abdul Nasser, a secular dictator repressing the Muslim Brotherhood, was in power in Egypt and his prestige was high throughout the Arab world? There were no "Islamic totalitarian movements" in Turkey (except perhaps the secular Pan Turks), Iran, or Pakistan at the time True, there were totalitarian and fascist elements in the ideology and the practice of the Muslim Brother-hood with its branches in various Arab countries. The Brotherhood had been quite strong in the late 1940s and early 50s, but after its repression by Nasser it amounted to very little. It was only with the fall of Nasser and the breakdown of Arab nationalism and communism that Islamism had its revival. While Halpern's observations were wrong (or to be precise not very relevant) at the time they were however to some extent prescient.

How helpful is the "Islamofascism" label at the present time with regard to the radical Islamists? There are striking parallels—the populism, the anti Westernism, the antiliberalism, the anti-Semitism, its aggressive, expansive, anti humanist character, the interpretation of Islam as both a religion and a totalitarian political-social order which provides answers to all problems of the contemporary world. It could be argued that while it lacks a Führer or a Duce, the supreme clerical leader (such as Khomeini) fulfills a similar role and while there is no political party which has a monopoly, the mosque fulfills a similar function as far as the mobilization of the masses and their indoctrination is concerned.

But at the same time there are differences that should not be overlooked. Fascism was an European phenomenon, dictatorships outside Europe (such as for instance the Japanese regime in the thirties and forties) were bound to develop on different lines according to historical tradition and political conditions. The age of fascism came to an end in 1945. Since then there has been neo-fascism and neo-Nazism which also differ in certain respects from its historical predecessors and models. Radical Islamism could be interpreted as a post fascist movement. But such a label tends to exaggerate the role of its European predecessor and to downplay the specific homegrown, in other words, the Islamist elements. Hitler did not engage in Jihad and he did not want to impose anything like the sharia.

Unfortunately, the fascist label has been used rather indiscriminately in the past; the German Social Democrats were called social fascists by the Communists at one time , Roosevelt and the New Deal were branded as fascist, so were de Gaulle, Barry Goldwater, Ronald Reagan, President Bush and a great many other political figures since World War II. Political movements and regimes can be barbarous and genocidal—Pol Pot's Cambodia might serve as an example, but this does not make them necessarily fascist. It would be much more accurate to define the present Iranian regime as a new (populist) form of oriental despotism than as fascist.

It is one of the ironies of the debate on Islamofascism that some of those who have argued that Islamic fundamentalism is at most a cultural but not a political or military challenge to the West have had fewer hesitations to call Christian fundamentalism in the U.S. and elsewhere at least "potentially fascist." It is another irony that one of the main arguments against the use of the term has been the allegation that it was deeply offensive to Muslims all over the world especially to Arabs.

But whereas "liberal" or "secular" might cause offense in the Arab world, the term Fascism (*al fashiye and al naziye*) has never been, nor have Hitler and Mussolini been considered great evildoers. The negative connotations

connected with fascism or Nazism are purely Western and have never
extended to Asia and Africa and least of all to the Middle East. There are
various good reasons to find the term Islamic Fascism wanting and unhelpful but the argument that it might cause offense outside Europe and North
America is not among them.

Islamophobia

If Islamic fascism is a dubious term so is, for different reasons, Islamophobia. It was first used in French in the 1980s but did not gain wide currency prior to the publication of a report by the British Runnymede Trust in 1998. This was followed by yet another report in 2004 by the Commission on British Muslims on Islamophobia. The report argued that Islamophobia, the discrimination and persecution of Muslims had become one of the major problems of Western societies. However, the new term soon came under criticism. There was no fear of Islam in any Western country.

Commentators identified eight components which they said define Islamophobia. Above all "Islam is seen as a monolithic bloc, static and unresponsive to change." But given the civil war in Iraq between Sunni and Shi'ites in Iraq and the many other conflicts between Muslim believers it will be difficult to find people in the West assuming that Islam is a "monolithic bloc." The other seven components are not less dubious—such as the belief that Islam is separate and "the other," that it is aggressive, a political ideology used for political advantage. True, there are people in the West who have reached such conclusions—as the result of reading the books of Sayed Qutb or listening to the speeches of the leaders of Iran who have been preaching precisely these doctrines. Another "component" is based on the complaint of exclusion of Muslims from mainstream society. Such emergence of alternative, separate societies in Europe is undeniable, but it is above all the result of the indoctrination of radical imams preaching "apartheid" as the only way to keep the commandments of their faith.

Islamic radicals too have criticized the term "Islamophobia" albeit for different reasons as an inadequate term. They suggest that a more accurate term would be "anti Islamic racism" which combines the elements of dislike of a religion and active discrimination against the people belonging to that religion. The political purpose underlying this alternative definition is obvious but it is based on the manifestly absurd assumption of an Islamic race including Muslims from Kosovo, Senegal, Indonesia not to mention converts to Islam in Britain, France and the United States. Muslim radicals have argued that Islamophobia is a new form of racism whereby Muslims are attacked not as a race but as a ethno-religious group, prejudice is no longer based on skin color but on notions of cultural superiority and otherness. This argument is equally feeble but even if it were true, it would still be wrong to use misleading terms (racism, ethnic group) that are clearly not applicable trying to define such prejudice.

If anything there has been indifference and lack of interest outside the Muslim world in Islam as a religion and its believers for a long time; paradoxically, such interest has grown in recent years, more copies of the Koran and books about Islam have been sold than ever before, there have been countless ecumenical dialogs and conferences sponsored by churches and other bodies. It is true that there has been growing fear of terror and those engaging in it, especially since 2001; terrorophobia would be a far more accurate term. There was and is also resentment against extremist movements aiming to impose their religious law and way of life on the rest of society. But this too hardly amounts to Islamophobia.

It is also true, that there has been xenophobia and also attacks against new immigrants at all times in many countries, but these attacks have not been on religious lines. In Germany, to give but one example, immigrants from Black Africa and the Far East have been attacked more often than Muslims, in Russia students from Black Africa and Christians from the Caucasus (Georgians and Armenians) have been attacked at least as often as those from Muslim Azerbaidjan. If there has been latent hostility towards Islam, India would probably be a better example. But Islamophobia has never been used in the Indian context, hence the suspicion that "Islamophobia" came into being as a public relations stratagem (partly as a counterweight to anti-Semitism) in the West in which it was expected to have a political impact in view of guilt feelings prevailing in these countries. This is not of course to deny the existence of tensions and conflicts but these were and are mutual and the term "Islamophobia" clearly intended to allocate responsibility and guilt to one side only.

Anti-Semitism

Anti-Semitism is in many ways yet another unfortunate term. That there has been hostility towards Jews as a people, a religion, a social or cultural group going back far into history and culminating in the mass murder during World War II is beyond dispute. But what is anti-Semitism? The term was coined according to many sources in 1879 by Wilhelm Marr, a German writer originally of the far left who later in life moved to the extreme right. (The word was in fact used before and it even appeared in encyclopedias but Marr certainly gave it wide currency as pointed out in my *The Changing Face of Antisemitism,* Oxford University Press, 2006). But what did it exactly mean? "Semitic" refers to such ancient and extinct languages as Phoenician and Accadian as well as many still widely used, including Arabic and Hebrew. But there is no Semitic religion or people or race and for this reason the use of the term has given rise to endless misunderstandings and deliberate distortion. Hannibal and Jesus Christ were speakers of Semitic languages but the anti-Semites clearly had nothing against them. Even the most rabid enemies of the Jews were not happy about the use of the term anti-Semitism; the Nazis did not want to antagonize their well wishers in the Middle East and during World War II Joseph Goebbels, Hitler's minister of propaganda gave instructions to use the term as little as possible. Muslim anti-Semites have routinely argued that they cannot possibly be anti-Semites because they are themselves Semites.

Since 1945 even confirmed anti-Semites have distanced themselves from the term using various forms of circumlocution (such as for instance "cosmo-politans" in Stalin's Russia); sometimes they have done so for legal reasons, (racialism being outlawed in some countries) without however changing their attitude towards Jews. Some quite obviously use "anti-Zionism" as a cover for anti-Jewish attacks, but others have claimed that it is false to paint all critics of Israel with the anti-Semitic brush.

In brief, Islamic fascism, Islamophobia, and anti-Semitism, each in its way, are imprecise terms we could well do without but it is doubtful whether they can be removed from our political lexicon.

Part 4

Terrorism

Postmodern Terrorism

As the nineteenth century ended, it seemed no one was safe from terrorist attack. In 1894 an Italian anarchist assassinated French President Sadi Carnot. In 1897 anarchists fatally stabbed Empress Elizabeth of Austria and killed Antonio Canovas, the Spanish prime minister. In 1900 Umberto I, the Italian king, fell in yet another anarchist attack; in 1901 an American anarchist killed William McKinley, president of the United States. Terrorism became the leading preoccupation of politicians, police chiefs, journalists, and writers from Dostoevsky to Henry James. If in the year 1900 the leaders of the main industrial powers had assembled, most of them would have insisted on giving terrorism top priority on their agenda, as President Clinton did at the Group of Seven meeting after the June bombing of the U.S. military compound in Dhahran, Saudi Arabia.

From this perspective the recent upsurge of terrorist activity is not particularly threatening. According to the State Department's annual report on the subject, fewer people died last year in incidents of international terrorism (165) than the year before (314). Such figures, however, are almost meaningless, because of both the incidents they disregard and those they count. Current definitions of terrorism fail to capture the magnitude of the problem worldwide. Terrorism has been defined as the substate application of violence or threatened violence intended to sow panic in a society, to weaken or even overthrow the incumbents, and to bring about political change. It shades on occasion into guerrilla warfare (although unlike guerrillas, terrorists are unable or unwilling to take or hold territory) and even a substitute for war between states. In its long history, terrorism has appeared in many guises; today society faces not one terrorism but many terrorisms.

Since 1900, terrorists' motivation, strategy, and weapons have changed to some extent. The anarchists and the left-wing terrorist groups that succeeded them, down through the Red Armies that operated in Germany, Italy, and Japan in the 1970s, have vanished; if anything, the initiative has passed to the extreme right. Most inter-national and domestic terrorism these days, however, is neither left nor right, but ethnic-separatist-religious in inspiration. Ethnic terrorists have more staying power than ideologically motivated ones, since they draw on a larger reservoir of public support.

The greatest change in recent decades is that terrorism is by no means militants' only strategy. The many-branched Muslim Brotherhood, the Palestinian Hamas, the Irish Republican Army (IRA), the Kurdish extremists in Turkey and Iraq, the Tamil Tigers of Sri Lanka, the Basque Homeland and Liberty (ETA) movement in Spain, and many other groups that have sprung up in this century have had political as well as terrorist wings from the beginning. The political arm provides social services and education, runs businesses, and contests elections, while the "military wing" engages in ambushes and assassinations. Such division of labor has advantages: the political leadership can publicly disassociate itself when the terrorists commit a particularly outrageous act or something goes wrong. The claimed lack of control can be quite real because the armed wing tends to become independent; the men and women with the guns and bombs often lose sight of the movement's wider aims and may end up doing more harm than good.

Terrorist operations have also changed somewhat. Airline hijackings have become rare, since hijacked planes cannot stay in the air forever and few countries today are willing to let them land, thereby incurring the stigma of openly supporting terrorism. Terrorists, too, saw diminishing returns on hijackings. The trend now seems to be away from attacking specific targets like the other side's officials and toward more indiscriminate killing. Furthermore, the dividing line between urban terrorism and other tactics has become less distinct, while the line between politically motivated terrorism and the operation of national and international crime syndicates is often impossible for outsiders to discern in the former Soviet Union, Latin America, and other parts of the world. But there is one fundamental difference between international crime and terrorism: mafias have no interest in overthrowing the government and decisively weakening society; in fact, they have a vested interest in a prosperous economy. Misapprehensions, not only semantic, surround the various forms of political violence. A terrorist is not a guerrilla, strictly speaking. There are fewer guerrillas, engaging in Maoist-style liberation of territories that become the base of a counter-society and a regular army fighting the central government—except in remote places like Afghanistan, Yemen, and the Philippines. The term "guerrilla" has had a long life partly because terrorists prefer the label, for its more positive connotations. It also persists because governments and media in other countries do not wish to offend terrorists by calling them terrorists. The French and British press would not dream of referring to their countries' native terrorists by any other name but call terrorists in other nations militants, activists, national liberation fighters, or even "gun persons."

The belief has gained ground that terrorist missions by volunteers bent on committing suicide constitute a radical new departure, dangerous because they are impossible to prevent. But that is a myth, like the many others in which terrorism has always been shrouded. The bomber willing and indeed eager to blow himself up has appeared in all eras and cultural traditions, espousing politics ranging from the leftism of the Baader-Meinhof Gang in 1970s Germany to rightist extremism. When the Japanese military wanted kamikaze pilots at the end of World War II, thousands of volunteers rushed to offer themselves. The young Arab bombers looking to be rewarded by the virgins in Paradise are a link in an old chain.

State-sponsored terrorism has not disappeared. Terrorists can no longer count on the Soviet Union and its Eastern European allies, but some Middle Eastern and North African countries still provide support. Tehran and Tripoli, however, are less eager to argue that they have a divine right to engage in terrorist operations outside their borders; the 1986 U.S. air strike against Libya and the various boycotts against Libya and Iran had an effect. No government today boasts about surrogate warfare it instigates and backs.

On the other hand, Sudan, without fanfare, has become for terrorists what the Barbary Coast was for pirates of another age: a safe haven. Politically isolated and presiding over a disastrous economy, the military government in Khartoum, backed by Muslim leaders, believes that no one wants to become involved in Sudan and thus it can get away with lending support to terrorists from many nations. Such confidence is justified so long as terrorism is only a nuisance. But if it becomes more than that, the rules of the game change, and both terrorists and their protectors come under great pressure.

Opportunities in Terrorism

History shows that terrorism more often than not has little political impact, and that when it has an effect it is often the opposite of the one desired. Terrorism in the 1980s and 1990s is no exception. The 1991 assassination of Rajiv Gandhi as he campaigned to retake the prime ministership neither hastened nor inhibited the decline of India's Congress Party. Hamas' and Hezbollah's stepped-up terrorism in Israel undoubtedly influenced the outcome of Israeli elections in May, but while it achieved its immediate objective of setting back the peace process on which Palestine Authority President Yasir Arafat has gambled his future, is a hard-line Likud government really in these groups' interests? On the other side, Yigal Amir, the right-wing orthodox Jewish student who assassinated Prime Minister Yitzhak Rabin last fall because he disapproved of the peace agreement with the Palestinians, might well have helped elect Rabin's dovish second-in-command, Shimon Peres, to a full term had Muslim terrorists not made Israeli security an issue again.

Terrorists caused disruption and destabilization in other parts of the world, such as Sri Lanka, where economic decline has accompanied the war between the government and the Tamil Tigers. But in Israel and in Spain, where Basque extremists have been staging attacks for decades, terrorism has had no effect on the economy. Even in Algeria, where terrorism has exacted the highest toll in human lives, Muslim extremists have made little

139

headway since 1992–93, when many predicted the demise of the unpopular military regime.

Some argue that terrorism must be effective because certain terrorist leaders have become president or prime minister of their country. In those cases, however, the terrorists had first forsworn violence and adjusted to the political process. Finally, the common wisdom holds that terrorism can spark a war or, at least, prevent peace. That is true, but only where there is much inflammable material: as in Sarajevo in 1914, so in the Middle East and elsewhere today. Nor can one ever say with certainty that the conflagration would not have occurred sooner or later in any case.

Nevertheless, terrorism's prospects, often overrated by the media, the public, and some politicians, are improving as its destructive potential increases. This has to do both with the rise of groups and individuals that practice or might take up terrorism and with the weapons available to them. The past few decades have witnessed the birth of dozens of aggressive movements espousing varieties of nationalism, religious fundamentalism, fascism, and apocalyptic millenarianism, from Hindu nationalists in India to neo-fascists in Europe and the developing world to the Branch Davidian cult of Waco, Texas. The earlier fascists believed in military aggression and engaged in a huge military buildup, but such a strategy has become too expensive even for superpowers. Now, mail-order catalogs tempt militants with readily available, far cheaper, un-conventional as well as conventional weapons—the poor man's nuclear bomb, Iranian President Ali Akbar Hashemi Rafsanjani called them.

In addition to nuclear arms, the weapons of mass destruction include biological agents and man-made chemical compounds that attack the nervous system, skin, or blood. Governments have engaged in the production of chemical weapons for almost a century and in the production of nuclear and biological weapons for many decades, during which time proliferation has been continuous and access ever easier. The means of delivery—ballistic missiles, cruise missiles, and aerosols—have also become far more effective. While in the past missiles were deployed only in wars between states, recently they have played a role in civil wars in Afghanistan and Yemen. Use by terrorist groups would be but one step further.

Until the 1970s most observers believed that stolen nuclear material constituted the greatest threat in the escalation of terrorist weapons, but many now think the danger could lie elsewhere. An April 1996 Defense Department report says that "most terrorist groups do not have the financial and technical resources to acquire nuclear weapons but could gather materials to make radiological dispersion devices and some biological and chemical agents." Some groups have state sponsors that possess or can obtain weapons of the latter three types. Terrorist groups themselves have investigated the use of poisons since the nineteenth century. The Aum Shinrikyo cult staged a poison gas attack in March 1995 in the Tokyo subway; exposure to the nerve gas sarin killed ten people and injured 5,000. Other, more amateurish attempts in the United States and abroad to experiment with chemical substances and biological agents for use in terrorism have involved the toxin that causes botulism, the poisonous protein ricin (twice), sarin (twice), bubonic plague bacteria, typhoid bacteria, hydrogen cyanide, vx (another nerve gas), and possibly the Ebola virus.

To Use or Not to Use?

If terrorists have used chemical weapons only once and nuclear material never, to some extent the reasons are technical. The scientific literature is replete with the technical problems inherent in the production, manufacture, storage, and delivery of each of the three classes of unconventional weapons.

The manufacture of nuclear weapons is not that simple, nor is delivery to their target. Nuclear material, of which a limited supply exists, is monitored by the U.N.-affiliated International Atomic Energy Agency. Only governments can legally procure it, so that even in this age of proliferation investigators could trace those abetting nuclear terrorists without great difficulty. Monitoring can overlook a more primitive nuclear weapon: nonfissile but radioactive nuclear material. Iranian agents in Turkey, Kazakhstan, and elsewhere are known to have tried to buy such material originating in the former Soviet Union.

Chemical agents are much easier to produce or obtain but not so easy to keep safely in stable condition, and their dispersal depends largely on climatic factors. The terrorists behind last year's attack in Tokyo chose a convenient target where crowds of people gather, but their sarin was apparently diluted. The biological agents are far and away the most dangerous: they could kill hundreds of thousands where chemicals might kill only thousands. They are relatively easy to procure, but storage and dispersal are even trickier than for nerve gases. The risk of contamination for the people handling them is high, and many of the most lethal bacteria and spores do not survive well outside the laboratory. Aum Shinrikyo reportedly released anthrax bacteria—among the most toxic agents known—on two occasions from a building in Tokyo without harming anyone. Given the technical difficulties, terrorists are probably less likely to use nuclear devices than chemical weapons, and least likely to attempt to use biological weapons. But difficulties could be overcome, and the choice of unconventional weapons will in the end come down to the specialties of the terrorists and their access to deadly substances.

The political arguments for shunning unconventional weapons are equally weighty. The risk of detection and subsequent severe retaliation or punishment is great, and while this may not deter terrorists, it may put off their sponsors and suppliers. Terrorists eager to use weapons of mass destruction may alienate at least some supporters, not so much because the dissenters hate the enemy less or have greater moral qualms but because they think the use of such violence counterproductive. Unconventional weapon strikes could render whole regions uninhabitable for long periods. Use of biological arms poses the additional risk of an uncontrollable epidemic.

And while terrorism seems to be tending toward more indiscriminate killing and mayhem, terrorists may draw the line at weapons of super-violence likely to harm both foes and large numbers of relatives and friends—say, Kurds in Turkey, Tamils in Sri Lanka, or Arabs in Israel. Furthermore, traditional terrorism rests on the heroic gesture, on the willingness to sacrifice one's own life as proof of one's idealism. Obviously there is not much heroism in spreading botulism or anthrax. Since most terrorist groups are as interested in publicity as in violence, and as publicity for a mass poisoning or nuclear bombing would be far more unfavorable than for a focused conventional attack, only terrorists who do not care about publicity will even consider the applications of unconventional weapons. Broadly speaking, terrorists will not engage in overkill if their traditional weapons—the submachine gun and the conventional bomb—are sufficient to continue the struggle and achieve their aims.

But the decision to use terrorist violence is not always a rational one; if it were, there would be much less terrorism, since terrorist activity seldom achieves its aims. What if, after years of armed struggle and the loss of many of their militants, terrorist groups see no progress?

Despair could lead to giving up the armed struggle, or to suicide. But it might also lead to a last desperate attempt to defeat the hated enemy by arms not tried before. As one of Racine's heroes said of himself, their "only hope lies in their despair."

Apocalypse Soon

Terrorists groups traditionally contain strong quasi-religious, fanatical elements, for only total certainty of belief (or total moral relativism) provides justification for taking lives. That element was strong among the prerevolutionary Russian terrorists and the Romanian fascists of the Iron Guard in the 1930s. Fanatical Muslims consider the killing of the enemies of God a religious commandment, and believe that the secularists at home as well as the State of Israel will be annihilated because it is Allah's will. Aum Shinrikyo doctrine held that murder could help both victim and murderer to salvation. Sectarian fanaticism has surged during the past decade, and in general, the smaller the group, the more fanatical.

As humankind approaches the end of the second millennium of the Christian era, apocalyptic movements are on the rise. The belief in the impending end of the world is probably as old as history, but for reasons not entirely clear, sects and movements preaching the end of the world gain influence toward the end of a century, and all the more at the close of a millennium. Most of the preachers of doom do not advocate violence, and some even herald a renaissance, the birth of a new kind of man and woman. Others, however, believe that the sooner the reign of the Antichrist is established, the sooner this corrupt world will be destroyed and the new heaven and earth foreseen by St. John in the Book of Revelation, Nostradamus, and a host of other prophets will be realized. Extremist millenarians would like to give history a push, helping create world-ending havoc replete with universal war, famine, pestilence, and other scourges. It is possible that members of certain Christian and Jewish sects that believe in Armageddon or Gog and Magog or the Muslims and Buddhists who harbor related extreme beliefs could attempt to play out a doomsday scenario. A small group of Israeli extremists, for instance, firmly believes that blowing up Temple Mount in Jerusalem would bring about a final (religious) war and the beginning of redemption with the coming of the Kingdom of God. The visions of Shoko Asahara, the charismatic leader of Aum Shinrikyo, grew increasingly apocalyptic, and David Koresh proclaimed the Last Day's arrival in the Branch Davidians' 1994 confrontation with Bureau of Alcohol, Tobacco, and Firearms agents.

Those who subscribe to such beliefs number in the hundreds of thousands and perhaps millions. They have their own subcultures, produce books and CDS by the thousands, and build temples and communities of whose existence most of their contemporaries are unaware. They have substantial financial means at their disposal. Although the more extreme apocalyptic groups are potentially terrorist, intelligence services have generally overlooked their activities; hence the shock over the subway attack in Tokyo and Rabin's assassination, to name but two recent events.

Apocalyptic elements crop up in contemporary intellectual fashions and extremist politics as well. For instance, extreme environmentalists, particularly the so-called restoration ecologists, believe that environmental disasters will destroy civilization as we know it—no loss, in their view—and regard the vast majority of human beings as expendable. From such beliefs and values it is not a large step to engaging in acts of terrorism to expedite the process. If the eradication of smallpox upset ecosystems, why not restore the balance by bringing back the virus?

The motto of *Chaos International*, one of many journals in this field, is a quotation from Hassan I Sabbah, the master of the Assassins, a medieval sect whose members killed Crusaders and others in a "religious" ecstasy; everything is permitted, the master says. The premodern world and postmodernism meet at this point.

Future Shock

Scanning the contemporary scene, one encounters a bewildering multiplicity of terrorist and potentially terrorist groups and sects. The practitioners of terrorism as we have known it to this point were nationalists and anarchists, extremists of the left and the right. But the new age has brought new inspiration for the users of violence along with the old.

In the past, terrorism was almost always the province of groups of militants that had the backing of political forces like the Irish and Russian social revolutionary movements of 1900. In the future, terrorists will be individuals or like-minded people working in very small groups, on the pattern of the technology-hating Unabomber, who apparently worked alone sending out parcel bombs over two decades, or the perpetrators of the 1995 bombing of the federal building in Oklahoma City.

An individual may possess the technical competence to steal, buy, or manufacture the weapons he or she needs for a terrorist purpose; he or she may or may not require help from one or two others in delivering these weapons to the designated target. The ideologies such individuals and minigroups espouse are likely to be even more aberrant than those of larger groups. And terrorists working alone or in very small groups will be more difficult to detect unless they make a major mistake or are discovered by accident.

Thus at one end of the scale, the lone terrorist has appeared, and at the other, state-sponsored terrorism is quietly flourishing in these days when wars of aggression have become too expensive and too risky. As the century draws to a close, terrorism is becoming the substitute for the great wars of the 1800s and early 1900s. Proliferation of the weapons of mass destruction does not mean that most terrorist groups are likely to use them in the foreseeable future, but some almost certainly will, in spite of all the reasons militating against it. Governments, however ruthless, ambitious, and ideologically extreme, will be reluctant to pass on unconventional weapons to terrorist groups over which they cannot have full control; the governments may be tempted to use such arms themselves in a first-strike, but it is more probable that they would employ them in blackmail than in actual warfare. Individuals and small groups, however, will not be bound by the constraints that hold back even the most reckless government.

Society has also become vulnerable to a new kind of terrorism, in which the destructive power of both the individual terrorist and terrorism as a tactic are infinitely greater. Earlier terrorists could kill kings or high officials, but others only too eager to inherit their mantle quickly stepped in. The advanced societies of today are more dependent every day on the electronic storage, retrieval, analysis, and transmission of information. Defense, the police, banking, trade, transportation, scientific work, and a large percentage of the government's and the private sector's transactions are on-line. That exposes enormous vital areas of national life to mischief or sabotage by any computer hacker, and concerted sabotage could render a country unable to function. Hence the growing speculation about infoterrorism and cyber-warfare.

An unnamed U.S. intelligence official has boasted that with $1 billion and 20 capable hackers, he could shut down America. What he could achieve, a terrorist could too. There is little secrecy in the wired society, and protective measures have proved of limited value: teenage hackers have penetrated highly secret systems in every field. The possibilities for creating chaos are almost unlimited even now, and vulnerability will almost certainly increase. Terrorists' targets will change: Why assassinate a politician or indiscriminately kill people when an attack on electronic switching will produce far more dramatic and lasting results? The switch at the Culpeper, Virginia, headquarters of the Federal Reserve's electronic network, which handles all federal funds and transactions, would be an obvious place to hit. If the new terrorism directs its energies toward information warfare, its destructive power will be exponentially greater than any it wielded in the past—greater even than it would be with biological and chemical weapons.

Still, the vulnerability of states and societies will be of less interest to most terrorists than to ordinary criminals and organized crime, disgruntled employees of big corporations, and, of course, spies and hostile governments. Electronic thieves, whether engaged in credit card fraud or industrial espionage, are part of the system, using it rather than destroying it; its destruction would cost them their livelihood. Politically motivated terrorist groups, above all separatists bent on establishing states of their own, have limited aims. The Kurdish Workers Party, the IRA, the Basque ETA, and the Tamil Tigers want to weaken their enemies and compel them to make far-reaching concessions, but they cannot realistically hope to destroy them. It is also possible, however, that terrorist groups on the verge of defeat or acting on apocalyptic visions may not hesitate to apply all destructive means at their disposal.

All that leads well beyond terrorism as we have known it. New definitions and new terms may have to be developed for new realities (such as the violent Islamist groups), and intelligence services and policy-makers must learn to discern the significant differences among terrorists' motivations, approaches, and aims. The Bible says that when the Old Testament hero Samson brought down the temple, burying himself along with the Philistines in the ruins, "the dead which he slew at his death were more than he slew in his life." The Samsons of a society have been relatively few in all ages. But with the new technologies and the changed nature of the world in which they operate, a handful of angry Samsons and disciples of apocalypse would suffice to cause havoc. Chances are that of 100 attempts at terrorist superviolence, 99 might fail. But the single successful one could claim many more victims, do more material damage, and unleash far greater panic than anything the world has yet experienced.

The Terrorism to Come

Terrorism has become over a number of years the topic of ceaseless comment, debate, controversy, and search for roots and motives, and it figures on top of the national and international agenda. It is also at present one of the most highly emotionally charged topics of public debate, though quite why this should be the case is not entirely clear, because the overwhelming majority of participants do not sympathize with terrorism.

Confusion prevails, but confusion alone does not explain the emotions. There is always confusion when a new international phenomenon appears on the scene. This was the case, for instance, when communism first appeared (it was thought to be aiming largely at the nationalization of women and the burning of priests) and also fascism. But terrorism is not an unprecedented phenomenon; it is as old as the hills.

Thirty years ago, when the terrorism debate got underway, it was widely asserted that terrorism was basically a left-wing revolutionary movement caused by oppression and exploitation. Hence the conclusion: Find a political and social solution, remedy the underlying evil—no oppression, no terrorism. The argument about the left-wing character of terrorism is no longer frequently heard. But the belief in a fatal link between poverty and violence has persisted. Whenever a major terrorist attack has taken place, one hears appeals from high and low to provide credits and loans, to deal at long last with the deeper, true causes of terrorism, the roots rather than the symptoms and outward manifestations. And these roots are believed to be poverty, unemployment, backwardness, and inequality.

It is not too difficult to examine whether there is such a correlation between poverty and terrorism, and all the investigations have shown that this is not the case. The experts have maintained for a long time that poverty does not cause terrorism and prosperity does not cure it. In the world's 50 poorest countries, there is little or no terrorism. A study by scholars Alan Krueger and Jitka Maleckova reached the conclusion that the terrorists are not poor people and do not come from poor societies. A Harvard economist has shown that economic growth is closely related to a society's ability to manage conflicts. More recently, a study of India has demonstrated that terrorism in the subcontinent has occurred in the most prosperous

(Punjab) and most egalitarian (Kashmir, with a poverty ratio of 3.5 compared with the national average of 26 percent) regions and that, on the other hand, the poorest regions such as North Bihar have been free of terrorism. In the Arab countries (such as Egypt and Saudi Arabia, but also in North Africa), the terrorists originated not in the poorest and most neglected districts but hailed from places with concentrations of radical preachers. The backwardness, if any, was intellectual and cultural—not economic and social.

These findings, however, have had little impact on public opinion (or on many politicians) and it is not difficult to see why. There is the general feeling that poverty and backwardness with all their concomitants are bad—and that there is an urgent need to do much more about these problems. Hence the inclination to couple the two issues and the belief that if the (comparatively) wealthy Western nations would contribute much more to the development and welfare of the less fortunate, in cooperation with their governments, this would be in a long-term perspective the best, perhaps the only, effective way to solve the terrorist problem.

Reducing poverty in the Third World is a moral as well as a political and economic imperative. But to expect from it a decisive change in the foreseeable future as far as terrorism is concerned is unrealistic, to say the least. It ignores both the causes of backwardness and poverty and the motives for terrorism.

Poverty combined with youth unemployment does create a social and psychological climate in which Islamism and various populist and religious sects flourish, which in turn provide some of the footfolk for violent groups in internal conflicts. According to some projections, the number of young unemployed in the Arab world and North Africa could reach 50 million in two decades. Such a situation will not be conducive to political stability; it will increase the demographic pressure on Europe, since according to polls a majority of these young people want to emigrate. Politically, the populist discontent will be directed against the rulers—Islamist in Iran, moderate in countries such as Egypt, Jordan, or Morocco. But how to help the failed economies of the Middle East and North Africa? What are the reasons for backwardness and stagnation in this part of the world? The countries that have made economic progress—such as China and India, Korea and Taiwan, Malaysia and Turkey—did so without massive foreign help.

All this points to a deep malaise and impending danger, but not to a direct link between the economic situation and international terrorism. There is of course a negative link: Terrorists will not hesitate to bring about a further aggravation in the situation; they certainly did great harm to the tourist industries in Bali and Egypt, in Palestine, Jordan, and Morocco. One of the main targets of terrorism in Iraq was the oil industry. It is no longer a secret that the carriers of international terrorism operating in Europe and America hail not from the poor, downtrodden, and unemployed but are usually of middle-class origin.

The Local Element

The link between terrorism and nationalist, ethnic, religious, and tribal conflict is far more tangible. These instances of terrorism are many and need not be enumerated in detail. Solving these conflicts would probably bring about a certain reduction in the incidence of terrorism. But the conflicts are many and if some of them have been defused in recent years, other, new ones have emerged. Nor are the issues usually clear cut or the bones of contention easy to define—let alone to solve.

If the issue at stake is a certain territory or the demand for autonomy, a compromise through negotiations might be achieved. But it ought to be recalled that al Qaeda was founded and September 11 occurred not because of a territorial dispute or the feeling of national oppression but because of a religious commandment—jihad and the establishment of *shari'ah*. Terrorist attacks in Central Asia and Morocco, in Saudi Arabia, Algeria, and partly in Iraq were directed against fellow Muslims, not against infidels. Appeasement may work in individual cases, but terrorist groups with global ambitions cannot be appeased by territorial concessions.

As in the war against poverty, the initiatives to solve local conflicts are overdue and should be welcomed. In an ideal world, the United Nations would be the main conflict resolver, but so far the record of the U.N. has been more than modest and it is unlikely that this will change in the foreseeable future. Making peace is not an easy option; it involves funds and in some cases the stationing of armed forces. There is no great international crush to join the ranks of the volunteers: China, Russia, and Europe do not want to be bothered, the United States is overstretched. In brief, as is so often the case, a fresh impetus is likely to occur only if the situation gets considerably worse and if the interests of some of the powers in restoring order happen to coincide.

Lastly, there should be no illusions with regard to the wider effect of a peaceful solution of one conflict or another. To give but one obvious example: Peace (or at least the absence of war) between Israel and the Palestinians would be a blessing for those concerned. It may be necessary to impose a solution since the chances of making any progress in this direction are nil but for some outside intervention. However, the assumption that a solution of a local conflict (even one of great symbolic importance) would have a dramatic effect in other parts of the world is unfounded. Osama bin Laden did not go to war because of Gaza and Nablus; he did not send his warriors to fight in Palestine. Even the disappearance of the "Zionist entity" would not have a significant impact on his supporters, except perhaps to provide encouragement for further action.

Such a warning against illusions is called for because there is a great deal of wishful thinking and naïveté in this respect—a belief in quick fixes and miracle solutions: If only there would be peace between Israelis and

Palestinians, all the other conflicts would become manageable. But the problems are as much in Europe, Asia, and Africa as in the Middle East; there is a great deal of free-floating aggression which could (and probably would) easily turn in other directions once one conflict has been defused.

It seems likely, for instance, that in the years to come, the struggle against the "near enemy" (the governments of the Arab and some Muslim countries) will again feature prominently. There has been for some time a truce on the part of al Qaeda and related groups, partly for strategic reasons (to concentrate on the fight against America and the West) and partly because attacks against fellow Muslims, even if they are considered apostates, are bound to be less popular than fighting the infidels. But this truce, as events in Saudi Arabia and elsewhere show, may be coming to an end.

Tackling these supposed sources of terrorism, even for the wrong reasons, will do no harm and may bring some good. But it does not bring us any nearer to an understanding of the real sources of terrorism, a field that has become something akin to a circus ground for riding hobbyhorses and peddling preconceived notions.

How to explain the fact that in an inordinate number of instances where there has been a great deal of explosive material, there has been no terrorism? The gypsies of Europe certainly had many grievances and the Dalits (untouchables) of India and other Asian countries even more. But there has been no terrorism on their part—just as the Chechens have been up in arms but not the Tartars of Russia, the Basque but not the Catalans. The list could easily be lengthened.

Accident may play a role (the absence or presence of a militant leadership). But there could also be a cultural–psychological predisposition. How to explain that out of 100 militants believing with equal intensity in the justice of their cause, only a very few will actually engage in terrorist actions? And out of this small minority even fewer will be willing to sacrifice their lives as suicide bombers? Imponderable factors might be involved: indoctrination but also psychological motives. Neither economic nor political analysis will be of much help to gain an understanding, and it may not be sheer accident that there has been great reluctance to explore this political-intellectual minefield.

The Focus on Islamist Terrorism

To make predictions about the future course of terrorism is even more risky than political predictions in general. We are dealing here not with mass movements but small—sometimes very small—groups of people, and there is no known way at present to account for the movement of small particles in either the physical world or in human societies.

It is certain that terrorism will continue to operate. At the present time almost all attention is focused on Islamist terrorism. But it is useful to remember from time to time that this was not always the case—even less than thirty years ago—and that there are a great many conflicts, perceived oppressions, and other causes calling for radical action in the world which may come to the fore in the years to come. These need not even be major conflicts, in an age in which small groups will have access to weapons of mass destruction.

At present, Islamist terrorism all but monopolizes our attention and it certainly has not yet run its course. But it is unlikely that its present fanaticism will last forever; religious-nationalist fervor does not constantly burn with the same intensity. There is a phenomenon known in Egypt as "Salafi burnout," the mellowing of radical young people, the weakening of the original fanatical impetus. Like all other movements in history, messianic groups are subject to routinization, to the circulation of generations, to changing political circumstances, and to sudden or gradual changes in the intensity of religious belief. This could happen as a result of either victories or defeats. One day, it might be possible to appease militant Islamism—though hardly in a period of burning aggression when confidence and faith in global victory have not yet been broken.

More likely the terrorist impetus will decline as a result of setbacks. Fanaticism, as history shows, is not easy to transfer from one generation to the next; attacks will continue, and some will be crowned with success (perhaps spectacular success), but many will not. When Alfred Nobel invented dynamite, many terrorists thought that this was the answer to their prayers, but theirs was a false hope. The trust put today in that new invincible weapon, namely suicide terrorism, may in the end be equally misplaced.

Even the use of weapons of mass destruction might not be the terror panacea some believe it will be. Perhaps their effect will be less deadly than anticipated, perhaps it will be so destructive as to be considered counterproductive. Statistics show that in the terrorist attacks over the past decade, considerably more Muslims were killed than infidels. Since terrorists do not operate in a vacuum, this is bound to lead to dissent among their followers and even among the fanatical preachers.

There are likely to be splits among the terrorist groups even though their structure is not highly centralized. In brief, there is a probability that a united terrorist front will not last. It is unlikely that Osama and his close followers will be challenged on theological grounds. But there has been criticism for tactical reasons: Assuming that America and the West in general are in a state of decline, why did he not have more patience? Why did he have to launch a big attack while the infidels were still in a position to retaliate massively?

Some leading students of Islam have argued for a long time that radical Islamism passed its peak years ago and that its downfall and disappearance are only a question of time, perhaps not much time. It is true that societies that were exposed to the rule of fundamentalist fanatics (such as Iran) or to radical Islamist attack (such as Algeria) have been immunized to a certain extent. However, in a country of 60 million, some fanatics can always be found; as these lines are written, volunteers for suicide missions are being enlisted in Teheran and other cities of Iran. In any case, many countries have not yet undergone such firsthand experience; for them the rule of the sharia and the restoration of the caliphate are still brilliant dreams. By and large, therefore, the predictions about the impending demise of Islamism have been premature, while no doubt correct in the long run. Nor do we know what will follow. An interesting study on what happens "when prophecy fails" (by Leon Festinger) was published not long after World War II. We now need a similar study on the likely circumstances and consequences of the failure of fanaticism. The history of religions (and political religions) offers some clues, as does the history of terrorism.

These, then, are the likely perspectives for the more distant future. But in a shorter-term perspective, the danger remains acute and may, in fact, grow. Where and when are terrorist attacks most likely to occur? They will not necessarily be directed against the greatest and most dangerous enemy as perceived by the terrorist gurus. Much depends on where terrorists are strong and believe the enemy to be weak. That terrorist attacks are likely to continue in the Middle East goes without saying; other main danger zones are Central Asia and, above all, Pakistan.

The founders of Pakistan were secular politicians. The religious establishment and in particular the extremists among the Indian Muslims had opposed the emergence of the state. But once Pakistan came into being, they began to try with considerable success to dominate it. Their alternative educational system, the many thousand madrassas, became the breeding ground for jihad fighters. Ayub Khan, the first military ruler, tried to break their stranglehold but failed. Subsequent rulers, military and civilian, have not even tried. It is more than doubtful whether Pervez Musharraf will have any success in limiting their power. The tens of thousands of graduates they annually produce formed the backbone of the Taliban. Their leaders will find employment for them at home and in Central Asia, even if there is a de-escalation in tensions with India over Kashmir. Their most radical leaders aim at the destruction of India. Given Pakistan's internal weakness, this may appear more than a little fanciful, but their destructive power is still considerable, and they can count on certain sympathies in the army and the intelligence service. A failed Pakistan with nuclear weapons at its disposal would be a major nightmare. Still, Pakistani terrorism—like Palestinian and Middle Eastern in general—is still territorial, likely to be limited to the subcontinent and Central Asia.

Battlefield Europe

Europe is probably the most vulnerable battlefield. To carry out operations in Europe and America, talents are needed not normally found among those who have no direct personal experience of life in the West. The Pakistani diaspora has not been very active in the terrorist field, except for a few militants in the United Kingdom.

Western Europe has become over a number of years the main base of terrorist support groups. This process has been facilitated by the growth of Muslim communities, the growing tensions with the native population, and the relative freedom with which radicals could organize in certain mosques and cultural organizations. Indoctrination was provided by militants who came to these countries as religious dignitaries. This freedom of action was considerably greater than that enjoyed in the Arab and Muslim world; not a few terrorists convicted of capital crimes in countries such as Egypt, Jordan, Morocco, and Algeria were given political asylum in Europe. True, there were some arrests and closer controls after September 11, but given the legal and political restrictions under which the European security services were laboring, effective counteraction was still exceedingly difficult.

West European governments have been frequently criticized for not having done enough to integrate Muslim newcomers into their societies. But cultural and social integration was certainly not what the newcomers wanted. They wanted to preserve their religious and ethnic identity and their way of life, and they resented intervention by secular authorities. In its great majority, the first generation of immigrants wanted to live in peace and quiet and to make a living for their families. But today they no longer have much control over their offspring.

This is a common phenomenon all over the world: the radicalization of the second generation of immigrants. This generation has been superficially acculturated (speaking fluently the language of the host country) yet at the same time feels resentment and hostility more acutely. It is not necessarily the power of the fundamentalist message (the young are not the most pious believers when it comes to carrying out all the religious commandments) which inspires many of the younger radical activists or sympathizers. It is the feeling of deep resentment because, unlike immigrants from other parts of the world, they could not successfully compete in the educational field, nor quite often make it at the work place. Feelings of being excluded, sexual repression (a taboo subject in this context), and other factors lead to free-floating aggression and crime directed against the authorities and their neighbors.

As a result, non-Muslims began to feel threatened in streets they could once walk without fear. They came to regard the new immigrants as antisocial elements who wanted to change the traditional character of their homeland and their way of life, and consequently tensions continued to increase. Pressure on European governments is growing from all sides, right and left, to stop immigration and to restore law and order.

This, in briefest outline, is the milieu in which Islamist terrorism and terrorist support groups in Western Europe developed. There is little reason to assume that this trend will fundamentally change in the near future. On the contrary, the more the young generation of immigrants asserts itself, the more violence occurs in the streets, and the more terrorist attacks take place, the greater the anti-Muslim resentment on the part of the rest of the population. The rapid demographic growth of the Muslim communities further strengthens the impression among the old residents that they are swamped and deprived of their rights in their own homeland, not even entitled to speak the truth about the prevailing situation (such as for instance to reveal the statistics of prison inmates with Muslim backgrounds). Hence the violent reaction in even the most liberal European countries such as the Netherlands, Belgium, and Denmark. The fear of the veil turns into the fear that in the foreseeable future they too, having become a minority, will be compelled to conform to the commandments of another religion and culture.

True, the number of extremists is still very small. Among British Muslims, for instance, only 13 percent have expressed sympathy and support for terrorist attacks. But this still amounts to several hundred thousands, far more than needed for staging a terrorist campaign. The figure is suspect in any case because not all of those sharing radical views will openly express them to strangers for reasons that hardly need be elaborated. Lastly, such a minority will not feel isolated in their own community as long as the majority remains silent—which has been the case in France and most other European countries.

The prospects for terrorism based on a substantial Islamist periphery could hardly appear to be more promising. But there are certain circumstances that make the picture appear somewhat less threatening. The tensions are not equally strong in all countries. They are less palpably felt in Germany and Britain than in France and the Netherlands. Muslims in Germany are predominantly of Turkish origin and have (always with some exceptions) shown less inclination to take violent action than communities mainly composed of Arab and North African immigrants.

If acculturation and integration has been a failure in the short run, prospects are less hopeless in a longer perspective. The temptations of Western civilization are corrosive; the young Muslims cannot be kept in a hermetically closed ghetto (even though a strong attempt is made). They are disgusted and repelled by alcohol, loose morals, general decadence, and all the other wickedness of the society facing them, but they are at the same time fascinated and attracted by them. This is bound to affect their activist fervor, and they will be exposed not only to the negative aspects of the world surrounding them but also its values. Other religions had to face these temptations over the ages and by and large have been fighting a losing battle.

It is often forgotten that only a relatively short period passed from the primitive beginnings of Islam in the Arabian desert to the splendor and luxury (and learning and poetry) of Harun al Rashid's Baghdad—from the austerity of the Koran to the not-so-austere Arabian Nights. The pulse of history in contemporary history is beating much faster, but is it beating fast enough? For it is a race against time. The advent of megaterrorism and the access to weapons of mass destruction is dangerous enough, but coupled with fanaticism, it generates scenarios too unpleasant even to contemplate.

Enduring Asymmetry

There can be no final victory in the fight against terrorism, for terrorism (rather than full-scale war) is the contemporary manifestation of conflict, and conflict will not disappear from earth as far as one can look ahead and human nature has not undergone a basic change. But it will be in our power to make life for terrorists and potential terrorists much more difficult.

Who ought to conduct the struggle against terrorism? Obviously, the military should play only a limited role in this context, not only because it has not been trained for this purpose. The military may have to be called in for restoring order in countries that have failed to function and have become terrorist havens. It may have to intervene to prevent or stop massacres. It may be needed to deliver blows against terrorist concentrations. But these are not the most typical or frequent terrorist situations.

The key role in asymmetric warfare (a redundant new term for something that has been known for many centuries) should be played by intelligence and security services that may need a military arm.

As far as terrorism and also guerrilla warfare are concerned, there can be no general, overall doctrine in the way that Clausewitz or Jomini and others developed a regular warfare philosophy. An airplane or a battleship do not change their character wherever they operate, but the character of terrorism and guerrilla warfare depends largely on the motivations of those engaging in it and the conditions under which it takes place. Over the past centuries, rules and laws of war have developed, and even earlier on there were certain rules that were by and large adhered to.

But terrorism cannot possibly accept these rules. It would be suicidal from their point of view if, to give but one example, they were to wear uniforms or other distinguishing marks. The essence of their operations rests on hiding their identities. On the other hand, they and their well-wishers insist that when captured, they should enjoy all the rights and benefits accorded to belligerents, that they be humanely treated, even paid some money and released after the end of hostilities. When regular soldiers do not stick to the rules of warfare, killing or maiming prisoners, carrying out massacres, taking hostages, or committing crimes against the civilian population, they will be treated as war criminals.

If terrorists behaved according to these norms they would have little if any chance of success; the essence of terrorist operations now is indiscriminate

155

attacks against civilians. But governments defending themselves against terrorism are widely expected not to behave in a similar way but to adhere to international law as it developed in conditions quite different from those prevailing today.

Terrorism does not accept laws and rules, whereas governments are bound by them; this, in briefest outline, is asymmetric warfare. If governments were to behave in a similar way, not feeling bound by existing rules and laws such as killing prisoners, this would be bitterly denounced. When the late Syrian President Hafez Assad faced an insurgency (and an attempted assassination) on the part of the Muslim Brotherhood in the city of Hama in 1980, his soldiers massacred some 20,000 inhabitants. This put an end to all ideas of terrorism and guerrilla warfare.

Such behavior on the part of democratic governments would be denounced as barbaric, a relapse into the practices of long-gone pre-civilized days. But if governments accept the principle of asymmetric warfare, they will be severely, possibly fatally, handicapped. They cannot accept that terrorists are protected by the Geneva Conventions, which would mean, among other things, that they should be paid a salary while in captivity. Should they be regarded like the pirates of a bygone age as *hostes generis humani*, enemies of humankind, and be treated according to the principle of *a un corsaire, un corsaire et demi*—"to catch a thief, it takes a thief," to quote one of Karl Marx's favorite sayings?

The problem will not arise if the terrorist group is small and not very dangerous. In this case, normal legal procedures will be sufficient to deal with the problem (but even this is not quite certain once weapons of mass destruction will be more readily accessible). Nor will the issue of shedding legal restraint arise if the issues at stake are of marginal importance, if in other words no core interests of the governments involved are concerned. If, on the other hand, the very survival of a society is at stake, it is most unlikely that governments will be impeded in their defense by laws and norms belonging to a bygone (and more humane) age.

It is often argued that such action is counterproductive because terrorism cannot be defeated by weapons alone, but is a struggle for the hearts and minds of people, a confrontation of ideas (or ideologies). If it were only that easy. It is not the terrorist ideas which cause the damage but their weapons. Each case is different, but many terrorist groups do not have any specific idea or ideology but a fervent belief, be it of a religious character or of a political religion. They fight for demands, territorial or otherwise, that seem to them self-evident, and they want to defeat their enemies. They are not open to dialogue or rational debate. When Mussolini was asked about his program by the socialists during the early days of fascism, he said that his program was to smash the skulls of the socialists.

Experience teaches that a little force is indeed counterproductive except in instances where small groups are involved. The use of massive, overwhelming force, on the other hand, usually is effective. But the use of massive force is almost always unpopular at home and abroad, and it will be applied only if core interests of the state are involved. To give but one example: The Russian government could deport the Chechens (or a significant portion), thus solving the problem according to the Stalinist pattern. If the Chechens were to threaten Moscow or St. Petersburg or the functioning of the Russian state or its fuel supply, there is but little doubt that such measures would be taken by the Russian or indeed any other government. But as long as the threat is only a marginal and peripheral one, the price to be paid for the application of massive force will be considered too high.

Two lessons follow: First, governments should launch an anti-terrorist campaign only if they are able and willing to apply massive force if need be. Second, terrorists have to ask themselves whether it is in their own best interest to cross the line between nuisance operations and attacks that threaten the vital interests of their enemies and will inevitably lead to massive counterblows.

Terrorists want total war—not in the sense that they will (or could) mobilize unlimited resources; in this respect their possibilities are limited. But they want their attacks be unfettered by laws, norms, regulations, and conventions. In the terrorist conception of warfare, there is no room for the Red Cross.

Love or Respect?

The why-do-they-hate-us question is raised in this context, along with the question of what could be done about it—that is, the use of soft power in combating terrorism. Disturbing figures have been published about the low (and decreasing) popularity of America in foreign parts. Yet it is too often forgotten that international relations is not a popularity contest, and that big and powerful countries have always been feared, resented, and envied; in short, they have not been loved. This has been the case since the days of the Assyrians and the Roman Empire.

Neither the Ottoman nor the Spanish Empire, the Chinese, the Russian, nor the Japanese was ever popular. British sports were emulated in the colonies and French culture impressed the local elites in North Africa and Indochina, but this did not lead to political support, let alone identification with the rulers. Had there been public opinion polls in the days of Alexander the Great (let alone Genghis Khan), the results, one suspects, would have been quite negative.

Big powers have been respected and feared but not loved for good reasons—even if benevolent, tactful, and on their best behavior, they were threatening simply because of their very existence. Smaller nations could not feel comfortable, especially if they were located close to them. This was the case even in times when there was more than one big power (which allowed for the possibility of playing one against the other). It is all the more so at a time when only one superpower is left and the perceived threat looms even larger.

There is no known way for a big power to reduce this feeling on the part of other, smaller countries—short of committing suicide or, at the very least, by somehow becoming weaker and less threatening. A moderate and intelligent policy on the part of the great power, concessions, and good deeds may mitigate somewhat the perceived threat, but it cannot remove it, because potentially the big power remains dangerous. It could always change its policy and become nasty, arrogant, and aggressive. These are the unfortunate facts of international life.

Soft power is important but has its limitations. Joseph S. Nye has described it as based on culture and political ideas, as influenced by the seductiveness of democracy, human rights, and individual opportunity. This is a powerful argument, and it is true that Washington has seldom used all its opportunities, the public diplomacy budget being about one quarter of one percentage point of the defense budget.

But the question is always to be asked: Who is to be influenced by our values and ideas? They could be quite effective in Europe, less so in a country like Russia, and not at all among the radical Islamists who abhor democracy (for all sovereignty rests with Allah rather than the people), who believe that human rights and tolerance are imperialist inventions, and who want to have nothing to do with deeper Western values which are not those of the Koran as they interpret it.

The work of the American radio stations during the Cold War ought to be recalled. They operated against much resistance at home but certainly had an impact on public opinion in Eastern Europe; according to evidence later received, even the Beatles had an influence on the younger generation in the Soviet Union. But, at present, radio and television has to be beamed to an audience 70 percent of which firmly believes that the operations of September 11 were staged by the Mossad. Such an audience will not be impressed by exposure to Western pop culture nor a truthful matter-of-fact coverage of the news. These societies may be vulnerable to covert manipulation of the kind conducted by the British government during World War II: black (or at least gray) propaganda, rumors, half-truths, and outright lies. Societies steeped in belief in conspiracy theories will give credence to even the wildest rumors. But it is easy to imagine how an attempt to generate such propaganda would be received at home: It would be utterly rejected. Democratic countries are not able to engage in such practices except in a case of a major emergency which at the present time has not yet arisen.

Big powers will never be loved, but in the terrorist context it is essential that they should be respected. As bin Laden's declarations prior to September 11 show, it was lack of respect for America that made him launch his attacks;

he felt certain that the risk he was running was small, for the United States was a paper tiger, lacking both the will and the capability to strike back. After all, the Americans ran from Beirut in the 1980s and from Mogadishu in 1993 after only a few attacks, and there was every reason to believe that they would do so again.

Response in Proportion to Threat

Life could be made more difficult for terrorists by imposing more controls and restrictions wherever useful. But neither the rules of national nor international law are adequate to deal with terrorism. Many terrorists or suspected terrorists have been detained in America and in Europe, but only a handful have been put on trial and convicted, because inadmissible evidence was submitted or the authorities were reluctant to reveal the sources of their information—and thus lose those sources. As a result, many who were almost certainly involved in terrorist operations were never arrested, while others were acquitted or released from detention.

As for those who are still detained, there have been loud protests against a violation of elementary human rights. Activists have argued that the real danger is not terrorism (the extent and the consequences of which have been greatly exaggerated) but the war against terrorism. Is it not true that American society could survive a disaster on the scale of September 11 even if it occurred once a year? Should free societies so easily give up their freedoms, which have been fought for and achieved over many centuries?

Some have foretold the coming of fascism in America (and to a lesser extent in Europe), others predicted an authoritarian regime gradually introduced by governments cleverly exploiting the present situation for their own anti-democratic purposes. And it is quite likely indeed that among those detained there have been and are innocent people and that some of the controls introduced have interfered with human rights. However, there is much reason to think that to effectively combat terrorism, considerably more stringent measures will be needed than those presently in force.

But these measures can be adopted only if there is overwhelming public support, and it would be unwise even to try to push them through until the learning process about the danger of terrorism in an age of weapons of mass destruction has made further progress. Time will tell. If devastating attacks do not occur, stringent antiterrorist measures will not be necessary. But if they do happen, the demand for effective countermeasures will be overwhelming. One could perhaps argue that further limitations of freedom are bound to be ineffective because terrorist groups are likely to be small or very small in the future and therefore likely to slip through safety nets. This is indeed a danger—but the advice to abstain from safety measures is a counsel of despair unlikely to be accepted.

There are political reasons to use these restrictions with caution, because Muslim groups are bound to be under special scrutiny and every precaution should be taken not to antagonize moderate elements in this community. Muslim organizations in Britain have complained that a young Pakistani or Arab is 10 times more likely to be stopped and interrogated by the police than other youths. The same is true for France and other countries. But the police, after all, have some reasons to be particularly interested in these young people rather than those from other groups. It will not be easy to find a just and easy way out of the dilemma, and those who have to deal with it are not to be envied.

It could well be that, as far as the recent past is concerned, that the danger of terrorism has been overstated. In the two world wars, more people were sometimes killed and more material damage caused in a few hours than through all the terrorist attacks in a recent year. True, our societies have since become more vulnerable and also far more sensitive regarding the loss of life. But the real issue at stake is not the attacks of the last few years but the coming dangers. Megaterrorism has not yet arrived; even 9-11 was a stage in between old-fashioned terrorism and the shape of things to come: the use of weapons of mass destruction.

The idea that such weapons should be used goes back at least 150 years. It was first enunciated by Karl Heinzen, a German radical—later a resident of Louisville, Kentucky, and Boston, Massachusetts—soon after some Irish militants considered the use of poison gas in the British Parliament. But these were fantasies by a few eccentrics, too farfetched even for the science fiction writers of the day. Today these have become real possibilities. For the first time in human history very small groups have, or will have, the potential to cause immense destruction. In a situation such as the present one, there is always the danger of focusing entirely on the situation at hand—radical nationalist or religious groups with whom political solutions may be found. There is a danger of concentrating on Islamism and forgetting that the problem is a far wider one. Political solutions to deal with their grievances may sometimes be possible, but frequently they are not. Today's terrorists, in their majority, are not diplomats eager to negotiate or to find compromises. And even if some of them would be satisfied with less than total victory and the annihilation of the enemy, there will always be a more radical group eager to continue the struggle.

This was always the case, but in the past, it mattered little: If some Irish radicals wanted to continue the struggle against the British in 1921–22, even after the mainstream rebels had signed a treaty with the British government which gave them a free state, they were quickly defeated. Today even small groups matter a great deal precisely because of their enormous potential destructive power, their relative independence, the fact that they are not rational actors, and the possibility that their motivation may not be political in the first place.

Perhaps the scenario is too pessimistic, perhaps the weapons of mass destruction for whatever reason will never be used. But it would be the first time in human history that such arms, once invented, had not been used. In the last resort, the problem is, of course, the human condition. In 1932, when Einstein attempted to induce Freud to support pacifism, Freud replied that there was no likelihood of suppressing humanity's aggressive tendencies. If there was any reason for hope, it was that people would turn away on rational grounds—that war had become too destructive, that there was no scope anymore in war for acts of heroism according to the old ideals.

Freud was partly correct: War (at least between great powers) has become far less likely for rational reasons. But his argument does not apply to terrorism motivated mainly not by political or economic interests, based not just on aggression but also on fanaticism with an admixture of madness.

Terrorism, therefore, will continue—not perhaps with the same intensity at all times, and some parts of the globe may be spared altogether. But there can be no victory, only an uphill struggle, at times successful, at others not.

The Ticking Clock

In his election campaign, President Barack Obama made several statements about terrorism. He dissociated himself from George W. Bush's "holistic approach" (whatever this meant) and the rhetoric about the "global war on terrorism." He promised a more substantial "security architecture." Head of this new architecture was the unfortunate Janet Napolitano, a former governor of Arizona, who went on record saying that the system had worked well after the barely failed attempt to bomb a plane over Detroit on Christmas Day.

Obama also promised to work closely with America's allies, to pay greater attention to civil rights and the constitution, to close Guantanamo and to deal with detainees attentive to due process. And he charged the Bush administration with failing adequately to confront nuclear terrorism.

Two days after his Inauguration, two presidential orders were signed, banning harsh interrogation and ordering Guantanamo Bay to be closed within a year. The official rhetoric during Obama's first year certainly changed: the inflammatory term "terrorism" was dropped and replaced by "man-caused disaster" (no credit was given to woman or child suicide bombers) and Islamism was no longer mentioned at all.

Looking back on Obama's first year and his handling of "man-caused disasters," I feel less surprised and shocked than some of those who have also followed these issues for a fairly long time. Obama's experience in Chicago had not been in this field, nor had I been greatly impressed by the handling of former presidents (and their advisers—always with some exceptions). Under Clinton and Bush, the main role in combating terrorism had been allocated to the military, but it was not really prepared for this task either by training or by the specific knowledge needed for this assignment. I had doubts about the continuation of the Afghan war after 2002, not because it was immoral or illegal but because victory in Afghanistan seemed out of reach. It involved an investment in manpower, other resources, and political will that did not exist in the U.S. and was almost wholly absent in Europe.

Public opinion in the U.S. and also in Europe was largely oblivious of the dangers ahead. After all, there had been no terrorist attack on the scale of 9/11 and relatively few smaller ones. The more successful counterterrorism was in preventing attacks, the greater the resistance against taking terrorism seriously—why devote enormous efforts to combating an enemy whose strength was probably greatly overestimated? The terrorist "danger" (it was argued) was overblown and overhyped. Why accept limitations on our civic liberties that in all probability were quite unnecessary? More and more such voices were heard on university campuses from Ohio State to Aberystwyth (home of the journal *Critical Studies on Terrorism*), in the media and among those assuming that warnings issued by their governments were a priori suspect and wrong.

Good advice was offered in books and articles, often by officials who, when in office, had not been notably successful at catching Osama bin Laden or weakening al-Qaeda in other ways. A Chicago professor named Robert Pape put forward an influential new theory explaining contemporary terrorism on the basis of elaborate and detailed statistics: it had nothing to do with Islamic fundamentalism but was the nationalist reaction to foreign invasion. This was accepted with enthusiasm not only by isolationists but also by some Washington policy-makers: leave the Middle East and there will be no terrorism. Sterling advice, but what had it to do with the real world? Of course, there has been nationalist terrorism in opposition to foreign invasion. But, at present, 95 percent (or more) of suicide terrorism has nothing to do with foreign invasion. The victims were and are fellow Muslims, be it in Pakistan or the Philippines, in Somalia or Turkey, in Yemen or Iraq. Some went further and claimed that a solution to the terrorist problem was very easy indeed: impose a peace settlement on Israel and the Palestinians and the price of oil will dramatically fall, failed states will prosper, the popularity of America and the West in general will skyrocket, bin Laden will retire to his agricultural projects in the Sudan, and terrorism will disappear from the face of the earth.

Judges in various Western countries regarded it as their main duty to limit the powers of the police and other agencies combating terrorism. Eagle-eyed lawyers were forever watching whether those trying to counteract terrorism were operating within the boundaries of international law and to take them to task if they did not. Not for them the philosophy underlying one of Karl Marx's favorite sayings: *à corsaire, corsaire et demi*.

In brief, the threat had been grossly inflated, there was no transcendental, existential challenge. There were a few terrorists, but they would fade away out of boredom or because they would realise that they could not achieve much. The real danger was not terrorism but counterterrorism, the idea of a "wartime president" with almost unlimited, undemocratic powers and a state of siege.

Obama's ideas about "outreach" and "engagement," negotiating and trying to reach compromises with even the worst enemies, seemed a little naive and unrealistic from the beginning and, seen in retrospect, have not been successful. But let us be fair: unless such approaches were made (and rebuffed), there would have been for decades to come a stream of complaints about "missed opportunities," broadly similar to the opportunities allegedly missed during the Cold War on which some historians (and not only historians) continue to harp to this day.

Finally, the economic downturn of 2008/9 created an important change in the order of priorities: unemployment became the cardinal political issue and is likely to remain so for some time to come. It did not come as a surprise that in his State of the Union address in late January, Obama devoted only the last few minutes to foreign policy and to terrorism just a sentence or two. It is an understandable reaction for a politician with an eye on forthcoming elections. But ultimately, as a Washington commentator noted recently, Obama's presidency will be judged not by health reform but by national security.

This is merely a brief outline of the political context in which the policy towards terrorism developed during Obama's first year in office. There was and still is a great deal of confusion, and I suspect that even a more clear-sighted president would not have been able to move too far ahead of public opinion. Why make sacrifices because of a danger which might or might not materialize at some future date? This, after all, is one of the well-known weaknesses of democratic societies—the Pearl Harbor syndrome. Only a major shock, a trauma, will act as a wake-up call, generate the awareness of threats and galvanize people into action. And sometimes more than one might be needed. It seems also to be true that in their private lives, people will take out insurance policies and take precautions against all manner of unlikely events, whereas as a group, they tend to ignore very real dangers.

After one year in office, Obama is a disillusioned man. Like all other presidents in recent memory, he came to power with the firm intention to deal first and foremost (and if possible exclusively) with domestic issues. Like all other presidents, he was largely prevented from doing so by an unquiet and meddlesome world. The issue at stake at present is how long his re-education will take and how far it will go, and this also refers of course to his advisers, admirers and many other like-minded people.

How much urgency is there? A great deal, according to those who have been studying the problem of WMD and who have had access to various sources of information. It could well be that in recent decades the danger of terrorism has been overstated. In the two World Wars, more people were killed and more material damage caused in certain weeks than in a decade of terrorist attacks. But even in the 1970s, experts noted that our societies were becoming more vulnerable as the result of the use of new weapons. The real issue at stake now is not the attacks of the past but the coming dangers. Megaterrorism has not yet arrived—even 9/11 was a stage between traditional terrorism and the shape of things to come.

What is our state of preparedness? A number of bipartisan committees appointed by the U.S. Congress have been dealing in recent years with these issues. So have books and scientific papers, such as the reports *World at Risk* (2008) and *The Clock is Ticking* (2009) and books by Graham Allison, Rolf Mowatt Larssen, Matthew Bunn, and others. Their findings were summarized in one sentence in *World at Risk*:

> Unless the world community acts decisively and with great urgency, it is more likely than not that a weapon of mass destruction will be used in a terrorist attack somewhere in the world by the end of 2013.

It seems more likely that Iran may pass on primitive (dirty) nuclear material to a client such as Hezbollah, on the assumption that it would emphatically deny its involvement, that such a transaction could not be easily traced, and that it would therefore not have to suffer major consequences. Iran would have international law on its side, because a majority of UN member states would ask for a careful investigation, which, needless to say, would lead nowhere. However, such a course of action is also not without its dangers. Once such weapons have been transferred to another party, the sponsor loses control. While the U.S. might be deflected from reacting immediately, Israel might have fewer inhibitions.

The arrival of an Iranian bomb now seems highly likely. But a nuclear Iran will almost certainly lead to the acquisition of WMD in other Middle Eastern countries. There is furthermore the worrisome issue of the Pakistani atomic bombs. There is an almost indefinite number of scenarios and while some countries are more likely targets than others, none can be certain that it will be exempt.

Graham Allison, a Harvard professor, asked in *Foreign Policy* why the failure to imagine the worst? If Obama, in his very first speech to the Security Council, was so outspoken about the likely consequences of exploding a single nuclear bomb, why has this not been followed up by action? Partly, no doubt, because he addressed the wrong audience. But what if he had spoken to NATO or the American people?

It is part of human nature to suppress unpleasant and painful information, especially if there is no certainty that impending danger can be prevented. Not all the arguments of the skeptics can be dismissed out of hand. To obtain fissile material is not easy, nor is the construction of a nuclear device. It is quite likely that the first attempts to construct a bomb and detonate it will fail—and this would set global alarm bells ringing. It is not certain that within three years terrorists will have a nuclear bomb and set it off. It may take five, or even seven, years. As Dr. Johnson said, nothing focuses the mind so much as the certain knowledge of a hanging. But if the period of grace is not a day, but five years, this does not necessarily focus the mind—perhaps something will turn up—especially not the awareness of politicians who are elected for only four years.

At this point the issue of leadership becomes of crucial importance. To gain time is important. Terrorism will not disappear in the foreseeable future but fanaticism does run in waves; it does not persist forever with equal intensity. A more conciliatory tone as suggested by Obama may be important but gaining respect is at least as decisive. Terrorists should not be led into temptation; they should not think that it is less risky to attack the U.S. than China or Russia.

Soft power is important and has been neglected in the past. It is certainly laudable to counter the ideology behind WMD terrorism. But this also means making use of the weaknesses of an antagonist. One such weakness is the almost unlimited willingness of the Islamists (and of fanatics in general) to believe in conspiracy theories, however absurd. About 70 per cent of Islamists believe that 9/11 was carried out by elements within the American government and that the suicide attacks in Pakistan are committed by the CIA (or Mossad or Indian intelligence) rather than the Taliban. Use can and should be made of this proclivity.

It is important to stop the Iranian and North Korean nuclear programs but it is also clear that Washington will not get much help from its allies or the UN. A "comprehensive policy towards Pakistan" would be exceedingly useful but no one has found a way to achieve this. In brief, it is far easier to recognize the dangers than to point to ways and means of averting them. Meanwhile, as the most recent progress report says, the clock is ticking.

Even the most radical skeptics do not claim that a terrorist attack with nuclear weapons is impossible and that it will never happen. Nor do those who think that such an attack is more likely than not maintain that the worst-case scenario is inevitable.

There is no certainty that it can be prevented. But it is certain that such an attempt could be made more difficult. The best way to this end is to make it as clear as possible what the reaction to such an attack would be.

Underestimating Terrorism

More than eight years have passed since the twin towers fell in New York City and the United States declared its global "war on terrorism." The president who spearheaded the initial phases of this endeavor has since left office, and a new president from another party is now in the White House.

Terrorism, nonetheless, remains high atop the national and international agenda and the subject of ceaseless comment and controversy. It also remains one of the most emotionally charged topics of public debate, though quite why this should be the case is not entirely clear, because the overwhelming majority of participants do not sympathize with terrorism.

Confusion prevails, but confusion alone does not explain the emotions. There is always confusion when a new international phenomenon appears on the scene. This was the case, for example, when communism first appeared, and also fascism. But terrorism is not an unprecedented phenomenon; it has been around since as far back as recorded history.

Sometimes, terrorism has wrought tremendous global tribulations, even sparking great wars such as World War I. At other times, it has receded into the background noise of world politics.

Something of a cottage industry has formed of late, mainly in academic departments, urging a wholesale reevaluation of terrorism; the thinking goes that the threat of terrorism is overblown and being overhyped. Some point out that death by lightning strike is far more likely than death by terrorism.

That may be true, but if a lightning strike was substituted with a devastating attack on a major Western city, perhaps with a weapon of mass destruction, the ramifications would be profound, likely altering the course of human history.

This is not to overstate the threat, merely to point out the costs of understatement. In any event, it is quite fair to ask: what is the current state of the terrorist threat, and is it being assessed correctly? Misdiagnosing the threat almost certainly means misapplying the responses.

To best understand present and future challenges, one must first try to make sense of the traditional misunderstandings that have prevailed in the study of terrorism, a field as beholden to passion, emotion, and confusion as any other.

Passionate Misconceptions over Root Causes

Some of the misunderstandings about the nature of terrorism are rooted in ideology. In the 1970s, when terrorism was predominantly left wing in inspiration—or at least in rhetoric—it was probably not surprising that commentators belonging to the same political persuasion would produce explanations that were, at the very least, not unsympathetic as far as the terrorists were concerned. Thus it was argued that terrorism always occurred when there was intolerable oppression, social or national, and that the terrorists had genuine, legitimate grievances. Thus the conclusion was that if these grievances were eradicated, terrorism would also disappear.

Terrorism was seen as a revolutionary phenomenon; it was carried out by poor and desperate human beings and therefore had to be confronted with sympathetic understanding.

The argument stressing the left-wing character of terrorism is no longer widely heard except perhaps among members of certain sects trying to establish a popular front with Islamists in whom sect members see a powerful ally in the struggle against imperialism, even if they do not agree with the Islamists' fundamentalist doctrine, which they may find primitive and sometimes embarrassing. But the belief in a fatal link between poverty and violence has persisted. Whenever a major terrorist attack takes place, one hears appeals from high and low to provide financial help, to deal at long last with the "true causes of terrorism"; the "roots" rather than their symptoms and outward manifestations. And these roots are believed to be poverty, unemployment backwardness, and inequality.

Investigations have shown that poverty does not cause terrorism and prosperity does not cure it. Most terrorists are not poor and do not come from poor societies. In the Indian subcontinent, terrorism has occurred in the most prosperous (Punjab) and the most egalitarian (Kashmir) regions. By contrast, the poorest regions such as North Bihar have been relatively free of terrorism. In Arab countries such as Egypt and Saudi Arabia and also in North Africa, the terrorists have originated not in the poorest and most neglected districts, but from places with concentrations of radical preachers. The backwardness, if any, has been intellectual and cultural, not economic and social.

These findings have had only a limited impact on public opinion and politicians, and it is not difficult to see why there has been resistance to accepting them. There is the general feeling that poverty and backwardness are bad and that there is an urgent need to do more about them.

Reducing poverty in the developing world may be a moral as well as a political and economic imperative, but to expect decisive change from it in the foreseeable future as far as terrorism is concerned is unrealistic. Such an expectation ignores both the causes of backwardness and poverty and the motives for terrorism. Poverty combined with youth unemployment does create a social and psychological climate in which Islamism and various populists and religious sects flourish. That climate, in turn, provides some of the foot folk for violent groups in internal conflicts. According to some projections, the number of young unemployed in the Arab world and North Africa could reach fifty million in less than two decades.

Such a situation will not be conducive to political stability. It will increase the demographic pressure on Europe, because, according to polls, a majority of these young people want to emigrate there. Politically, the populist discontent will be directed against the rulers—the Islamists in Iran and the moderates in countries such as Egypt, Jordan, or Morocco. But how to help the failed economies of the Middle East and North Africa? What are the reasons for the backwardness and stagnation in that part of the world? The countries that have made substantial economic progress, such as China and India, South Korea and Taiwan, Malaysia and Turkey, did so without massive foreign assistance.

All of this points to a deep malaise and even an impending danger, but not to a direct link between the economic situation and international terrorism. There is a negative correlation: terrorists will not hesitate to bring about a further aggravation in the situation by, for example, causing great harm to the tourist industries in North Africa, Egypt, and Bali. Terrorism has spread to the Maldives in the Indian Ocean not because of poverty (it has the highest per capita gross national product in South East Asia, thanks to its tourism industry), but because Islamic preachers of violence were permitted to act freely.

One of the main targets of terrorism in Iraq has been the oil industry. Sometimes it is argued that resolving religious, nationalist, and ethnic grievances would eradicate terrorism. If the issue at stake is the conflict over a certain territory or the demand for more autonomy, a compromise through negotiations seems a possibility. But recall that al-Qaeda was founded and 9/11 occurred not because of a territorial dispute or the feeling of national oppression but because of a religious commandment—the establishment of sharia through jihad.

As in the war against poverty, the initiatives to solve local conflicts are overdue and should be welcomed. Easing these conflicts would probably bring about a certain reduction in the incidence of terrorism. But the conflicts are many, and even if some of them have been defused in recent years, new ones have emerged. Nor are the issues usually clear-cut or the bones of contention easy to define—let alone solve.

And there should be no illusions about the wider effects of a peaceful solution of one conflict on another. To give but one obvious example: peace (or at least the absence of war) between Israel and the Palestinians would be a blessing for those concerned. However, the assumption that the solution of a local conflict (even one of great symbolic importance) would have a dramatic effect in other parts of the world is unfounded. Osama bin Laden did not go to war because of Gaza and Nablus; he did not send his warriors to fight in Palestine.

Even the disappearance of the "Zionist entity" would not have a significant impact on his supporters, except perhaps to provide encouragement for further action.

Such a warning against illusions is called for because there is much wishful thinking and naiveté in this respect—a belief in quick fixes and miracle solutions. Some say, if only there could be peace between Israelis and Palestinians, all the other conflicts would become manageable. But the problems are as much in Europe, Asia, and Africa as in the Middle East; there is a great deal of free-floating aggression that could (and probably would) easily turn in other directions once one conflict has been defused.

Tackling these supposed sources of terrorism, even for the wrong reasons, will do no harm and may bring some good. But it will not bring analysts any closer to a comprehensive understanding of the sources of terrorism, let alone a capacity to respond effectively.

Nature of the Threat: Now and in Future

It is always risky to make predictions about the future of terrorism, even more so than about political trends in general. It is certain, however, that terrorism will not disappear from the earth: at a time when full-scale war has become too dangerous and too expensive, terrorism has become the prevailing mode of conflict. As long as conflict persists among groups of human beings, so will terrorism.

Today, nearly all attention is focused on Islamic terrorism, but it is useful to remember from time to time that this has not always been the case—even less than thirty years ago—and that a great many conflicts, perceived oppressions, and other causes are calling for radical action in the world, which also may lead to terrorism in the years to come. These need not be even major conflicts in an era in which small groups will have access to weapons of mass destruction.

Islamic terrorism has certainly not yet run its full course, but it is unlikely that its present fanaticism will last forever; religious-nationalist fervor does not constantly burn with the same intensity. There is a phenomenon known in Egypt as "Salafi burnout," the mellowing of radical young people, the weakening of the original fanatical impetus. Like all other movements in history, messianic groups are subject to routinization, to the circulation of generations, to changing political circumstances, and to sudden or gradual changes in religious belief. This could happen as the result of either victory or defeat. One day it might be possible to appease militant Islamism—though hardly in a period of burning aggression when confidence and faith in global victory have not yet been broken.

172

The terrorist impetus is likely to decline as the result of setbacks. Attacks will continue, some will be crowned with success, perhaps spectacular success, but many will not. When Alfred Nobel invented dynamite many terrorists thought that it was the answer to their prayers. But theirs was a false hope. The trust put today in that invincible weapon, suicide terrorism may in the end be equally misplaced. Even the use of weapons of mass destruction might not be the panacea some terrorists believe it will be. Perhaps the effect of such a weapon will be less deadly than anticipated, perhaps it will be so destructive as to be considered counterproductive. Statistics show that in the terrorist attacks over the past decade, considerably more Muslims were killed than infidels. Because terrorists do not operate in a vacuum, this situation is bound to lead to dissent among their followers and even among the fanatical preachers. In brief, a united terrorist front, if ever established, may not last. It is unlikely that bin Laden and his close followers will be frontally challenged on theological or ideological grounds, but there has been criticism for political and tactical reasons such as the attacks against Muslim civilians, both Sunni and Shiite, and the failure to anticipate the massive retaliation of the West following the attacks of 9/11.

Some leading students of Islam have argued that radical Islamism reached its peak years ago and that its downfall and disappearance are only a question of time, perhaps not much time. Although some societies have been exposed to the rule of fundamentalist fanatics (such as Iran) or to radical Islamist attacks (such as Algeria), many Muslim countries have yet to undergo such firsthand experience; for them, sharia rule and the restoration of the caliphate are still brilliant dreams.

These, then, are the likely perspectives for the more distant future. But in a shorter-term perspective the danger remains acute and may, in fact, grow. Where and when are terrorist attacks most likely to occur? They will not necessarily be directed against the greatest and most dangerous enemy perceived by the terrorist leaders. Much depends on where the terrorists are strong and believe the enemy to be weak. That terrorist attacks are likely to continue in the Middle East goes without saying; other primary danger zones are central Asia, particularly Pakistan, and, more recently, nearly all of Western Europe.

Pakistan certainly remains at risk. Its madrassas continue to serve as breeding grounds for jihad fighters, and radical leaders can count on certain sympathies in the army and intelligence services. A failed Pakistan with nuclear weapons at its disposal would be a major nightmare.

Yet Europe is perhaps the most vulnerable battlefield, having become over the years the main base of terrorist support groups from the Middle East, North Africa, and Pakistan. This process has been facilitated by the growth of Muslim communities (and growing tensions with the local population), which have provided a reservoir of new recruits. The freedom of action for radicals to organize and indoctrinate in Western Europe is considerably greater than in the Arab and Muslim world. True, there were some arrests and closer controls after the events of 9/11 and the attacks in Madrid and London, but because of the legal and political restrictions under which European security services labor, effective counteraction remains exceedingly difficult.

For decades, Western European governments have been frequently criticized for not doing enough to integrate Muslim communities, but cultural and social integration are not what many immigrants want, and their preachers have constantly warned against it. Immigrants have wanted to preserve their political, cultural, and religious identities and their ways of life, and have resented interference by secular authorities. And yet the vast majority of first-generation immigrants simply wanted to live in peace and quiet and make a living for their families. But today they no longer have much control over their more radical offspring.

The radicalization of second-generation immigrants is a common phenomenon in general and is certainly the case in Western Europe. This generation has been superficially acculturated, speaking fluently the language of the land, and yet feeling resentment and hostility more acutely. It is not necessarily the power of the fundamentalist message that inspires many of the younger radical activists or sympathizers; they are by no means the most pious believers when it comes to carrying out all the religious commandments. The British suicide bombers in 2005, for example, were not known for their religious orthodoxy; most of them did not pray regularly. Rather, it is the feeling of deep resentment because, unlike immigrants from other parts of the world, Muslim immigrants in Europe often find themselves unable to compete successfully in the classroom or the workplace. Feelings of being excluded, sexual repression (a taboo subject in this context), and other factors have led to free-floating aggression and higher rates of criminal behavior directed against the authorities and the neighbors.

As a result, non-Muslims in Europe have felt threatened in the streets they could once walk without fear. They have come to regard the new immigrants as antisocial elements who wanted to impose on non-Muslim Europeans their way of life. Pressure on the European governments has been growing from all sides, right and left, to stop immigration and restore law and order.

This, in brief, is the milieu in which Islamist terrorism and terrorist support groups in Western Europe have developed. There is little reason to assume that this trend will change fundamentally in the near future. On the contrary, the more the young generation of immigrants asserts itself, the more violence occurs in the streets, and the more terrorist attacks take place, the greater will be the anti-Muslim resentment of the rest of the population. The rapid demographic growth of the Muslim communities further strengthens the impression among original residents that they are being deprived of their rights in their own homeland, not even entitled to speak the truth about the prevailing situation (such as revealing how many prison inmates have Muslim back-grounds). Thus violent reactions to Muslims are on view in even the most liberal European countries such as the Netherlands, Belgium, and Denmark.

True, the number of extremists is still quite small. Among British Muslims, fewer than 20 percent have expressed sympathy and support for terrorist attacks. But this percentage still translates into several hundred thousand, far more than is needed for staging a terrorist campaign. Furthermore, such statistics do not take into account the growth of Muslim communities and Western Europe's continuing need for immigrants because of their low and declining birthrates. There is already great pressure on Southern and Western Europe to absorb the growing legions of unemployed in North Africa and the Middle East.

If acculturation and integration have been a failure in the short run, prospects are less hopeless from a long-term perspective. Young Muslims cannot be kept forever in hermetically sealed ghettos, even if their preachers make a valiant effort to do so. The young people are disgusted and repelled by alcohol, loose morals, general decadence, and all the other wickedness of the society surrounding them—as indoctrinated by their preachers—but at the same time, they are fascinated and attracted by them. As one Berlin imam put it: the road to the mosque is long, and the temptations are many. This environment is bound to affect young people's activist fervor, and they will be exposed to not only the negative aspects of the society around them but also its values. Other religions had to face these temptations over the ages and often fought a losing battle.

Suicide Terrorism

No other phenomenon in our time has generated so much shock and horror as suicide terrorism. And no other, alas, has generated so much misunderstanding and misinterpretation. Not by accident perhaps, because in this post heroic age many are bound to find it inexplicable that young people should be willing to sacrifice their lives to inflict indiscriminate harm on their enemies. In secular societies, ideological passions seem a spent force and fanaticism has become a phenomenon restricted to small, marginal groups. It is now widely believed that suicide terrorism is something quite unprecedented in the history of mankind, that the motive is religious fanaticism, that it is carried out by the poorest of the poor, the most oppressed and humiliated, those who lost all hope, and that furthermore it is an invincible strategy.

There is certainly nothing new about suicide terrorism. Until a few decades ago, most terrorism was suicide terrorism. The tyrannicides in ancient Greece, the Assassins and the regicides in the Middle Ages were suicide terrorists. As long as the weapon of the terrorist was the dagger, the short-range pistol, or an unstable bomb, more likely than not to explode in his own hands, he had no chance to get away alive. The kings and queens, the ministers and generals were well guarded, most of the assailants did not even try to escape.

There has been a cult of sacrificial death in battle in the history of most peoples all through recorded history. The Nordic sagas deal with little but such acts of heroism, those who had died were taken to Asgard, the palace of the gods with 540 doors where they were reported to lead a very comfortable existence. After a short interval during the Enlightenment, the cult of the fallen heroes came back with a vengeance during the age of romanticism. As Theodor Koerner wrote on the eve of a battle in the war against Napoleon, "Happiness lies only in sacrificial death." Koerner died in battle, he was a great patriot but not a great poet, the idea of sacrificial death was, however, widely shared at the time. Hölderlin had written well before a poem "Death for the fatherland," more or less in the same vein which had been pioneered by Horace

Review of Christoph Reuter, Mein Leben ist eine Waffe. *Selbstmordattentaeter-Psychogramm eines Phaenomens* (Munich, 2002), pp. 448.

two thousand years earlier in his "Dulce et Decorum est." It was not just honorable to die for one's country, it was also sweet, and Homer had said it before.

Nazism gave a strong impetus to this cult, the heroes were not really dead but living in eternity. It was customary among German as well as Romanian Nazis that when the list of those present were read out at a gathering, those who had been killed were included and someone was saying "present." when their names were called. Thousands of kamikaze pilots were writing home in 1944/45 that if they had seven lives they would gladly sacrifice them to smite the enemy. True, some of them went on their last mission out of a feeling of duty rather than conviction and yet others (as we now know) went most reluctantly but had been conditioned by their training not to question orders. Contemporary suicide terrorism to quote Mr. Reuter's path breaking book on the subject is a modern phenomenon only in part, it is a mixture of the battle of Kerbela (where Ali, Mohammed's son in law perished in heroic battle) and cable TV, a synthesis of old myths and new media.

Which leads to the question of the religious background and motivation of suicide terrorism. It has been practiced in recent decades by more than a dozen terrorist movements and however often jihad is invoked, it certainly cannot be explained with reference to any specific religion.

Suicide terrorism has been practiced by groups and groupuscules of the extreme right and the extreme left as well as nationalist separatist groups such as the Kurdish PKK. The classic case of suicide terrorism for many years was the LTTE (the Tamil Tigers) in Sri Lanka, a secular political movement. The Tamil separatists want a state of their own, and considering that there are no more than million Tamils living near the Jaffna peninsula, the stronghold of the Tigers, they have carried out for twenty years far more such attacks than anyone else. (There has been an armistice between the Tigers and the Colombo government since the beginning of the year).

The Tamil Tiger's doctrine does not refer to holy writs, and it claims to be "beyond religion," but there still is an elaborate symbolism of death and resurrection and a mystical sacrificial commitment to the nation. The Tigers venerate their martyrs on five distinct holidays during the year. There is in their doctrine the same emphasis on blind, absolute obedience as in the last instructions of Muhammed Atta to his comrades—and as there was in the early days of the Jesuit order; the members of the order have to obey their superiors *perinde ac si cadaver essent*—as if they were corpses. There is one important difference between the Tigers and the Hamas, the Islamic Jihad and al Qa'eda and its allies—the Tigers are very proud of their actions which are listed on many monuments, but attacks against civilians do not count. Attacks against civilians are terrorism, and they do not want to be considered terrorists but fighters for national liberation.

There is no clear dividing line between religion and fanatical nationalism as far as the motivation is concerned and this is true with regard to the Middle East as well as other parts of the world where suicide terrorism has been practiced. When suicide terrorism first appeared in Lebanon in 1983 many observers thought that it was a specific Shi'ite phenomenon, but this was quite mistaken even at the time and Mr. Reuter rightly notes that after the experience of many years of fundamentalist rule one will look in vain in Iran for candidates for such missions—disillusion has been too strong.

If the role of religion is less clear than commonly assumed, what of poverty and oppression? Many years ago a Dutch historian of Islamic radicalism noted that poverty does not cause terrorism and prosperity does not cure it, but his was a voice calling in the wilderness. More recently Kofi Annan has observed that one should not add to the suffering of the poor of the third world by regarding them as potential terrorists. There is no terrorism in the fifty countries listed as the poorest and least developed by the United Nations.

True, happy people are unlikely candidates for suicide terrorism, and refugee camps and personal experience of national oppression appear a likely breeding ground for terrorist militants. But this does not account for the Tamil Tigers or many other groups. It certainly does not explain the motives of those who hijacked the planes and crashed them in New York and Washington a year ago. These young Saudis had never experienced poverty or lived under foreign occupation.

Attempts have been made to establish a psychological profile of suicide bombers but this has not been easy because terrorism varies so much from country to country. Furthermore, those going to blow themselves up are usually unwilling to submit to psychological tests and interviews. On the other hand, enough of them have been captured and interrogated to find at least some common features. They grow up in closed societies with the emphasis on obeisance, a critical attitude so dear to the West in modern times is absent. The individual counts for very little, the collective is all important.

Indoctrination is of key importance. It often begins at a very early age—signs on the walls of Hamas kindergarten in the occupied territories read "the children are the holy martyrs of tomorrow." Such indoctrination is quite frequent in the annals of history. In our time the issue of brainwashing has figured prominently in various cults and sects; some of these sects have induced their members to commit collective suicide, with equal ease they can be made to engage in suicide terrorism. The evidence shows that wherever terrorism occurs religious preachers or nationalist propagandists (or, as in Sri Lanka a charismatic leader) play a crucial role in creating a climate conducive to such action.

Some Muslim preachers have argued that preaching jihad is not indoctrination but a religious obligation. This is true but jihad can be interpreted in various ways. Nor does it explain why only a minority of ardent believers in a cause become terrorists and of the terrorists only a few volunteer (or are selected) for suicide missions. In other words, an objective cause is needed as well as firm religious belief or extreme nationalism or another ideology appealing to some deep seated urges such as the feeling of oppression and/or a mission. Intensive indoctrination is a precondition but also a psychological predisposition which turns some young people into terrorists and others not. Those willing to blow themselves up in a supermarket or a cafeteria, are young people in search of a message, they want to believe and not to ask questions, they are naïve not skeptical, there is a surfeit of idealism but the critical sense is underdeveloped and the personality is weak, easily given to persuasion. In the last resort they go to their death because they have been educated to be true believers, conditioned to assume that it is the most natural thing of the world and that it is their duty before god (or their leader).

We are as yet a long way from fully understanding the various manifestations of suicide terrorism and its motives, but the present book is an important contribution. Mr. Reuter, a young German journalist, has traveled for years through Arab countries, the Middle East, and Central Asia; he is also an Orientalist by training and thus able to talk more or less freely to people and to read texts usually not accessible to the average foreign correspondent. His account of suicide terrorism is to the best of my knowledge the first in any language—not to count the papers submitted at a conference a year ago and a few articles.

Mr. Reuter sheds light on the views of Muslim theological authorities concerning suicide terrorism; some give it full support, others are vacillating or justify it in certain conditions only. He is fascinated by the strong impact of conspiracy theories of history on suicide terrorism, which is particularly strong in the Muslim world. It will be recalled that many of those who welcomed the attacks of September 11 claimed, at the same time, that they were carried out by the Israeli Mossad, not an easy feat of imagination. He discusses the issue of awards bestowed on the martyr such as the virgins waiting for him in paradise and puts them into proper perspective.

Mr. Reuter is, of course, aware that suicide terrorism and martyrdom did not start in Lebanon in 1983. He does deal with the Kamikaze, the Tamil Tigers, and the others but rather briefly. Most of this substantial book still deals with the Palestinians and Osama Bin Laden which is understandable because they have been in the limelight of late more than all others. Nevertheless, such heavy concentration on just one strand of this phenomenon is dangerous, for generalizing on the basis of one species of suicide terrorism is bound to lead to conclusions that could be one-sided and even misleading.

One of the basic differences between the " classic terrorism" (until roughly three or four decades ago) and the new terrorism is that most of the former was directed against leading figures in state and society, whereas the new terrorism, especially outside Europe, has become quite indiscriminate in the choice of its targets. To explain this, Mr. Reuter refers to philosophical nihilism, to Nietzsche and Ernst Jünger who also wrote that the deep luck of human beings consisted in being sacrificed. But Osama bin Laden, whatever his other failings, is not a nihilist. For the real explanation of the lack of restraints and the atrocities of these groups in comparison with earlier generations of terrorists, one ought to look to the cultural traditions, the mentality and the values of the society in which these groups have emerged.

How successful is suicide terrorism? Mr. Reuter seems to share, at least in part, the currently fashionable belief in the near invincibility of the suicide bombers. Once such a bomber is on his way, there is no stopping him. True enough, but the bomber is only the last link in a long chain. There is no random, spontaneous suicide terrorism, the candidates do not set out on their mission when they feel like it. They are indoctrinated, trained and directed by people with a clear political agenda, and these are certainly not invulnerable. Of the dozen or so groups who engaged in suicide terrorism, most have gone out of business including the Tamil Tigers and the Lebanese Hezbollah. It is now practiced only by a few Islamic groups in Kashmir, Chechnya, by al Qaeda and allied groups and above all in Israel/Palestine. It has been successful in Palestine/Israel mainly because of the strategic and tactical mistakes of Israeli authorities in the occupied territories. Israel has the most sophisticated defensive installations, but so far these have been for export only. They have not been used locally because it would have meant giving up most of the territories and dividing Jerusalem; the Israeli losses have been the price that had to be paid.

Suicide terrorism is asymmetric warfare par excellence—a new term for something that has existed for many centuries. It means that the terrorists are not bound by any restraints, moral, or others, whereas a state has to observe the law of the land as well as international conventions. Flushed by success (as for instance in Latin America in the 1970s) terrorists tend to forget that once they become a real danger to the target state or society, their victims will retaliate in kind, brutally and indiscriminately, and that even a weak state is usually stronger than a effective terrorist group. The time may arrive when terrorists will have access to weapons of mass destruction. But this day has not come yet, and these weapons, furthermore, are problematic from the terrorists' point of view. Terrorists can in certain circumstances trigger off a war; they did so in Sarajevo in 1914, but the results, seen in the perspective of 2002, were certainly not those that were expected.

We have it on the authority of Tertullian that the blood of the martyrs is the seed of the church. But suicide terrorism is not a church, those conducting it do not want to spread their gospel but to destroy the enemy. Enthusiasm for martyrdom persists as long as there is a reasonable chance that it will lead to victory. What if after years of such missions and hundreds of martyrs the bombers and their dispatchers do not feel nearer to their goal, what if martyrdom fails? How to keep up the momentum in the long run? When dynamite was invented, some nineteenth-century terrorists thought that this was the answer to their prayers. Now some feel the same about suicide terrorism, and they are again mistaken.

Fanaticism

As recently as 1975 there was virtually no literature about terrorism except for some very readable thrillers on the pattern of *Day of the Jackal*. But during the last decade, it has grown exponentially (Amazon lists more than 5.500 books about the subject), and if one adds the literature on Iraq, Islamism and related topics, there is standing room only and not much of that either. This is true in particular with regard to the United States, and in some respects this enormous growth is to be welcomed for it shows intellectual curiosity. Many who even a year ago did not know the difference between zakat and jihad now write with confidence about some finer points in the theology of Ibn Taimiyya and the Koran exegesis of Sayyid Qutb.

But some of the issues involved are complicated and cannot be mastered within a year or even two. Furthermore, there is a tendency among authors (not only among the political science professors among them) not just to describe and analyze an important and fascinating phenomenon but to establish a general theory of terrorism and political violence. So far no such theory has emerged and it is more than doubtful whether it ever will. At best such theory building helps to explain the emergence of terrorism in certain countries at a certain period. But they are quite useless and even misleading with regard to other places and periods.

This is true in particular with regard to the question of motivation and it is therefore more than welcome to come occasionally across new studies which, while far from providing conclusive answers, take the discussion to a higher level.

Dr. Conzen, a practicing German psychoanalyst and the biographer of Erik Erikson is primarily concerned with the phenomenon of fanaticism, and it is of course true that terrorism, whatever its political or religious orientation, is bound to be fanatical; happy, contented people seldom kill. The author is well aware of the problems involved in "analysis in absentia," of the transfer

Review of Marc Sageman, *Understanding Terror Networks* (Philadelphia: University of Pennsylvania Press, 2004), pp. 220 and Peter Conzen, *Fanatismus.: Psychoanalyse eines unheimlichen Phaenomens.* (Stuttgart: Kohlhammer, 2005), pp. 300

of insights gained from single patients to historical processes, especially if they take place in cultures other than our own.

But, with all this, psychology can make a contribution towards the investigation of political and religious violence. Social and political factors should not be neglected, but they can take us only up to a certain point and not further. They cannot explain why of a group of people believing with equal intensity in their cause, feeling equally aggrieved, oppressed, antagonized, downtrodden, marginalized and so on, only a few will become terrorists whereas the others will not. Are these who opt for violent action the bravest or the most sensitive or the most consistent in their beliefs, are they the ones who feel hatred most acutely? (But this raises more questions concerning the origin of hatred). Is there such a thing as a human disposition towards fanaticism or even a fanatical personality? This, of course, is hotly contested by many who claim that terrorists (or fanatics) are just people like you and me. But if this were true there should be some six or seven billion terrorists around, which quite obviously is not the case. In other words, there must be in certain groups for whatever reasons a greater inclination than in others toward paranoia, a belief in holy terror, a world full of distrust, dishonesty, and destruction. There must be an inclination towards fanaticism.

Conzen devotes considerable space to the fanaticism of Hitler and his cronies; fanaticism was one of Hitler's favorite terms, often used in his speeches—he wanted his followers to be more fanatical. But the Nazi story is a different one and an analysis of the mental make up of the German terrorists of the 1970s (the RAF) also sheds only limited light on the Islamist terrorism of our days. The leading members of the RAF had all reasonable happy childhoods (which neither Hitler nor Stalin had), only one or two came from Nazi families, which could account for the revolt against the generation of the parents. But there still was a fear of love and intimacy among them, which has nothing to do with either generational revolt or the Vietnam war.

Fanaticism cannot be explained easily with reference to childhood experiences—or a longing in later years for a feeling of absolute security and harmony. There is no clear profile of the German terrorists, some came from the drug scene, in some cases, megalomania may have played a certain role—some adopted a bourgeois life style after the terrorist interlude. Having shed the radical left wing beliefs of their youth, some went later on all the way to neo-fascism and extreme nationalism.

Certain common features can be detected, such as the inclination towards finding a home in a group (a trend even more strongly stressed in Dr. Sageman's book), the feeling of absolute loyalty towards their comrades in arms, great enthusiasm and passionate visionarism. But in the end there simply is no accounting, for the thoughts and feelings of a handful of people out of seventy millions.

There is another insurmountable difficulty on the road of composing a psychological profile—the immense differences between terrorist groups even in the nineteenth and twentieth centuries. One cannot possibly attribute sadism (to give but one example) to the Russian terrorists or the anarchists of the late nineteenth and early twentieth centuries, they went out of their way not to hurt innocents. On the other hand, sadism and a destructive impulse are quite obviously an important factor in the activities of various contemporary groups such as, for instance, Algerian terrorism in the 1990s or Zarqawi's group in Iraq. It is not enough to kill indiscriminately, which has become common practice, the enemy should not just be murdered, he should be tortured and made to suffer. As some of Zarqawi's followers reproached him—you have been cutting throats too fast.

This is a feature which has greatly baffled psychiatrists and forensic scientists who have shrunk away from dealing with the issue of mass murder be it serial murder or crimes against humanity or indiscriminate terrorism. It is not an illness, nor are the perpetrators disturbed in a clinical sense, sociopaths do not fit into existing schemes so they are not included in DSM-IV the standard diagnostic manual of American psychiatrists. As Mme Julia Kristeva, a leading French analyst once noted—medieval men and women would have found it easier to accept the notion of evil than modern man including forensic scientists. Some of them at least until recently have regarded evil an absurd notion for which there was no room in their discipline.

Perhaps the most interesting part of Conzen's study is the summing up of past attempts to explain fanaticism. There were, of course a variety of subspecies—the fanaticism of a threatened collective, the fanaticism of social disintegration and above all fanaticism in the service of an idea or an ideal such as a religion or a secular political religion. Conzen stresses the importance of the group and of group pressure in fanatical movements. Members may regard themselves as instruments of God simply carrying out his will, but the same phenomenon of blind obeisance can be found also in groups which are not at all religious—the subservience to the leader, be it Ocalan of the Kurdish terrorists now in prison or Prabhakaran, the head of the Tamil Tigers in Sri Lanka.

Can fanaticism be reduced? If aggression is part of the human condition, can it be directed to constructive outlets? This problem has preoccupied psychologists and not only them, for a long time and while Dr. Conzen poses the question seeing the need, he has no more answers than others before him.

Dr. Sageman, now a practicing psychiatrist with a training also in political sociology, worked with Islamists (apparently in Pakistan) on behalf of the CIA from 1986–89. He does not think much of psychoanalysis (psychodynamics) but believes in empiricism. He dismisses a variety of mistaken notions about the motives and origins of Islamic terrorism—it is not rooted in childhood trauma, the relative deprivation concept is not of much help nor the frustration-aggression thesis. He is sarcastic of the insights of the "authoritarian personality" school, for which he finds no evidence among the practitioners of jihad. Nor does he find evidence for a paranoid disposition; in this respect, he clearly goes too far, for paranoid beliefs are clearly widespread among terrorist individuals and groups. If one were to prepare a world map of paranoia such as manifested for instance in conspiracy theories, one would find that while these can be found in every country, they are clearly more manifest in some than in others, with the Islamic extremists on top of the line.

As he sees it, there is a fundamental difference between, on one hand, the global jihadists pursuing jihad, foreign volunteers groups such as Al Qaeda—and, on the other, the fighters of Taliban and other local groups including the Palestinians. But what motivated the foreign volunteers? Broadly speaking, a common doctrine (Salafi Islamism), sharing a common social background, a common psychological makeup and being in a particular situation at the time of recruitment.

But there is one issue even more important than all these factors and also more important than a common ideology and this is the crucial role of social bonds at a time when such bonds in society have decreased or disappeared. This refers to friendship, the role of street gangs, social cliques. (Dr. Sageman uses fashionable terms such as "networks" "nodes" and "hubs" rather too often in this context). The author sees this activism as born in cliques of confused young people in need of a message, recruited at the periphery of radical mosques; in these circumstance very little brainwashing may be needed. But for his aversion to psychoanalysis he could have added that these are young people with a weak ego. He also notes in passing the growing impact of the Internet in this context, but this is a operational technicality rather than a motive.

What follows from these insights is rather obvious, that there is not much point in arresting the small fry but that one ought to go for the hub of the cliques (or the network) and that the penetration of the ranks of the jihadists is essential.

What is one to make of these arguments? The emphasis on the role of the gang or clique is very important and has been overlooked in the past—except perhaps by those focusing on street crime. This issue is probably central with regard to the groups which the author knows best, namely the Islamist volunteers in Europe, it does not necessarily apply to the same degree to terrorism in other places and times. Societal bonds are very important, but whether they are more crucial than ideology and an inclination towards hatred and fanaticism (about which so far we know very little) is doubtful. And so the search for motivation continues.

Part 5

Heroes and Antiheroes

Hans Paasche: Eccentric and Martyr

If there were an entry for Hans Paasche in a "Who Was Who" or similar work of reference (which I believe, there is not), it would read approximately as follows:

Hans Paasche b. Rostock 1881, son of Dr. Hermann P., member of National Liberal Party, deputy president of the Reichstag, mother Elfriede. Primary and secondary education in Rostock and Berlin. (Joachimsthalsche Gymnasium). Joined Imperial Navy 1899, 1901 midshipman, 1902, lieutenant. Eventually lieutenant commander. Participated in suppression (1905) of native rebellion (Maji Maji) in German East Africa, decorated for bravery. Resigns from navy 1909. Married December 1908 Ellen nee Witting, daughter of Richard Witting (Witkowski), mayor of Posen, director of major banks. Niece of Maximilian Harden, most famous journalist in Wilhelmian Germany. Three sons, one daughter. Paasche worked as gentleman farmer in Germany during 1909–14, joined various reform movements (temperance, vegetarianism, etc), lecturer, author of books on traveling and hunting in East Africa and a satire of contemporary German society (*Lukanga Mukara*). Volunteered for military service with outbreak of war, was forced to resign because of pacifist propaganda and the refusal to serve as a judge in a court martial. Continues pacifist activities, arrested in October 1917, kept in prison and sanatorium, released after November revolution 1918. Was active in revolutionary committees, joined various political associations. Killed in May 1920 by "Black Reichswehr" (extreme right-wing military group) "while trying to escape" during a search on his farm in East Germany. One of many political murders (*Fehmemorde*) committed during the early postwar period.

Such an entry contains the essential dates and facts concerning the life of Hans Paasche; it does not shed light on his motives and character nor about the fact that there has been a Paasche renaissance in recent years and that *Lukanga Mukara* is still in print (both legally and pirated) almost a hundred years after it was first published. Nor does it relate the strange and fascinating tale of Paasche's (and the Witting's) descendants.

189

Paasche was a sensitive, probably a hypersensitive child, a rebel at a time when there were a great many young rebels in Germany, against parental control, the tyranny of school, and the conventions of society. His formative years were the last decade of the nineteenth century and the years after the turn of the century. Germany had made unprecedented economic progress, its urbanization proceeded by leaps and bounds, and the country had emerged as the strongest military power on the continent. But there was a feeling of unease and dissatisfaction in many sections of the society and in particular among the young generation. It found its expression in new, revolutionary directions in literature and the art, in the growth of social democracy, and in a feeling of cultural pessimism and even apocalyptic forebodings. It was the period when the youth movement was born as well as various reform movements based on the belief that society and the individual could be decisively improved by adopting a different way of life. This included the temperance movement as well as naturism, new/old religious cults, the initiative to establish new communal settlements, vegetarianism, and others. A variety of strange sects and prophets made their appearance at the time on the German scene.

***

Hans Paasche became known to a wider public with the publication of *Lukanga Mukara* in 1912. Paasche knew Africa well; he had served with the *Schutztruppe*, the small military occupation force in East Africa, in parts in which few white people had appeared before, and he was one of the few officers who had a working knowledge of Swahili. He decided to spend his honeymoon on an expedition, all on foot, from the coast to Lake Victoria and the sources of the Nile, which lasted for almost eleven months. He was, in brief, more familiar than most with the life and customs of the black tribes in what was then Kenya and Tanganyika, and is now Kenya and Tanzania and Rwanda.

Lukanga Mukara (Lukanga from the island of Mukara in Lake Victoria) is the fictional account in the form of a series of letters to his king of a native of East Africa of his first visit to the country of the Wasungu (the Europeans, in this case the Germans). Lukanga complains about the unbearable smoke engulfing the cities in the country of the Wasungu. He is amazed by the fact that the locals are forever in a hurry to make money, in order to buy unnecessary things. He is appalled by the factories in which they do the same boring work for years and decades. He is amused by the fact that they are always dressed up even while bathing in the sea or in a lake. He writes to the king that if he would be seen in the public in the nude, he would be hunted down.

A great deal of space is devoted to the dress; if someone were seen without a hat, people would congregate and make fun of him. The hat is a symbol of dignity even if it is a dirty and sweaty bunch of material.

The dresses in the country of the Wasungu are made in such a way that all individuals look alike, a strong man looks like a weak person. The women marry the suit not the man, most marry without knowing how they look naked. Around the neck, the Wasungu wear a stiff ring made of plant fiber; their toes are pressed together in their socks and shoes. In these outfits, the Wasungu are incapable to run, and many look and move like fattened hippopotami.

The women do not appear nude even when they work in the fields; their figures are artificially deformed, and new figures are created by a contraption called stays (corsets), which divide their body into two parts, only loosely connected. Lukanga thinks that this was originally an idea of the Wasungu men to subjugate their women so as to reduce their health and stamina, making them the weaker sex. In a similar way the men invented cooking in kitchens so that the women would have no time to think. The only time when the women can be seen nearly naked is in the evening after dinner when dancing.

In contrast to the Africans, the Wasungu do not eat when they are hungry but according to their time pointers (watches). Lukanga ridicules the barbaric, unhealthy, and unaesthetic habits of the Wasungu such as the use of smoke sticks (cigarettes and cigars) as well as the consumption of alcohol, which makes them half crazy. They write letters, use cars, and drive on railways for no good purpose, all these activities seem to him self-generating. All the Wasungu know how to read and write because their laws demand it, but there are no laws against writing bad and harmful things and books more often than not serve as a means for keeping the people in ignorance.

In other letters Lukanga deals with the idiocies of the economy of the Wasungu, and the way they celebrate their king. The only positive and hopeful note is struck in his very last letter (most are dated 1912) when he visits a large meeting of the young generation on the Hohe Meissner mountain. This refers to a three-day convention that took place in 1913 on a mountain plateau in Thuringia on which occasion a famous formula was accepted to define the aspirations of the German Youth Movement. It was meant to lead to some form of organizational unity between the various groups, but this initiative was not crowned by success.

The first part of *Lukanga Mukara* was published in a journal entitled *Vortrupp* of which Paasche was the coeditor and which was mainly devoted to the struggle against alcoholism. It later appeared in *Vorwaerts*, the national daily of German Social Democracy, and was eventually brought out as a book. It was widely read and admired and translated into several foreign languages and has been in print to the present day. Since the book was frequently pirated, it is difficult to know how many copies appeared altogether, but the figure is certainly in excess of a hundred thousand.

The idea to depict the society and culture of a country through the perspective of foreigners had a hallowed tradition; the most famous example of the genre was Montesquieu's *Lettres Persanes* first published anonymously in 1721. It was an ideal vehicle for the author to criticize personalities and structures in his country; thus he wrote about Louis XIV: "I have investigated his character and found contradictions for which I have no answer—he had a minister aged eighteen and a mistress aged eighty." Before Montesquieu, there had been Dufresny in whose book conditions in Europe were described as seen by a Siamese visitor, after Montesquieu Francoise de Graffigny used a fictitious Peruvian lady for the same purpose. A similar book by Cadalso, a contemporary Spanish writer using a Moroccan visitor as his chief witness, was read widely at the time. There were many others: Joseph Addison, the greatest publicist of his time related the impressions of four (American) Indian kings visiting London; Oliver Goldsmith, conveyed the letters of a Chinese philosopher resident in the British capital; and Frederic II of Prussia (following in the footsteps of Diderot and Voltaire who had engaged in similar exercises), reproduced the reports of Phihu, an emissary of the emperor of China in Europe.

A contemporary of Paasche named Erich Scheurmann was even more successful as far as a wider public was concerned with a book entitled *Der Papalagi*. As a professional writer, Scheurmann had left for Samoa just before the outbreak of World War I, spent about a year on this German island colony in the Pacific and the rest of the war as lecturer on the South Pacific in the United States. He returned to Germany and wrote several novels of no great literary merit, and his books appeared during the Nazi era in the publishing house of Erich Ludendorff, Hitler's early collaborator. *Papalagi*, the book which made him famous among the public, appeared first in 1921 and pretended to render the speeches of Tuiavi, a Samoan chieftain, who believes that the greatest error committed by his people was to be influenced by Western civilization. Scheurmann's *Papalagi* deal with the same topics as Paasche such as the stupid pursuit of money and the way the Europeans dress and behave, and the author was charged by some critics with plagiarism. He certainly must have known Paasche's book and was influenced by it. There are important differences inasmuch as *Papalagi* had greater literary pretensions and lacked a sense of humor. (While rejecting European civilization, Scheurmann hoped that German colonial rule would continue in Samoa even after 1918.) But the book also had its cult, is still in print, and sold over the years hundreds of thousands of copies. It had a renaissance with the emergence of the ecological movement of the 1970s and is read now mainly by very young people.

The German Reform Movement which emerged during the last quarter of the nineteenth century aimed at basic change not just and not mainly in political institutions but in the whole approach to life, hence its German name

Lebensreform. It consisted not of one broad movement or party or association but of a great variety of groups, big and small, advocating such causes as the protection of nature and animals, anti-alcoholism, vegetarianism, the emancipation of women, the cultural revolt of the young generation, naturism, fundamental changes in the clothes worn by men and women, social and racial hygiene (*Eugenik*), and the establishment of rural settlements (in opposition to life in the big cities. It envisaged far reaching changes in education (free schools) and the establishment of adult education. On the spiritual level there were reform movements in the established churches as well as the emergence of new religions and cults; some Germanic–Aryan in inspiration, others drawing their inspiration from different directions such as the Far East and various anthroposophical schools.

This reform movement was by no means identical with the avant-garde impulses in literature and art that appeared after the turn of the century even though these two movements did on occasion meet such as in the famous Monte Verità colony in Ascona., Switzerland.

Most of these initiatives were not restricted to Germany; they could be found in one form or another in Britain and Scandinavia, but seldom, if ever, in France and the Mediterranean countries. Anti-alcoholism, for instance, was stronger in the United States at the time than in Germany, whereas nudism was largely a German discovery. Few adherents subscribed to all these, sometimes contradictory, new initiatives even though they shared a common belief in a more natural, healthier life. On the contrary, there was a tendency on the part of the various groups to believe that their cause was by far the most important and that the others, while positive and even desirable, would have to take second place.

Thus, to give but one example, the temperance movement genuinely believed (and Paasche shared this belief for years) that abstinence would solve most, if not all, political and social as well as medical and psychological problems.

The reform movement was the reaction against the negative outgrowths of the stormy urbanization which Germany had witnessed since the middle of the nineteenth century, as well as various social ills, the ossification of society, and the strictness of manners and conventions. It felt acutely a spiritual emptiness which established religions and ideologies could not fill, and it was in some respects neo-romantic in character inasmuch as it saw salvation not in a future order but in a glorious past which had been destroyed but could perhaps in one way or another be reconstructed. Paasche quotes Faust in this context in which the return to agricultural labor and a simple life in general as a means to rejuvenation is advocated; the advice, alas, was given by Mephisto!

Complaints about despoliating nature were, of course, not new. In Germany, the tocsin had been sounded even in the early years of the nineteenth century concerning deforestation and the establishment of sewage systems that poisoned rivers and lakes. The demand to limit the consumption of alcohol had been voiced by the churches and even the monarchy, not to mention the medical profession (Hufeland, for instance) even earlier on. When the second German temperance congress was held in Berlin in 1845, the anti-alcoholism movement had more than seventeen hundred branches in the country. But it is also true that interest in the temperance movement declined in Germany during the second half of the nineteenth century, very much in contrast to other countries such as Britain and Scandinavia

However, for Paasche and his fellow fighters of the *Vortrupp* (which had a circulation of about three hundred thousand), the campaign against alcoholism and smoking and other such vices was not just a much needed act of social hygiene, it was the central issue *tout court*. As Paasche put it more than once—*Lebensreform* was a world vision leading into a new world. The difference between Paasche and the youth movement was that he saw in the abstinence from alcohol and nicotine the main issue, whereas for the Wandervogel, it was an important challenge but only one of several, the means toward an end.

Such an extreme position was bound to lead Paasche into isolation; the great majority of his countrymen and women were not alcoholics, but they tended to take a dim view of extremists trying to ban (or ostracize) the consumption of wine altogether. (There is some reason to believe that Paasche himself did not always live up to his own extreme demands.) What had induced him to take such an extreme position? To a certain extent, it was aesthetic revulsion; it was difficult to imagine, Paasche once wrote, the Apostle Paulus smoking a cigar. In part, it was a question of character, an innate tendency toward the absolute and the extreme, an unwillingness to make concessions. It was triggered off by his experience during the service in the navy; while on the whole consumption of alcohol was frowned upon, the order of the day on Emperor's birthday was to get drunk. Above all, he was influenced by the drunken orgies he had witnessed in the colonies, and it is of course well known that Europeans in the tropics driven by boredom were often drinking to excess. Paasche noted that the native rebellions in the colonies were largely generated by alcoholism and that the producers of alcohol should be made to pay for the restoration of public order—a somewhat simplified explanation for a complex phenomenon.

Even during the early phase of the World War I, Paasche tended to consider alcoholism the main plague and danger facing the country and possibly the main obstacle to an early victory. But very soon he was to undergo an ideological conversion and no one disappointed him more than some of his fellow fighters from the *Vortrupp* days such as Hermann Poppert. Poppert was a judge in a rural area in Northern Germany, and his *Helmut*

Harringa was the cult book of the youth movement and much wider circles. It is one of the books which has now become virtually unreadable, its pathos unbearable, and its tragic character has become embarrassing and tragicomic. (The hero's brother after a night of drinking to excess meets a prostitute, contracts syphilis, and commits suicide.) All this is accompanied by an all-pervasive invocation of the mission of the Nordic race which in a final battle will destroy its enemies belonging to inferior races. The Germanic peoples, Poppert wrote, had given mankind the idea of freedom. Jews, for once, are not mentioned in this context, but then Poppert seems to have been in part of Jewish extraction.

The juxtaposition of Paasche and Poppert is of such interest and importance because it clearly shows the Janus face of Life reform of the pre-1914 era; it could lead to the extreme right as well as to the radical left. While Poppert died before the Nazis came to power (and they had not much use for him in any case), he had been an extreme militarist during the World War I, and many of the life reformers constituted the human reservoir in which the early Nazi movement found its first supporters. Hitler, it will be recalled, was a teetotaler, vegetarian, and nonsmoker, but he was reluctant to impose his lifestyle on others; on the other hand, it is difficult to imagine SA social evenings, let alone the meetings in the Munich Hofbraeuhaus, without the liberal consumption of beer and schnapps.

Not long after the outbreak of the war, to which Paasche had volunteered but was given a wholly unimportant, perhaps deliberately insulting command, pacifism became for him the central issue, the mission of his life. In 1917, he wrote a friend that the temperance movement (once so close to his heart) was a matter of total indifference unless it also brought an awareness of freedom. Those who abstained from drinking among the German youth had failed as miserably as the drinkers. And he continued: "When German youth awakens it is pan German, anti-Semitic, following the swastika. The German bourgeoisie is the scum of the earth, it ought to be destroyed." These were prophetic words indeed, but they were also typical Paasche, as far as the hyperbole was concerned. No political thinker at the time, however radical, would call for the destruction of the bourgeoisie which, in any case, while a pillar of the existing order, was not the driving political force.

Paasche had not become a radical pacifist overnight, just as he was not born an animal protectionist. He had been a passionate hunter; there are many pictures showing him in a proud pose with the big game he had shot. He was an excellent marksman, and even after he had forsworn hunting and switched to animal photography, he made an exception for crocodiles, of which he apparently shot a few hundred because they had been responsible for the death of some of his friends and native soldiers. He had not just been a competent soldier in Africa but a very daring and enterprising one, and some of his military actions had been foolhardy; he was awarded the royal

Kronenorden mit Schwertern, a much coveted distinction given to officers who had distinguished themselves by action of outstanding valor.

In battle he had engaged in practices that were war crimes in international law such as an order to kill prisoners who could not be transported. And it is quite immaterial that these were common practices in Africa at the time. With all his love for Africa and his admiration for the natives and their way of life, he did believe in the German (and Western) civilizing mission.

Was Paasche converted when he watched the human suffering, the dying and the corpses in Africa? Perhaps, in part, but this did not prevent him from volunteering in 1914 because he thought like virtually everyone else in Germany at the time that the war was just and had been forced on Germany. Serving on some forsaken lighthouse, he did not witness the horrors of the world war firsthand.

Paasche became a pacifist partly because he was a born rebel against authority but also because like some other officers who went through a similar conversion his horizon had been broadened as the result of long stays abroad.

It has been pointed out that others who became pacifists such as generals von Schoenaich, Montgelas, and von Deimling or colonels von Sonnenburg and von Tepper Laski had widely traveled or had been stationed abroad as military attaché or some similar capacity. Yet others like Colonel von Egidy or Captain Persius had intellectual interests far beyond the narrow world of the average professional officer. All these undermined the extreme nationalist motivation shared by and large by the officer corps. While Paasche was highly emotional in his mental makeup, anything but a systematical thinker, he reached his pacifist views largely as the result of thinking about the war.

Paasche was anything but a political animal. His belief in the mission of life reform and above all the temperance movement strikes one as naive but perhaps less so now than thirty or forty years ago when "scientific socialism" was still in fashion. While reaching extreme conclusions about the need for pacifism and even a revolution, the idea to join a political party and generally speaking of collective political action seems not to have occurred to him. Perhaps it was the example of his father that deterred him, a typical mainstream parliamentarian of the Wilhelmian era who, moreover, combined political activity and private business in a way that was ethically questionable. But this explanation may not be sufficient, because there was also the example of his father-in-law, Richard Witting, who was also in politics and business and whom Paasche admired.

Once he had the opportunity to be active in a politically important position immediately after the revolution of November 1918 as a member of the Great Berlin soldiers council and other committees, Paasche did not make use of it but almost immediately withdrew from such activities. It might have been connected, with the sudden death of his wife in December

1918. But he probably would have retired from active politics in any case; he was essentially a lone wolf, not an organization man, incapable to work in a larger framework.

The murder of Hans Paasche on his farm named Waldfrieden in Eastern Germany during a search for arms following a denunciation that a big cache of arms was hidden on his farm (which was wholly untrue) was not only a tragedy, it was a political scandal, for those responsible for the crime, though known by name, were never brought to trial. Such behavior would have been unthinkable in virtually any other European country. It showed the weakness of the republic, and it was boding ill for its long-term survival. There were many obituaries, critical editorials, and a poem by Kurt Tucholsky entitled "Paasche." Many came to his funeral and a lime tree at Burg Ludwigstein, where the archives of the German Youth Movement are located, was named after him.

But the memory of this stormy petrel giving his life for the emergence of better Germany was not entirely forgotten, partly through the efforts of his family and friends even during the years of Weimar and the Third Reich. He was rediscovered by the pacifists and the Greens in the 1970s and 1980s, and even some East German historians put a claim to him as a comrade in arms of Karl Liebknecht and Rosa Luxemburg. But he was not made of the stuff to bow to party discipline; had he lived, he would not have lasted a day in the Communist party just as Liebknecht and Luxemburg would have been thrown out as deviationists.

Paasche was not a systematic political thinker. He was far too restless, too much given to sudden changes of mood be it enthusiasm or despair. Maximilian Harden wrote in his obituary that even in his fortieth year he had remained a youngster (*Knabe*), often wrong in his views, someone who is easily manipulated. During the World War I, from her prison cell, Rose Luxemburg wrote her friend Clara Zetkin that she was reading *Fremdenlegionaer Kirsch*, a book written by Paasche a year or two earlier, which had become a bestseller. She read it because she had heard about Paasche's arrest and was greatly encouraged by the fact that there were human beings even in circles in which one least suspected them. *Fremdenlegionaer Kirsch* was the story of a young adventurous German who made his way by way of West Africa and service in the French army on the Western front to the German trenches in order to serve his country. Paasche had meant to show that there could be a patriotism free of chauvinism, but it is doubtful whether the hundreds of thousands who read the book, brought out by August Scherl, the right-wing publishing house, understood the message; for them it was simply yet another fascinating account of highly motivated young man following the call of patriotic duty in the face of overwhelming obstacles.

When Paasche first came to the Wittings to ask for the hand of their daughter ten years his junior, they noted that the groom was not really grown up, and this lack of maturity was also noted by others. It was Paasche's weakness but also his great charm and strength. Perhaps he was afraid to grow up because only youth, as he saw it, contained true idealism and promise, whereas maturity was a synonym for compromise and the acceptance of the *status quo.*

Paasche's true importance was that of a figure all too rare in recent German history, a pure and very brave man, a firm believer in human dignity, skeptical of authority and the conventions of society, and willing to live and to die for his ideals. He was out of the stuff martyrs were made. He did not pioneer a new ideology nor did he establish a political movement. But he served and will serve as a true youthful hero not in wars of conquest but in the battle for humanity and a better life.

Paasche had four children, Helga, the only girl, became a writer and dedicated her life to the memory of her father. Jochen, his son, married Maria, a daughter of General von Hammerstein-Equord, the head of the German army general staff in 1932/34. The couple survived the war in Japan and later lived in the United States.

Many of Maria's friends were young Zionists in Berlin, and she and her husband spent some time in Givat Brenner, a Kibbutz in southern Israel. The circle of Maria's sisters was equally unconventional as far as their family background was concerned; her maternal grandfather was General Luettwitz, of the Kapp Luettwitz putsch fame. This circle consisted of young Communists, including those who had split from the party for ideological reasons such as Werner Scholem, Arkadi Maslow, Leo Roth, names very familiar to students of German Communism between the two world wars. While Jochen Paasche's grandmother (Hans Paasche's mother) became toward the end of her life a fanatic reactionary and anti-Semite, in the story of his wife's family names of persons of Jewish provenance and left-wing views abound. Thus in the history of one single family, we encounter the extreme political and ideological cross currents of German history of the last hundred years. For this reason, too, the Paasche saga might be remembered for a long time.

Ernst Nolte

Some forty years ago I was sent a book on Nazi Germany for review which was of more than ordinary interest. The author was Ernst Nolte, a Heidegger student who after serving in the German army had taught at high school. The book (*Three faces of fascism*) showed a very good knowledge of various aspects of fascism, and even if some of the statements seemed far fetched and exaggerated, the critics showed attention and respect. A number of further studies by Nolte followed on Nazism and comparative fascism which were useful and significantly contributed to the study of fascism, which was in those years only at the beginning.

Later books by Nolte were on a variety of subjects—the Cold War, Soviet Communism, and the Jews and the Holocaust—fields in which Nolte was not equally at home, but expressed strong opinions. He thought that Nazism had not been an absolute evil and that justice should be done even to Hitler.

These opinions were exhaustively commented upon, mainly in Germany but also outside; it led to the famous "historian's dispute" (*Historikerstreit*). No contemporary German historian has been discussed more widely and intensively. Why he was so intensely debated is not entirely clear, for some of his theses were manifestly absurd—that Hitler's war against Russia was defensive in character; that when he committed atrocities, this was simply copying Stalin; that the Jews had declared war on Germany; and that this explained the Holocaust. It was not really the work of a historian sticking to facts but that of a trial lawyer looking for facts (often quite doubtful), which could fortify his argumentation.

It was a sad story of a person who had once made a notable contribution to our knowledge and who in later years was taken less and less seriously. In 2006 Nolte declared that if he had left another ten years of work, he would devote them to intensive occupation with Islamism, the third major phenomenon of our time besides Communism and fascism which negated modernity and liberal (*Liberalistisch*) American society. This was yet another surprising formulation for so far Nolte had not interpreted fascism and communism as primarily anti-American.

It took Nolte a mere three years, not ten, to confront Islamism and to present his findings. But there were problems from the very beginning because Islam and Islamism are not exactly terra incognita but subjects which have been studied by experts for a long time and which involved linguistic and historical knowledge which Nolte did not have. Hence it was not perhaps surprising that the reader of the new work was to be told much about Marxism, Nazism, the author's life story, his critics, about Jews, Israel, and anti-Zionism, so much indeed that at stages the impression was created that the author had become so fascinated by these subjects that he seriously considered conversion to Judaism.

Only when we reach page 221, the origins of Islamism are first mentioned but even thereafter Nolte returns again and again to Nazism, Communism, and above all Zionism. He has much more to say about Hitler's speech in front of German industrialists in 1932 than the Muslim Brotherhood, Taliban, or Hizb ut-Tahrir.

This fascination with Zionism makes it virtually impossible to gain a wider understanding of Islamism, its origins, and consequences. The conflict between Israel and its Arab neighbors is a tragedy, and a peaceful resolution would be highly desirable. But Theodor Herzl and Dr. Chaim Weizman are not the alpha and omega of Islamism and do not explain it. The overwhelming majority of Muslims are not Palestinians, but Pakistanis, Indonesians, Central Asians, Africans, etc. Islamism is now a danger above all in Pakistan, Afghanistan, Yemen, Somalia—countries in which neither Herzl nor Weizman played a significant role.

What generated Islamism and how does it manifest itself? The Islamists have an explanation which may satisfy the post-colonialists but is not really convincing: It is all the fault of Western colonialism, but countries like Syria, Iraq, Palestine, and even Egypt were only a few decades under colonial rule. If there was Western tyranny and exploitation, it was of very short duration. For many centuries they belonged to the Muslim Ottoman Empire.

How to explain therefore the decline and weakness of the Muslim world?

Islamism manifests itself in more than five daily prayers and the pilgrimage to Mecca. But Nolte is mainly preoccupied with ideology not realities—fanaticism and intolerance are mentioned only in passing, and this is also true about the surfeit of aggression (toward each other even more than toward the unbelievers). How to explain that outside Europe, wherever Muslims are in a minority from Nigeria to the Philippines, conditions bordering on civil war prevail? Answers will not be found in this book.

Nolte says in the beginning of this work that it is not the assignment of the historian to play the judge; he sticks to his principles as far as fascism and Islamism are concerned but not with regard to Communism and Zionism. The way he proceeds is strange and often tiresome. A claim is reported—the Americans (Bush and the CIA) had initiated 9/11; the reasons for and against this theory are discussed at length, but having wasted much time and space, Nolte reaches the conclusion that the assertion may after all not be entirely credible if formulated in this way. But perhaps the Mossad was prominently involved? This theory ought to be taken more seriously believes Nolte. But in the end he does not think it tenable either. If so, why waste so much time and mental effort?

The syndrome gets even worse when Nolte turns to his favorite topic—the Jews. Sharon, he reports, said that America is an Israeli colony and the Americans knew it. When and where did he say it and to whom? Nolte is not entirely certain, apparently the statement could be found in an obscure Hungarian newspaper.

There are two main crown witnesses in this narrative. One survived the Holocaust in a Polish ghetto, the suffering clearly affected his mental balance. He saw the source of the evil not in Zionism but the Jewish religion, the Old Testament and the Talmud; a professor of chemistry at Hebrew University became a Jewish anti-Semite. The other, Nathan Weinstock, a younger man, was a French Trotskyite who in the 1970s wrote a bitter attack against Israel entitled *The False Messias*. If Nolte would have investigated the subsequent career of his star witness, he would have found that this anti-Zionist Saulus turned into a pro-Zionist Paulus, who forbade the republication of his book which, he said, rested on incredible naiveté for which there was no possible excuse and could serve only to absolve the conscience of anti-Semites. The demonization of Israel, Weinstock now argues, rests mainly on lies. In brief, not a strong witness.

True, Nolte could have found another witness; anti-Zionism has become fashionable, and there is no dearth of purveyors. But this case and others in this book show that caution in this field is imperative and a study of three years devoted to these complicated issues may be insufficient. The truly decisive issues are not discussed: If it should be correct that Zionism had a great impact on Islamism, how to explain it? Were there strong religious or political motives? Was there a great fear of the Jews or a great hatred? This seems unlikely, Jews lived in the Muslim world for many centuries, and they were considered second-rate citizens of no particular importance.

How to explain then the great anti-Israeli protest demonstrations in Europe whereas Russian operations in Chechnya in which after all more than a hundred thousand perished did not provoke any reaction? How to account for the fact that Pakistani complaints against India (to give but one other example) generated no sympathy, nor did the fate of the Chinese Muslims? The answer seems obvious. Israel is a small country, of no particular strategic importance, with no significant oil fields or other mineral resources. To attack Israel is not very risky, whereas to come out against a great power such as Russia, India, or China could be dangerous. There is in the Muslim world a great deal of aggression against nonbelievers, but the direction it takes depends from pragmatic considerations.

What can we learn from Nolte? His book on Islamism gave him an opportunity to restate some of his old theories. It does not deal with the main trends in contemporary Islam. To do this, knowledge of Arabic is needed, possibly also of Farsi and Urdu and of course of the massive literature on political Islam, past and present. Was the intention of the author to define the place of Islamism among the great political ideologies of our time? This would have been a serious endeavor. But would it have added much to our knowledge? To find a common denominator for the great political movements of our time is very difficult without simplifying their doctrines and political practice. Generalizations in this context do not necessarily add to our understanding.

There are parallels between Islamism and the European fascist movements—anti-Westernism, populism, hostility toward liberalism, contempt for democracy, anti-Semitism, and the conviction that the own ideology provides answers to all the problems of our age.

But does Islamism live up to what political scientists call the "fascist minimum"? It has no Fuehrer or Duce, no political party. European fascism was a political religion but not a religion in a wider transcendental sense. Neither Hitler nor Mussolini had a *sharia* nor did they conduct a jihad.

Talking of "Islamic fascism" (Nolte also mentions the possibility of an Islamic communism) means to overrate the European roots of Islamism and to underrate the specific Muslim roots. All these movements tried to be totalitarian but none achieved this aim and Islamism will not succeed either. Religious-political fanaticism does not last forever. Its impetus is almost always limited to a generation or two. Only hundred years passed from the ascetic origins of Islam in the desert to the luxury (and the high culture, the tolerance, and the temptations) of Harun al Rashid's Baghdad. In our age, the pulse of history is beating even quicker.

The Orientalist

Habent sua fata auctores—of all the strange fates of twentieth century writers that of Mohammed Essad Bey may well have been the most extraordinary. Cometlike he appeared on the Berlin literary firmament in the nineteen twenties, an Oriental prince suitably adorned—a flowing robe, a turban and, of course, an enormous dagger which would have been the envy of Crocodile Dundee, in his belt. Within a few months he became the expert of leading newspapers and literary magazines for the mysterious East, the rise and fall and reemergence of Islam, eastern philosophy and religion, the oilfields, the Russian soul, Camels and oases, dark betrayal, fiendish murder—in brief, everything north and east of Constantinople. By the age of thirty he had written biographies of Stalin, the prophet Mohammed, Tsar Nicholas II, Reza Khan of Persia, as well as a history of the Caucasus but also the story of the Cheka, the Soviet secret police, the fate of the White Russian emigration, the geopolitical importance of oil. He had predicted the coming victory of Muslim fundamentalism (Wahhabism) and the renaissance of the Arab world. He had written a love story (*Nino and Ali* which became a cult book but also "Was Tolstoi epileptic?": His books were successful and translated into many languages.

Who was this Essad Bey? Leon Trotsky asked in a letter to his son. The answer could be found in an autobiography entitled *Blood and Oil in the Caucasus* written at the age of twenty five.

This was a foolhardy enterprise because among the Russian colony in Berlin there were a great many who knew that Essad Bey had been born Lev Nussimbaum in Baku in 1905, that his father was not a Muslim nobleman but a Jewish merchant, that his mother Bertha Slutzkin was not a Russian aristocrat either and that Stalin was not (as he claimed) a frequent house guest in their home in Baku.

Essad Bey attended the Russian high school in Berlin where some of the Nabokovs and Pasternaks had been his contemporaries. Aged seventeen he had converted to Islam and studied Persian and Arabic in his spare time at the Orientalist seminar of Berlin University. Turkish he had picked up as a

---

Review of Tom Reiss, *The Orientalist. In Search of a Man Caught Between East and West*. (London: Chatto & Windus, 2005).

boy in Baku, his Arabic was apparently uncertain. He constantly refers to the hero in "Ali and Nino" as *majnoun* which he thinks means ardent lover but in fact means madman.

The autobiography, almost entirely fantasy, inevitably caused a scandal, Essad Bey's literary career seemed at an end and there was even the danger that, being stateless, he would be expelled from Germany. But he had powerful supporters, was permitted to stay and the fame of the exotic prince outside Germany was not at all affected. His books, scored at the time very high marks on the part of the TLS reviewers, they were entertaining, refreshingly unusual, exceedingly interesting. If there were occasional inaccuracies there was an "atoning accuracy of spirit" (TLS June 2, 1932, and March 22, 1934). For a historian the style was a bit too sensational, he was "occasionally abandoning the typewriter for the equally effective long bow of medieval romance." The reviewer of his autobiography did not disbelieve the story of the oil lord father with the beautiful Nihilist wife who had rescued her from prison after seeing her face for a moment through the bars of her cell. But he was a little more skeptical about Essad Bey's claim to have organized a strike in the oilfields at the age of ten. Essad Bey's account of the Bolshevist Minister of War in Baku (in 1917/8) was also accepted. According to Essad Bey the minister, having emerged from a lunatic asylum proposed (anticipating "Animal Farm") that the portfolio of Veterinary affairs should be entrusted to a representative of the oppressed animals and that a donkey with cabinet rank should be invited to assist in its deliberations. (But the reviewer (*TLS*, June 18, 1931). regretted that no dates were given for these events.) Elsewhere he got even better reviews.

Essad Bey was permitted to publish well into the Nazi era having become a member of the professional organization of German-Aryan writers; the Nazis were aware that there was something dubious about Essad Bey-Nussimbaum but somehow never came around to investigate his antecedents more closely until the late nineteen thirties.

But Essad Bey was not an ordinary impostor nor could all his books simply be dismissed as trash. He seems genuinely to have persuaded himself of his Oriental heritage and suppressed his real origins. It was apparently a case of controlled schizophrenia which at a certain stage went out of control, a mental affliction not unique in the annals of psychiatry. Essad Bey was, in fact, in medical treatment in Berlin but on this part of his life even his indefatigable biographer has not been able to shed light.

In retrospect, his books were of uneven value; some were quite worthless, others entertaining on the level of *haute vulgarisation*.

He was widely read, had studied the Koran and Near Eastern history. He wrote well in his adopted language, his style was a bit too colorful. What he lacked in respect of factual knowledge he compensated with a wonderful imagination; if things had not quite happened as he described them, they easily could have happened that way. His Mohammed biography was praised by some of the experts as one of the best popular works on the subject and has remained in print for many decades. What he wrote about Stalin was neither more nor less insightful than other books published at the time.

In his politics Essad Bey was a true innocent; he lacked understanding and had no deep convictions but believed that one had to suspend judgment with regard to Hitler—after all, he had saved the Western world from disaster. He closely associated with dubious characters. At one time he was a follower of Kazem Bek, a Russian emigré fascist who returned to the Soviet Union as a penitent sinner in the nineteen fifties. His closest associate in America was George Sylvester Viereck, the Nazis' most eloquent advocate in the United States, and he was about to join Ezra Pound broadcasting anti-Allied propaganda from wartime fascist Italy when he died. Had he lived, he would have found himself facing a military tribunal.

He left the United States in 1935 where had had been wined and dined as a great exotic author and where he would have been reasonably well off and returned to Europe where he lived and died in great misery. His wife absconded in America with another leading faction writer of that day, Rene Fülöp Miller, but this seems not to have been the main reason for his return to Europe.

He next moved to Austria where he wrote Ali and Nino a Romeo and Juliet style love story with a civil war Azerbaijani background which in later years became a cult book. It was published under yet another pseudonym (Kurban Bey) which caused endless confusion; the Azerbaijanis were so proud of it that they claimed that only one of them could have written it. An Austrian baroness also claimed to have been the author or co author but this, for a variety of reasons, seems to be unlikely.

His last station was Italy. He admired Mussolini and offered his services as a biographer. Having enlisted Giovanni Gentile, the powerful ideologue of the regime to approach the Duce, he almost succeeded. But as on earlier occasions, information about his unsavory racial background reached the Duce and while he was not arrested, he was kept in forced residence in Positano near Naples. Even his radio set and typewriter were seized. He lived in dire poverty and, suffering from an incurable disease, died in 1942 not yet thirty-eight years of age. During the last year the locals who took pity on the poor "Muslim" as they called him had provided some food and the local pharmacist increasing doses of morphium.

The only person who took care of him was the old half crazy nursemaid from Baku who stuck with him to the end; his father had remained in Vienna, was deported to Poland and killed there. His neighbor, the German emigré writer Armin T. Wegner wrote soon after his death—"the horrible story of a young, unhappy Jewish apostate who made a fairy story out of his life in order to escape the sad reality. He played the comedy up to the very end." There was a long obituary in Oriente Moderno, the leading orientalist journal. It said that Essad Bey was 50 percent Russian, 24 percent Iranian and 24 percent Turkoman—two percent remained unaccounted for.

Wegner called him a typical literary swindler, but this was inaccurate for Essad Bey was quite untypical; he seems to have truly believed that all he said and wrote was true, if not literally, then on a deeper level of truth. He is buried as "Mohammed Essad Bey" in Positano, the grave is positioned towards Mecca and a small statue shows a turban.

I came across some of the books by Essad Bey aged fourteen in Nazi Germany. The catalogue said "Lev Nussimbaum" in brackets so there seems to have been no mystery about the identity of the author even then. But no one knew in later years what had become of him except an East German historian named Gerhard Hoepp whose articles in specialized journals were not widely read. Tom Reiss, a New York journalist devoted many years to the search in many countries for the real Essad Bey (if there ever was such a person) and he succeeded admirably. His book would have been even better had it been a third shorter; there are long digressions on the history of the Caucasus, on Weimar Germany, the study of Orientalism and other subjects, which are more or less correct but unnecessary, hold up the narrative and do not add anything significant to our knowledge. But the story of the man, more tragedy than comedy, had to be told and it has been told well in this book.

Arthur Koestler

The work of Arthur Koestler born in Budapest a hundred years ago has not remotely fared as well as that of Sartre whose centenary it also is. There were no lengthy television programs commemorating Koestler's oeuvre; the central square in St. Germain des Pres is now called after Sartre and de Beauvoir but no street or place in London or Paris or Budapest or anywhere else bears Koestler's name. No chief of state had come to pay his last respects after his death and the number of people attending the funeral was considerably less than 50.000. (Correction 2010: I have been told that there now is a statue of Koestler in Budapest's sixth district which was unveiled by the Mayor in 2009).

Various reasons could be adduced. Orwell who was on the whole friendly disposed towards Koestler noted that *The Gladiators* and *Arrival and Departure* were not satisfactory books even when they were first published; they and other novels have not worn well over time. The same could be argued with regard to some of Sartre's and de Beauvoir's writings, but they had a "family," a school, many disciples and even more admirers and of course an influential literary magazine. Sartre, furthermore, has his firm place in the repertory of the French stage and de Beauvoir the almost unswerving support of the feminists except the most radical among them. Koestler's few attempts as a playwright were feeble and for good reasons he had no chance to become an icon of feminism. Unlike Sartre, Koestler never read Husserl and Heidegger. Koestler was a lone wolf, better in annoying and offending people than making and keeping friends.

There are political reasons: Sartre's politics became something of an embarrassment even to his most ardent admirers even in his lifetime. But on the whole French intellectuals found it easy to forgive him his many and

---

Review of Arthur Koestler, *Arrow in the Blue* (London: Vintage, 2005), pp. 414
Arthur Koestler, *The Invisible Writing* (London: Vintage, 2005), pp. 526;
Michel Laval, *L'homme sans concessions. Arthur Koestler et son siècle.* (Paris: Calmann-Levy, 2005), pp. 706; and
Christian Buckard, *Arthur Koestler; ein extremes Leben.* (Munich: C. H. Beck, 2004)

often outrageous misjudgments whereas Koestler's anti-Communism left a great deal of bad blood even after the Cold War had ended precisely because he had been right prematurely.

Koestler's work after the nineteen fifties when he left politics is not now highly thought off. Few can make sense of his "Holonic concepts" or his work on parapsychology, he did not become (as he thought he might) the Darwin of the twentieth century. Where his work is more appreciated such as in the history of science and his campaign for the abolition of the death penalty, his contribution was not as unique and outstanding as his earlier literary work.

But with all this Koestler has not been forgotten. Some of his work has been republished on the occasion of his centenary in this country as well as in France and Germany and elsewhere. This goes above all for his autobiographical writings. *Arrow in the Blue* and *The Invisible Writing* which certainly belong to the finest in this genre published in the last century. It is also true with regard to *Darkness at Noon* which has become a classic.

There have been some more biographical studies of Koestler this year, above all Michel Laval's massive *L'homme sans concessions* which was many years in the making. The author is well informed about the European Left in the nineteen thirties and forties, probably better than any earlier biographer. He gives an excellent panorama of the cultural and political ambiance in which Koestler's work was rooted. But, as the subtitle indicates, the book deals more with his friends and enemies and the general background than with the writer and his work.

On the whole Koestler has not fared very well with his biographers—with one partial exception about which more below. (This was written before the publication of Michael Scammell's biography in 2009—a definitive work). The books by Ian Hamilton and Debray Ritzen with all their undoubted value are long essays rather than full scale biographies. Professor Cesarani had access to Koestler's papers but the picture that emerged was not balanced. He dealt in considerable detail with Koestler's sex life and his attitude to women in general which was deplorable. But was he a monster?

Again a comparison with Sartre and de Beauvoir is instructive; recent publications such as Hazel Rowley's *Tete a Tete, Simone de Beauvoir and Jean Paul Sartre* and Bianca Lamblin's *Memoires d'une jeune fille derangée* have shed some new light on the subject and make Koestler appear in comparison almost a paragon of openness and honesty. That Koestler was a bully devoid of even a minimum of self-discipline, is well known. Yet despite all the drunken brawls and the ugly aggression he was not mendacious in his relations with sexual partners, holding in contempt those he professed to love as Sartre and de Beauvoir did. Nor did he specialize in attracting disturbed young girls. He was a disturbed man and neither anti-depressants nor psychoanalysis greatly helped him. But there was no more evil in him than in most other human beings. He was capable of love, often romantic love, which is perhaps more than can be said about Sartre and de Beauvoir.

When Koestler's name is mentioned these days it is more often than not in connection with *Darkness at Noon,* the novel about the Moscow trials in the 1930s. The confessions of old Bolsheviks according to which they had committed unspeakable crimes (which they could not possibly have committed) were a psychological riddle at the time and Koestler's basic assumption in his novel was wrong—as we now know. But it still remains one of the greatest political novels of the last century. The confessions were not made because the instigators of the trials appealed to the iron party discipline of old Bolsheviks and their belief that the party is never wrong and that the party demanded their sacrifice. The interrogators were far less subtle and sophisticated, they were torturing and beating and blackmailing the victims to get their confessions. But if Koestler's theory was wrong with regard to those appearing in the trials it still applied to a large extent to many other Communists in the Soviet Union and the West who continued to justify the show trials for many years after.

Christian Buckard's recently published life of Koestler is neither a full scale biography nor a literary appraisal; it focuses on Koestler's` attitude to Judaism, Zionism and Palestine/Israel. It is far more detailed than any previous study on his early life—as a boy in Budapest, student in Vienna and above all in Palestine first as a loafer, down and out in Haifa and Tel Aviv, later as a young journalist in the nineteen twenties. The author disinterred Koestler's articles (in various languages) from this period and they make interesting, sometimes fascinating reading. One would look in vain for ideological consistency in the politics of this young man. A follower of Jabotinsky, the very talented right wing Zionist leader, he decided nevertheless to join a left wing Kibbutz in Palestine. Koestler, the ardent Zionist had only very limited interest in Jewish tradition, history and culture—like Theodor Herzl, the founder of political Zionism, before him and his transition to Communism in the early thirties did not perhaps come as a total surprise.

Koestler's stay in a kibbutz lasted a few weeks only, he was too much of an individualist to fit in and not a good agricultural worker. He was asked to leave and spent the next year in all kind of unlikely pursuits such as getting advertisements for a new Hebrew language newspaper, as a surveyor and the author of fairy tales. (He never mastered the language.) He often starved and slept on the floor of offices belonging to friends. Then there came a sudden breakthrough—an offer to write for leading German and Austrian newspapers. Within a couple of years he became what he wanted to be—a star journalist. He wrote well and went out of his way to deal with unusual subjects—be it a monastery in the Sinai desert or a whore house in Beirut.

On Middle Eastern politics he knew little but still wrote with great confidence about Jordan, Egypt and Iraq; he even had a few scoops. He pointed to religious fanaticism (Wahhabism at the time) and pan-Arab nationalism which he thought had a great future, because of the widespread inclination to believe that all that had gone wrong in the Middle East was the fault of Western colonialism. He attacked the policy of the Zionist leadership which he found too meek, always willing to compromise. But he still did not feel at home, Jerusalem depressed him and the coffee houses of Tel Aviv were not remotely in the same league compared with those of Vienna and Budapest. And so he left Palestine in 1929 and in view of his early journalistic successes he was made correspondent of a leading German newspaper in Paris. Soon after he joined the Communists.

Koestler's subsequent career has been well documented. Auden once advised him to drop writing novels and to write only autobiography—but this, in a way, he almost always did: in prison under a death sentence in Spain (*Spanish Testament* later entitled *Dialogue with Death*), his stay in a French internment camp (*Scum of the Earth*).

His interest in Palestine was reawakened during the years prior to the establishment of the state of Israel; he revisited Israel in the 1930s and again in 1945–49, sometimes for long periods.

But the old inconsistencies persisted. He had greater sympathies for the terrorists of the forties (Irgun and the Stern gang) than for his old friends of the kibbutz; yet on other occasions he would declare that Zionism was nonsense and that the Jews in the diaspora should all assimilate. Once the state had been established there was a parting of ways. The new country was too provincial for Koestler, the European intellectual, and there was other criticism for instance of cultural Levantinism—it simply did not greatly interest him. But when the existence of the country seemed to be at stake (in 1973) he was greatly upset and if he did not revisit Israel it could well be that he was afraid of the emotional shock. For all his scientific bent he was a deeply emotional being.

He returned to the subject of Judaism only once, twenty years later with the *Thirteenth Tribe*, a strange little book in which he tried to prove that the Jews were not of Palestinian but Caucasian origin (The tenth century Khazar empire). This caused disbelief and some anger, I remember an agitated Isaiah Berlin telling me at a chance meeting at the London Library that Koestler had deliberately wanted to annoy his fellow Jews. It is true that the Koestler version of the origins of the Jewish people has since become part of the anti-Semitic arsenal, but I am not certain even now what his motives were; the thesis was quite obviously nonsensical and of what political relevance was it anyway?

What of Koestler's oeuvre will remain? His books were uneven, but this is true also of greater writers. Even the best were rooted in an age that has long passed—the Spanish Civil War, the Moscow trials, the holocaust. But they deal with moral issues that have not gone away such as the question of means and the end in politics. A leading contemporary critic (Harold Bloom) called

Darkness at Noon a period piece likely to last three generations and then to disappear for good. Maybe so, but in the meantime Mr. Bloom has edited a book containing critical interpretations of *Darkness at Noon* in a series also containing volumes on the *Iliad, As You Like It*, and *Great Expectations.* Koestler would have been amused had he known that this book continued to annoy post-colonialists sixty years after it was written. In brief, some of his works still stir up passions and this is more than can be said about some venerable classics.

Koestler: Scum of the Earth (Postface 2006)

When Arthur Koestler was arrested as an undesirable (possibly dangerous) alien in Paris on October 4, 1939, he was thirty-four years of age. He had already made a name for himself as a talented and versatile journalist albeit not of the front rank. Born in a Budapest Jewish family, he had grown up and studied some technical subjects in Vienna. Being a committed Zionist he moved on to Palestine in 1926, a British mandatory territory at the time. He joined a Kibbutz but his interest in and aptitude for agricultural labor was limited and he moved on to occasional work as a journalist, first as a stringer later as a foreign correspondent for a variety of leading German newspapers.

This took him back to Vienna and Berlin in 1929 and during the years that followed he traveled a great deal all over Europe ranging from a flight with the dirigible Graf Zeppelin over the North Pole to a long stay in the Soviet Union. He became a Communist in 1931 and remained in the party up to the time of the Moscow purges and show trials (1936–38) described in the novel which made him world famous, *Darkness at Noon.* (This novel was written in fact between Koestler's first arrest in Paris and his second in spring 1940.)

In between Koestler had also covered the Spanish Civil War for the London liberal daily *News Chronicle* and had been arrested by the forces of General Franco. Had it not been for the intervention of influential friends in Britain he would not have been released after a few months and he might have been executed; at that time human lives did not count for very much in Spain. He later described his time in prison in *Spanish Testament.* About half of Koestler's novels take place in prison or on the eve of detention.

There was a freshness and intensity to Koestler's writing and an ability to focus on the leading political and ideological issues of the time in a way that was neither boring nor doctrinaire, talents rare at any time. His critics probably outnumbered his admirers and also in his later life; a man of short stature he was pugnacious, especially when slightly drunk which happened not infrequently. He was not given to compromises in discussion and action, often overstated his case and being a premature anti-Communist did not make him popular in many circles.

With all this he was one of the most interesting writers of his time, more often right than wrong, always likely to provoke heated discussion, sometimes unnecessarily.

Paris where Koestler lived at the time was the center of the political emigration from Germany and other European dictatorships. There was no logical reason why Koestler should have been arrested, as a Jew and a man of the left his anti Nazi credentials were above suspicion. But for the French police which had disliked the presence of the many emigrants the war was a welcome opportunity to get rid of them. Hundreds of unwelcome writers and political figures were arrested at the time; many of them managed to hide after the German invasion of France, other succeeded to reach Britain or more often the United States. Some were caught in the trap, committed suicide or were deported to Germany where they were murdered. Koestler should not have been among those arrested because he was Hungarian and Hungary was a neutral country at the time; but this might not have been known to the local Paris police, or if it was known it was ignored.

The French behavior to these political exiles was disgraceful, but it was not unique. In Britain under wartime regulation 18B thousands of anti-Nazi Germans (not to mention a few hundred Italian waiters from Soho) were arrested and shipped to the Isle of Man. Many were released after several months, others deported to Canada and Australia and a few hundred perished on the journey. In the United States few German and Italian anti Nazis were arrested but thousands of Nisei, Americans of Japanese extraction mainly in California. It took several decades for an official apology and some amends to be made.

Koestler's group was sent to Le Vernet, a camp in the foothill of the Pyrenees. Those in charge of the camp had not the faintest idea about the identity of the inmates (no one was ever interrogated) except that they were the scum of the earth. The treatment was not particularly cruel, not comparable with a German concentration camp. What bothered the inmates above all was the idiocy of it all and the uncertainty—how long would they be kept, and what would be their fate in the case of a French defeat? These fears were by no means unjustified, for later on during the war Le Vernet became for some of those kept there the starting point of a journey which ended in Nazi gas chambers.

Today Le Vernet is a little resort ("un joli petit village" according to the travel agencies), there is even a small museum reminding visitors of the existence of a camp at one time very long ago. A few years ago the French president unveiled a statue meant to commemorate the camp and its unfortunate inmates.

Koestler was, as he describes, among the fortunate to be released after a few months; subsequently he made his way to Britain where he joined first the Pioneer Corps and later worked for the BBC and became part of the London literary scene. To what extent was his attitude to France shaped by his stay in Le Vernet? Less perhaps than should be assumed, partly because he had no great illusions to begin with as to how he and his fellow emigrés were regarded by many Frenchmen. The French collapse and the widespread collaboration did not come to him (as it did to some others) as a total surprise. On the other hand there were features of French life and culture which very much appealed to him. After the war he returned frequently to Paris and at one stage even bought a house not far from the capital. It was in France that *Darkness at Noon* had greater success than anywhere else selling close to a million copies. As for Koestler's book on Le Vernet, it was published in France after the war but not widely read and commented upon and it has been out of print now for a long time. It is not difficult to divine why demand for it in France has remained so limited.

Victor Serge:
The Revolutionary

Victor Serge who died in Mexico City in 1947 had been forgotten for a while; the *Village Voice* published an article in the nineteen eighties entitled "Who is Victor Serge?" But in recent years there has been a Serge revival in France and, to a certain extent in the English speaking world. There have been biographical studies, dissertations as well as articles about him, there is now a Victor Serge Foundation, a Victor Serge library offering revolutionary literature in Moscow, and his books are republished in several countries. A leading French publisher recently put out a massive volume of Serge's non fiction. This revival has been largely the work of a small number of devoted admirers one of which is Ms. Weissman, the author of the most recent Serge biography.[1]

Serge (the real name was Kibalchich) was born in Brussels in 1890 in a family of poor Russian political refugees. His uncle had been a key figure (and the main bomb expert) of the Russian terrorists of 1879 vintage (the Narodnaya Volya). He grew up mainly in Belgium, never had a systematic education but was taught science by his father, literature by his mother and read an enormous lot. The parents separated and from the age of fifteen Serge lived alone, first in Belgium later in France. He worked as a photographer's apprentice and from a very young age was active in anarchist circles. Even in his teens he lectured and contributed to anarchist periodicals. In 1912 he was arrested in Paris as the alleged brains of the "bande Bonnot." This was a strange, semi criminal group of militants specializing in bank robberies. They killed a number of people in the process, some of the proceeds went to their cause, part to their own pockets.

Serge was considered by the police the inspiration of the gang and given a five years sentence. That he had been involved with the group is beyond doubt, but the extent of his activity is unclear. Had he truly been the brain

Review of Susan Weissman, *Victor Serge: The Course is Set on Hope* (London, New York: Verso, 2001), 364 pp. and Victor Serge, *Memoires d'un revolutionnaire et autres ecrits* (Paris: Robert Laffont, 2001), 1047 pp.

of the gang, the sentence would have been much more severe. Serge's biographers have not tried very hard to go into this more deeply because they were apparently not very interested in the libertarian period of his life. This is regrettable because Serge was an ardent revolutionary but never really a faithful party man. All his life he remained an anarchist at heart, which is born out both in his novels and in his political behavior. Party discipline did not come to him naturally—he was a born rebel.

Serge was released from prison in early 1917 and deported from France. He spent some time in Spain and then found his way to revolutionary Russia; in later years he wrote a fascinating account of the *Year One of the Russian Revolution*. Serge's attitude toward Bolshevism was critical almost from the beginning, or to be precise from Kronstadt (1921), the uprising of the sailors against the Soviet government which was suppressed by Trotsky. Serge joined the Russian Leftwing opposition early on but for a number of years was sent to missions on behalf of the Communist International in Berlin and Vienna where he made the acquaintance of most leading Communist intellectuals and political leaders of the day. He returned to Moscow in 1926 and witnessed the growth of Stalinism and the destruction of the various oppositions. He was excluded from the party, put under surveillance and eventually arrested. Most of his friends and relations disappeared in the 1930s.

His fate would not have been different but for the fact that his friends in France launched a massive campaign demanding his liberation. This campaign lasted for years, the Serge case became a major embarrassment for the Communists and for Soviet policy in Western Europe, eager to advocate a popular front in the mid-thirties. Serge's friends enlisted Andre Gide and even Romain Rolland who intervened with Stalin on his behalf. Thus, alone among all the oppositionists he was released from prison just before the great purges came under way. The fact that he was originally of foreign nationality might have helped the Soviet authorities to let him leave the country (minus his manuscripts) while saving their face. Serge was considered in Moscow not so much a political figure but a litterateur and this could also have been of importance in Stalin's unprecedented magnanimity.

The next few years Serge spent in France; Weissman's biography contains many interesting details about his meetings with defectors from the Soviet Union such as Ignaz Reiss and Walter Krivitski as well as Trotsky's assistants which included Mark Zborowski, a leading Soviet spy in these circles. Serge was also in touch with many independent figures of the far left and his portraits of the leftwing opposition in Russia, of Soviet writers of the twenties many of whom he knew intimately and of his revolutionary friends in Western Europe are of considerable historical importance.

Serge admired Trotsky and joined the Trotskyites in France but for a little while only. Whereas Trotsky wanted to create a Fourth International at the time, Serge thought the timing altogether bad since the left in Europe was in full retreat. Trotsky turned his full invective against this "coquettish moralist," even though Serge had been close to him and had translated six of his books into French. Serge (Trotsky wrote) was a poet, that is to say not a person to be taken seriously, a "bridge from revolution to reaction." Serge did not reply. The whole affair turned into an ad hominem attack and Weissman notes that when Serge published in Partisan Review an article about "Marxism in our time," (*Partisan Review*, August/September 1938) Trotsky wrote about it "without any evidence of having read it." Serge faced social and political ostracism during the Paris years; most publishers did not want his books. When he wanted to find work as a proof reader the Communist unions tried to declare a strike.

On the day the Germans entered Paris Serge left for the south of France together with his son Vlady; like so many others he was helped by Varian Fry in Marseilles. Another life line, according to the biographers, was the *Partisan Review* Fund for European writers and artists established in the main by Nancy and Dwight Macdonald. It was Serge's fourth exile and seventh flight in twenty years. The stay in Marseilles lasted far longer than anticipated. It proved to be impossible to get even an U.S. transit visa for him because of his anarchist past; having been a member of the CPSU, a member of the executive of the Communist International and even the Red Army General staff (during the civil war in Russia) may have been less of an hindrance after the Soviet Union became an ally. Serge left Marseilles in 1941 and after some further adventures lasting several months reached Mexico by way of Martinique and the Dominican Republic.

The fall of France is described in one of his novels (The long Dusk) written in Marseilles while waiting for his visa; it was the only of his novels published in English in his life time. A very young Irving Howe reviewed it in *Partisan Review* saying that Serge was one of the still responsive survivors of a destroyed generation who had retained his socialist convictions always tempered by a warming humanism. Howe did not think very highly of the literary value of the book ('neither his political work nor his novels are as significant as the man himself") but he concluded "Other will write better novels on these themes but too few will we respond so warmly." Serge's life in Mexico was anything but trouble free. Like all his life he lived in dire poverty, small fees from articles published in the U.S. (*Politics, Partisan Review, New Leader* and *Modern Review)* were almost his only income, he felt very lonely and the Stalinists, as before, were out to get him. He spent a considerable amount of his time defending himself against various Stalinist calumnies.

Serge continued to write novels as well as on politics (mainly on the Soviet Union and its future) but he had no certainty that what he wrote would have any impact, indeed would be read outside a small circle of friends. He died of a heart attack in Mexico City in November 1947; his family believed that he might have been poisoned or murdered in some other way.

The present Serge revival is deserved in every way, he was a very brave and honest man at a time when so many intellectuals in Europe compromised and collaborated. He belongs to a very small group of survivors, the revolutionaries of World War I vintage. He was an eyewitness of events of world historical importance, of great hope and even greater tragedy. His political recollections are very important, because they reflect so well the mood of this lost generation. His novels will find readers now because they help to get an understanding of the aftermath of the Russian revolution and its impact on militants and intellectuals, a world of yesterday almost as distant from subsequent generations as the Napoleonic wars.

The revival of the interest in Victor Serge has to do in large part with the desire of present day Trotskyite sympathizers to find a cultural icon; throughout its long history Trotskyism attracted a great many intellectuals but could not keep them for any length of time. While Trotsky lived, his personality served as a rallying point. True, his later theoretical and political writings, the obsessive endeavor to give a Marxist explanations for developments in the Soviet Union and the world at large, were neither particularly innovative nor persuasive. But his strong personality, his tragic fate in exile and eventually his assassination attracted many intellectuals.

Trotskyism after Trotsky is a different story, in the age of Pablo and Posadas, of Tony Cliff and Ernest Mandel there was room in the movement for enthusiasts and true believers but not for those with more than a superficial knowledge of history, politics, economics, or sociology, let alone for critical spirits. The Trotskyites in France, and to a lesser degree in Britain would attract generations of students, but these would invariably drop out within a short time.[2] The Trotskyites had a golden opportunity to make headway following the decline of the appeal of Soviet Communism and eventually its demise. But their sectarian quarrels and splits, their growing detachment from the real world and their egregious political misjudgments (including the "critical support" for Ayatollah Khomeini and even the Taliban) antagonized all but the hardiest and most obtuse spirits.

In this situation the figure of Victor Serge must have seemed exceedingly attractive in the search for figures giving the movement historical and moral legitimacy, but there were certain difficulties to overcome. To begin with, Serge in his divergencies with Trotsky (who treated him almost with contempt) was more often right than the "old man." This fact is acknowledged by Ms. Weissman, and it provoked the ire of some of the more orthodox Trotskyite reviewers of her book.

More important yet, it has to be proved that with all his harsh criticism of the Soviet Union, he would, had he lived, never have become a Cold Warrior and renegade. Thus the Trotskyites (as does Ms. Weissman) compare

Koestler's *Darkness at Noon* unfavorably with Serge's *Case of Comrade Tulayev* and *Midnight in the Century*. In fact, both Koestler and Serge were wrong with their explanations of Stalinism and the purges. Koestler argued that the "enemies of the people" confessed because Stalin appealed to party discipline whereas for Serge the case of Tulayev was more or less an accident. As Serge saw it Stalin was a tool of the bureaucracy which, as we now know, was very far from historical truth. Koestler is rejected by the Trotskyites not so much because of what he wrote at the time but because (to quote Ms. Weissman) he became one of the god-that-failed anti communists. She also calls his book "a pure statement of Stalinist thinking." Serge, in contrast, we are told, kept his hope despite all that had happened and all that he had witnessed. I have a strong suspicion that with all this, Koestler would have been acceptable to the Trotskyites had he died, like Serge in 1947.

Ms. Weisman and others have been struggling valiantly to make Serge posthumously one of them, a revolutionary who never wavered, not perhaps a faithful member of the movement but an outstanding fellow traveler. It is a struggle against overwhelming odds. He contributed after his escape from France almost exclusively to social democratic journals and some which were not socialist at all. And this not just because others would not publish him, his views had changed as the result of his experiences. The socialism he envisaged during the last fifteen years of his life had little to do with traditional Marxism, let alone Marxism Leninism, but was based on radical rethinking and revaluation, it had moved far from the old doctrines. It included an emphasis on freedom and humanism, in some ways it was a return to the libertarian socialism of his youth.

He praised the Mensheviks and strongly recommended their writings, for their understanding of the Soviet danger was far more astute than that of his old political friends of the far left. All this appears not just from his articles published in the United States but most strikingly from his letters in 1945/6 to his old friend Emanuel Mounier, a leftwing Catholic leader and founder of the influential French monthly *Esprit*.[3]

Serge early on called the Soviet Union and the various Communist parties "totalitarian," a term considered today Cold War-ish and unforgivable in some circles, and considerable energy is invested by Serge's present day promoters to show that "totalitarian" meant something different then. But there is no escape from the fact that Serge was an ardent Cold Warrior even before the Cold War had really come under way.

Seen in retrospect it could not have been different. He had lived more than fifteen years in the Soviet Union, he had witnessed Communist ideology and Communist reality from a close angle, in contrast to some of his comrades in the West he could not possibly consider Stalinism a mere aberration. For him the Soviet Union and Communism was the most important issue in world politics and, after the destruction of fascism, also the greatest threat. The debates whether the Soviet regime was bureaucratic collectivist or state monopoly capitalist or other such hair splitting must have appeared to him either ridiculous or incomprehensible.

And yet, with all this one owes a debt of gratitude to those who, for whatever motives, are resurrecting the work of Victor Serge. His articles and books speak for themselves and we would be poorer without them.

Burckhardt and the Red Cross

Jacob Carl Burckhardt, a scion of a Basel patrician family, was a major figure on the European cultural scene between the two world wars, a friend of Hugo von Hofmannsthal and Rainer Maria Rilke, connected with the Stefan George circle but also a confidant of leading French writers. He was a professor of history whose three-volume biography of Richelieu also appeared in English. He had a political career as the chief representative of the League of Nations in Danzig in the 1930s. He met Hitler, Himmler, Heydrich, and their underlings and was given the opportunity to visit some concentration camps. He was the chief Swiss diplomatic envoi to France after World War II, and lastly and most importantly, he was president of the International Committee of the Red Cross. He was a highly educated man, good-looking, impressive in his appearance, a grand seigneur, and to use the overworked term—charismatic.

I became first interested in Burckhardt because of his Red Cross activities. What did he know about the mass murder of Jews, when did he know it, and how did he react? I tried to do some research in the Red Cross archives in Geneva but was not given access to the relevant sources. A few years later the International Committee of the Red Cross commissioned a Geneva historian to write an official account of the ICCR; but it was not very happy with his book either because Professor Favez did not stress sufficiently all the mitigating circumstances explaining its behavior—meaning its lack of action. It was only in 1997 that the Red Cross (through its archives director) admitted moral failure having kept silent about the Holocaust.

It will be recalled that during the war years, certainly up to 1943, Switzerland like Sweden was under considerable pressure on the part of Germany. There were frequent threats, and moreover, according to its statutes, the Red Cross was not obliged to deal with civilians; its main purpose was to take care of prisoners of war. (But it did help civilians—for instance in Greece which suffered from starvation during the later years of the war). It is clear that the International Committee could have done more, officially and unofficially, at least by making the information about the mass murder of Jews known that it had received from many sources.

Why did it keep silent? It was my feeling at the time that there must have been reasons beyond the Nazi threat, and my interest focused on Burckhardt about whom little was available apart from what he had written himself. Together with Philip Etter, a minister in the Swiss government, Burckhardt actually prevented the ICCR in October 1942 from publishing a resolution which, though in the most cautious way, would have protested against the mass murder of civilians. The great majority of the ICCR steering committee was in favor, but Burckhardt and Etter argued that this would unnecessarily provoke the Germans and negatively affect the work of the Red Cross in other fields.

I studied Burckhardt's earlier and later writings and found some of them impressive, even prophetic, for instance, some of the letters written to Hofmannsthal in the twenties about Italy, Germany, fascism, and the future of Europe. True, I came, in England, across a few contemporaries who had known him before and during the war and who called him a typical appeaser, who wanted to prevent war at any price. I refer specifically to the journalist and historian Elizabeth Wiskeman who had served in Switzerland during the war as a diplomat; Burckhardt retaliated by calling her a German–Jewish refugee, even though she was neither German nor Jewish nor a refugee. British diplomats did not trust him because of what they considered excessive Germanophilia. By and large it seemed, however, a little unfair to focus on Burckhardt and the Red Cross at a time when American and British statesmen who were not under similar pressures were behaving worse, certainly as far as the fate of European Jewry was concerned.

It was only many years after Burckhardt's death in 1956 that more light was shed about his attitude during the war and his apparent motives. Some of his letters were published, and a fellow Swiss diplomat Paul Stauffer published several biographical studies.

I found of particular interest a letter (first published in 1999) written by Burckhardt in June 1933 to a friend, Leopold Baron von Adrian (1875–1951), an Austrian diplomat and cultural figure of some renown. (He was the grandson of Giacomo Meyerbeer, the son of Meyerbeer's daughter Caecilie and a close friend of Hugo von Hofmannsthal.) In this letter, he explained why he found it difficult to generate any sympathy let alone help for the persecuted German Jews. He made it clear that he had known some "pure" Jews with the highest moral standards. But there could be no doubt that the German Jews had produced a Berlin culture which was deeply amoral and degenerate and which would have provoked a reaction by any healthy people, not just the Nazis. There might have been some violent transgressions committed by the Nazis, but this happened in every revolution, and in Germany, in 1933, there was probably less of it than in any other. In any case, there were all these rich Jews arriving abroad in their fine cars and living in the best hotels who could take care of their fellow Jews, and since all the world press were in the hands of the Jews, they needed no outside help. And on he went—attacking not only the rich Jews but also the Jewish Communists. He also hinted at the Jews's responsibility for the crucifixion of Christ. In any case, the tragedy of the German Jews was hardly comparable with what had happened to the Russian upper class after 1917 and to the Armenians in World War I.

A lawyer for the defense could argue that such attitudes toward Jews were frequent at the time, probably even the rule and not only in Switzerland and that 1933 was not 1943. In the letters of Burckhardt's kinsman, the famous historian of the renaissance Jacob Burckhardt, one finds expressions not just of Judeophobia but of racialist anti-Semitism well before racialism became fashionable in central Europe in the last third of the nineteenth century. He was not willing, for instance, to go to the theatre or staying in certain Swiss resorts because of the presence of Jews.

It could well be that some of the wealthy Jews who stayed in Swiss luxury hotels in the 1920s were too loud and ostentatious and annoyed other guests. Perhaps the Jewish tourists should not have come in the most expensive cars such as Maybach and Horch but more modest ones—assuming that this allegation was true.

But did Burckhardt become less anti-Semitic in the years after Hitler's rise to power, and how did he in retrospect (after the end of the war) consider his behavior? There certainly is no evidence that he was aware of any misjudgment or misbehavior on his own part. True, he seems to have been appalled by certain manifestations of anti-Semitism—if they occurred in Communist regimes such as the Prague trials of 1952.

Burckhardt seems to have felt resentment against the Jews even after the war because they were looking, as he saw it, for revenge against Germany. Furthermore, he tried to make the Jews to a great extent responsible for the outbreak of the World War II—the second and fatal European civil war. He truly thought that the war could have been prevented (and that he could have played a leading role in this) but that the systematic incitement in the West, to a large extent generated by the Jewish media, made this impossible. He believed that Hitler and his companions could have been persuaded to mend their ways or might have been amenable to some sort of psychological treatment as Stauffer puts it. In any case the Third Reich was no more than an episode and would eventually have disappeared.

Committing atrocities, Burckhardt wrote, was not a German monopoly; it had been done by both sides and was typical, for the present generation. In his postwar comments, Burckhardt always played down the specific horrors committed against the Jews, relativizing and trivializing the sho'ah. The Jews must be aware that they bore at least some of the guilt for what happened.

Klaus Harpprecht, the biographer of Marion Countess Doenhoff, editor of the leading German weekly *Die Zeit* and a close friend of Burckhardt during the last two decades of his life, wrote about him that he was essentially a creature of the nineteenth century and for this reason incapable to understand a movement such as Nazism. This could be part of the explanation but certainly not all of it. Churchill's roots, not to mention many others, were even more rooted in and formed by the world before 1914 but they did understand evil when they faced it. Burckhardt, on the other hand, who thought of himself as a man of the highest moral principles, belonged to a different species. He was not only politically a neutral, understandable and justifiable considering the circumstances of his birth, existence, and the context of his activities, he was also neutral between good and evil without ever admitting it, probably without being aware of it. He saw positive features in Hitlerism and even more in Italian fascism, and while he did not frequently publicize these views in the postwar period, he certainly did not repudiate them. The Allies, he maintained, had an equal if not greater responsibility for the outbreak of the World War II.

The position taken by Burckhardt in the von Ossietzky case was not untypical. The prominent German publicist and pacifist had been thrown in a concentration camp where, suffering from TB, he was mistreated. One hundred and twenty-one Swiss parliamentarians suggested that Ossietzky be awarded the Nobel peace price which he was eventually given. Burckhardt criticized this initiative of his countrymen which, he said, "Had not helped at all but only caused Nazi attacks against Switzerland." But it did help; the massive propaganda campaign induced the Nazis to release Ossietzky—a few months before his death.

The dilemma facing Burckhardt all along was whether he should give his hand to initiatives aiming at "going public"—to confirm even in the most cautious way the information of the mass murder of the Jews in Eastern Europe. He always decided against it because, as he claimed, such publicity could only provoke attacks by the German government against Switzerland and the Red Cross. He claimed that Germany might even revoke the Geneva conventions if pressed too hard. The only effective way was quiet diplomacy. However, there are few indications that Burckhardt tried quiet diplomacy, partly because the fate of the Jews was not on the top of his priorities and also because he must have known that quiet diplomacy would have no effect. The only known successful case seems to have been the one concerning a Polish countess—apparently an unpolitical affair—who following Burckhardt's quiet diplomacy, was released from prison or a prison camp by Nazi state security.

On one occasion in 1942, Burckhardt told an academic colleague in Geneva, Professor Paul Guggenheim, that he had heard from two trustworthy German officials that there was a Hitler order that Germany ought to be *judenfrei,* free of Jews, next year. He repeated, when asked to do so, this statement in a somewhat weakened form in a conversation with Paul

Squire, U.S. consul in Geneva, and this was subsequently transmitted to Washington. However, he did apparently not pass on this information to his colleagues from the ICCR. But as far as is known, he never repeated this or any similar statement; it seemed too risky and was bound to lead to awkward questions—what was the Red Cross doing facing this threat?

Nor was he the most truthful of contemporaries, to put it as mildly as possible. From the massive historical studies written by Stauffer (above all *Zwischen Hofmannsthal und Hitler: Carl Burckhardt. Facetten einer aussergewoehnlichen Existenz* pp. 338 Zuerich 1991 *and Sechs furchtbare Jahre. Auf den Spuren Carl J. Burckhardts durch den zweiten Weltkrieg* pp 514 Zürich 1998) emerges what had been on occasion been suspected by other contemporaries—that very little of what Burckhardt wrote could be believed without further checking. (This referred even to his letters to Hofmannsthal which I had admired for their prophetic predictions—it appeared that the letters had been doctored prior to publication). It refers to his travelogues to Turkey and Greece after World War I, to the account of his activities as League of Nations High Commissioner in Danzig. It applies to his reports about his long meetings with Hitler and other Nazi officials. Some of the statements made by Hitler are most unlikely, were almost certainly invented. It applied even to his Richelieu biography. Some contemporaries tended to take a charitable view—"Burckhardt," they said, "was inclined to 'fabulieren.'" This is a German term difficult to translate—it is something between embellishing a story, telling fibs and outright lies.

A lawyer for the defense could argue that autobiographical accounts are seldom if ever wholly truthful. There is always the desire to explain and justify one's behavior *ex posteriori*. This is perfectly true; few such books were written to denigrate one's actions and to depict oneself in a bad light.

But Burckhardt's writings on his activities go well beyond what can be explained and excused or what can be considered a temporary aberration. In the case of Burckhardt such practices of not telling the truth were systematic, almost methodical.

It could be claimed that Burckhardt acted under considerable pressure—the unfortunate fate of a neutral in time of war. There could have been some personal, hereditary explanations for these strains and stresses; Burckhardt's father committed suicide, and his mother spent years in mental institutions. But does this explain Burckhardt's politics? Philip Etter, his collaborator in suppressing the ICCR announcement of October 1942 and a kindred soul, was according to all evidence the most stolid and mentally balanced of Swiss citizens, yet he and many others shared Burckhardt's views with regard to the Jews, the Nazis—and Switzerland's duty to keep au dessus *de la melee.*

There were exceptions as far as Burckhardt's animosity against Jews was concerned. Hitler's anti-Semitism (he wrote) was "proletarian" (Burckhardt's term), whereas his own was apparently that of an aristocrat. He would not have greatly minded if the Jews would have disappeared from Europe, but he did not approve of Hitler's means. He even had some Jewish friends, mostly half Jews (like von Hofmannsthal or Baron von Adrian) or non-Jewish Jews.

Burckhardt was, to quote Jean Claude Favez, a complex even contradictory personality: arrogant, charming, a worrier, easygoing but at bottom a pessimist. He knew little about England and the United States and thought like many other leading Swiss politicians that Germany would win the war—long after it should have been clear that this was most unlikely. This misjudgment influenced no doubt his policy and that of the International Red Cross, which continued to be one of great caution—and fear of Germany.

According to Favez most contemporaries had nothing but praise for his farsightedness. When after the war the Weizmann Institute in Rehovot, Israel, made him an honorary fellow. The citation said that this was done as a reward "for bringing succor to people in distress, especially the Jewish people." It was an undeserved encomium, unlikely to be shared by future historians.

Montefiore—King of the Jews

Moses Montefiore, the best known and most admired Jew of the nineteenth century was virtually forgotten in the century after. The name Montefiore survived with a hospital in the Bronx, another in Pittsburgh, a Jewish quarter in Jerusalem just outside the Old City with its famous windmill as a landmark, a pugnacious Anglican bishop and a few distant descendants of which the author of this fine biography is one.

Born in Livorno in 1787 to an Italian Jewish family with British connections, they moved to London when Montefiore was a small child. There he had a most spectacular career, married into the Rothschild family, made at an early age a great fortune at the stock exchange, was accepted by the best clubs and families, even became a member of the Royal Society. He was knighted and made sheriff of the city of London, a largely ceremonious but highly prestigious office. He had a reputation of utmost probity; there might have been a slightly darker side—philandering—at least according to the strict official standards of the early Victorian period. But it cannot have been very important and we know virtually nothing about it because his private correspondence was burned after his death.

He was a good man; much as he liked making money, he liked even more giving it away to those who needed it more than he did. And so, at what will now be considered early middle age he retired from business and devoted the rest of his life (he died at the age of 101) to acting as a one person first aid flying brigade traveling to places where his brethren in faith were persecuted—from Morocco to Palestine and Damascus, to Russia and Rumania. He became a folk hero of the persecuted who attributed to him extraordinary powers. He seems to have liked traveling at a time when it was far more strenuous than now; few people went on their honeymoon to Jerusalem at a time when steam ships had just been invented. He was ninety-one when he went to the Holy City for the last time, braving cholera, pirates and numerous other plagues.

Review of Abigail Green, *Moses Montefiore. Jewish Liberator, Imperial Hero.* (Cambridge, MA: Harvard University Press, 2010).

He became roving foreign minister and emissary extraordinary of a people without a state. In many places they called him "sar"—a minister, a person of extraordinary influence, attributing to him almost magical powers—there was nothing Montefiore could not achieve. He was the Jewish lobby—such as it was.

The belief in Montefiore's omnipotence was somewhat exaggerated, not all his missions were successful—he could hardly influence harsh Tsarist policy towards their Jewish subjects and there were narrow limits what he could achieve in the Ottoman Empire even in its weakened state in the nineteenth century. But even symbolism was important—the fact that Montefiore had been received for an audience by Tsar Nicholas I, not known as a philo-Semite, did matter. The Tsar had given orders that on this occasion the guard in front of the palace should be constituted of Jewish soldiers, whom he praised as brave as the Maccabeans. In any case Montefiore's intervention (together with the Frenchman Cremieux) helped at the time of the Damascus scandal (1840), a blood libel when local Jews were accused of ritual slaughter (slaughtering Christian clergymen to use their blood for Passover)—some of them were tortured and killed. He alleviated the misery in Palestine, Morocco and other places. On occasion Montefiore tended to be a little naïve, but on the whole took a rather cautious, often pessimistic view especially in old age of his achievements.

To what did he owe his successes? He was a man of imposing stature and great dignity. Britain at the time was a great power and he was known to have influential friends in the highest circles. All this great helped but there must have been in addition some personal qualities which made him likeable, persuasive, an important person not to be ignored or trifled with.

Montefiore had not been particularly religious in his younger years but became more observant later on and Jerusalem was closest to his heart. On his four poster bed in Ramsgate there was the inscription "If I forget thee, O Jerusalem (Psalms 137). The city was a miserable place at the time—and remained so for years after. The situation of the Jews, living in abject poverty was even more miserable, the great majority lived from handouts by their more fortunate and pious coreligionists in Europe. Montefiore tried to help in many ways such as building alms houses, and, perhaps most importantly, buying land to encourage young Jews to engage in productive labor. At one stage there seems to have been a chance for obtaining from the Sublime Porte something approaching political autonomy, provided European Jews would come with their money and help developing the country. But Montefiore ruefully admitted that he did not know a single Jew in Britain who would settle in the country.

Abigail Green is a professional historian, an Oxford don; in this excellent biography she left hardly a stone unturned concerning Montefiore's life and times. The book is mercifully free of theoretical discussions on the development of philanthropy in modern history, on colonialism, on whether Montefiore was a Zionist, a proto Zionist or no Zionist at all. I am not sure whether he really was an "Imperial hero." It is exactly what a good biography should be. If anything, she is a little too self conscious, seemingly afraid of being charged with writing a hagiography. But he was a genuinely good man, their number in history is not very substantial, and praise should be given where it is due.

Three Witnesses: The Legacy of Viktor Klemperer, Willy Cohn, and Richard Koch

For understanding what life was like under a modern dictatorship, diaries are invaluable. Yet few diaries were written in such regimes and even fewer have survived. To write and keep a diary is exceedingly dangerous. It is difficult to hide, there is always the risk of discovery and the punishment could well be death. Thus it comes as no surprise that whereas many thousands of books and even more articles have been written by survivors of the Holocaust, only about one hundred and twenty diaries written by Jews in Nazi-occupied Europe have been published; most of them cover only a limited period and few of them, to the best of my knowledge, are very detailed. In addition, we know of some 300–400 unpublished diaries, or fragments of diaries.

Other sources on this tragic period are often more dubious as far as their authenticity is concerned. The writers might be perfectly honest, but in books written years or decades after the event, it is impossible to discard the benefits of hindsight, and human memory is always selective. Even letters and similar such documents, important as they are, frequently lack the same authenticity. They are usually written with a specific intention and with the psychology of the reader in mind. In the case of a diary such considerations do not play a decisive role, especially when it seemed doubtful whether writer and diary would physically survive, when the writing of the diary was a psychological need. Diaries written in these circumstances tell us what their authors thought and what they felt at the time, something which even great historians cannot tell us with total certainty. Diaries are not scholarly in character; they lack footnotes and are subjective and impressionistic.

Of the diaries in the Warsaw Jewish Historical Institute and in Yad Vashem, some were written by children, others by Jewish policemen, rabbis, some by Orthodox Jews, others by unbelievers, some by leaders in the ghettos, others by marginal figures. The perspective of the writer is almost always limited: he knows and describes what happened in his immediate surroundings. And this, precisely, is their great value for posterity.

All this refers to the victims rather than the pillars of the regime. In Nazi Germany and Fascist Italy, a few leaders did write diaries, Goebbels and Ciano being obvious examples. They are of interest to the student of politics, but they do not add to our knowledge from any other point of view. Under the Soviet regime, there were hardly any diaries by either the leaders or the led except perhaps by some literary figures such as Kornei Chukovsky. Since he expected at any time the visit of the secret police, he was very cautious in what he put on paper. There is a much-quoted paragraph in his diaries about how he and Pasternak were overjoyed watching Stalin at a meeting in 1936. The Russian term for prudent techniques of this land is *perestrakhovka*—reinsurance.

Of the diaries written under Nazi rule that of Anne Frank is of course the best known, but it tells the reader little except about the mood and feelings of a young girl and how she felt about the other persons sharing the small hiding place. Among those which have reached us from Poland are those by Adam Czemiakow, Emanuel Ringelblum, Chaim Kaplan, and, in greatest detail, Ludwik Landau, but Czemiakow was too busy (and too exposed) to be very outspoken and detailed, while Ringelblum covers a relatively short period only.

Compared with these and others, the diaries of Viktor Klemperer on which I focus are a category apart not because of their literary merits or because he survived but rather because of their sheer length and abundance of detail. This is also one of the very few diaries to have reached us from Germany rather than Poland or France.

Born in 1883 in a small town on the German-Polish border, Viktor Klemperer was the ninth child of a reform rabbi who preferred to be known as a "preacher" rather than a *Rabbiner*. Two of Viktor's brothers became well known physicians in Germany. George was called to Moscow to attend to Lenin in 1922; he later emigrated to the United States, where many of the descendants of the family now live. Otto, the conductor, was a first cousin. Viktor went to school in Berlin, studied literature, and tried his hand at journalism and literature without outstanding success. At age twenty-nine he returned to the university and eventually became a professor of romance languages and literature. His history of French literature was well received in the 1920s in France and Germany and he also wrote books on Corneille and Montesquieu. He married Eva, a non-Jewish pianist; they had no children. He taught in Naples before the First World War and for a time was Benedetto Croce's assistant. Later he served in the German army on the Western Front as well as in the East.

Politically, he was a liberal and a German patriot, more in the cultural than in the political sense. He converted to Protestantism when as a young man he did his army service; he declared himself a Jew when he got married a few years later, but again registered as a Protestant when he re-entered the university. To all intents and purposes he thought of himself as a Christian in later life. Until recently, his best known book was *LTI* (*Lingua terti tmperii*) an interesting study of the language fostered by the Third Reich; it was written after 1933 but could, of course, be published only after 1945. In 1987, his two-volume autobiography, *Curriculum*, appeared in East Berlin; this too had been written during his enforced rest after 1933 and it ran to some 1,400 pages. It concludes at the end of World War I. The author does not emerge as a particularly likable, harmonious human being, but a man full of complexes and resentment vis-à-vis his family and virtually everyone else.

This is particularly noteworthy in his relationship to his older brother George, the physician. In fact, from another recently published book, George emerges not as a monster but as an intelligent man, a good doctor, a shrewd observer and generous to a fault. Viktor's autobiography is still an interesting document but deals with ground well covered before.

The recently published diaries, on the other hand (*Ich will Zeugnis ablegen bis zum Letzten*, Berlin 1995; 2 vols. of about 1,600 pages, yet only a part of the original manuscript of five thousand typewritten pages), are one of the truly important documents of our time. Klemperer was an inveterate writer of diaries, a pursuit he had begun at age sixteen. Yet he was forever doubting whether this was not a futile instinct, an exercise in vanity and a very dangerous one at that. Was it not wholly pointless to start and go on writing out of a feeling of duty, was he not deceiving himself, or at best, getting immersed in writing as others would take to alcohol or drugs? Whatever the deeper motives, even if it was a form of vanity, we ought to be grateful that it prevailed over the pessimism for it resulted in a truly amazing achievement.

Why did it take fifty years to publish them? The brief answer is that Klemperer lived and died (in 1960) in East Germany, and while he was a highly esteemed citizen of that country, a member of the prestigious Academy of Sciences, what he said about Nazism and Communism, and above all the heavy preoccupation with things Jewish was not at all in accordance with the party line. His autobiography came out only in 1987, the diaries only after the DDR had collapsed. What is so extraordinary about this account is the description in infinite detail of what he saw in his immediate vicinity, the mentioning of names and places, the description of his mood and that of others.

Since he had been a *Frontsoldat* in World War I, he was chased away from the university not in 1933 but only two years later. Shortly before he had *had* like all others, to swear an oath of allegiance to the *Führer.* He had little money and constantly complained about his poverty, but he did not starve until the war broke out; in fact, he received a small pension to the very end. He suffered from growing depression: many of his acquaintances and friends emigrated, including most of his family. Then he was denied access to his beloved libraries, they took his house away, and he had to move to one of the so called "Jewish houses"; later he lost his telephone and his car; finally he was forbidden even to buy a daily newspaper. Many former colleagues and non-Jewish acquaintances shunned him, including those who were anything but fanatical Nazis; who could blame them, it became too dangerous. Then he could no longer use public transport and walk on certain streets (or certain sides of the streets). During the war, rationing of food and clothing was introduced, and the Jewish rations were much smaller than those of others, so that eventually he was constantly hungry. He describes how he stole a little bread and sugar from a neighbor; he felt deeply ashamed but his hunger overcame him.

With all this he could still receive letters, parcels, and even money from America almost up to Pearl Harbor, and from relations in Sweden even later. Since his wife was Aryan, she could travel sometimes on his behalf and obtain some extra food in neighboring villages. When in 1941 the Jewish star became obligatory, he suffered what he called a hysterical breakdown; for sixty years he had tried to escape the Jewish stigma. After that, venturing out of the home became a major trial in day time, and after eight in the evening, Jews had to be home in any case.

All this would have been easier to bear if there had been an end in sight, but there was not. Up to 1938, there were constant rumors about the impending collapse of the Nazi regime, but with the great political and military victories the belief in Hider's invincibility grew all the time. Beginning with the defeat of the German offensive against Moscow in winter 1941, and more dramatically after Stalingrad and the Axis defeat in North Africa, there was hope that the war would not end with a German victory. But also it became clear with the deportations beginning in late 1941 that in the meantime Europe's Jews would be destroyed. One by one Klemperer's Jewish acquaintances in Dresden disappeared and were not heard of again—only holders of the Iron Cross (first class) and those living in mixed marriages remained. It seemed only a question of time until they too would be deported to a fate that became more and more certain.

In the meantime, during the fairly regular Gestapo visits, the Klemperers, like others were beaten and even more of their few possessions taken. They were threatened: why are you still here, why have you not committed suicide? Klemperer describes a scene with a Gestapo official reading the letter from her daughter received by an old lady about to be deported—"perhaps by way of a miracle we shall meet again"—with the Gestapo officer commenting: "as far as you are concerned there won't be any miracles." The postwar movie and television caricatures of Gestapo officials seem not to have been far from the truth.

The decision not to destroy the diary in these circumstances was an act of great courage. Klemperer kept it in the little bundle with clothes that was always ready to be taken to the bomb shelter at the time of an alert. But since the manuscript was growing and growing, his wife had to take it every few months to an Aryan friend of the family, a physician in Pima, a town not far from Dresden, who was, however, herself under suspicion in view of her known lack of pro-Nazi enthusiasm. If with all this Klemperer did not give up, it was not so much that he hoped to live to the day that this diary of despair would ever be published: all other considerations apart, he was in bad health and thought he had only a short while to live. Rather, writing gave his otherwise purposeless life a certain sense. He had been good, but not outstanding in his profession. His *Weltanschauung* had collapsed ("My whole national ideology has been shipwrecked," January 11, 1938); he had no children; who would mourn him? He was not a practical man and almost useless in the primitive conditions in which he now found himself. He was only too painfully aware of his shortcomings: others were far better at obtaining a little food and, generally speaking, making the best of a horrible situation. And so he went on writing, the witness who could not really hope that his evidence would ever be read by anyone.

The diaries are a rich mine in many respects, but only a few issues can be briefly mentioned in the following: Klemperer's observations about Jews and Judaism, the attitude of the German population towards the Jews as he experienced it in daily life, and last, the question of what he and his fellow victims knew about the fate the Nazis had in store for them.

Klemperer and his family had consciously opted long before for Germany; to be Jewish seemed an anachronism, an impediment towards being wholly German. He was not a religious believer in the first place and his reservations about the Jewish religion were not greater than those vis-à-vis Christianity, especially after he realized that the Protestant church was not willing to lift a finger to help Christian Jews like him. He had a strong aversion to *Ostjuden*, not on a personal basis (some of the more likeable characters in his account belong to this category), but to the *Ostjuden* as a phenomenon. He had served during the First World War in Ober Ost (Lithuania and Northern Poland) and whereas for some other German Jews this experience had been a positive shock of recognition, not so for Klemperer. Much has been written about the negative attitude of the *Kaiserjuden* (as Weizmann called them) towards their less fortunate brethren from the East But it was not, of course, only snobbery and the fear of being reminded of their origins in the ghetto. It was also the frequent absence of an aesthetic sense on the part of the *Ostjuden*, their innate sense, imported from Eastern Europe, that the state and the authorities were an enemy, and the feeling among some that Germany was a cow to be milked—and deserted as soon as no more gain was to be expected. It would be foolish to deny that these features did exist, that there was an *Ostjuden* problem in Germany, mainly perhaps, in view of their concentration in certain places. In Leipzig, for instance, they constituted after 1918 the majority in the Jewish community. Klemperer opposed uncontrolled immigration and would have introduced a "cultural test" before granting permission to settle in Germany. In the final analysis, he felt uncomfortable because the Ostjuden, a few intellectuals apart, did not even want to be Germans. If so, why had they settled in Germany, rather than emigrating to Palestine? He realized with horror that even in his own family, the (positive) German characteristics were disappearing under Nazi rule and the (negative) narrowly Jewish features reasserted themselves. One day his sister told him: "You merely believe you are a German." Was she perhaps right?

In brief, Klemperer was anything but a good Jew. But it would be wrong to see in him nothing but a self-hating Jew and a traitor to his people: He could not betray something in which he did not believe; he belonged to the assimilationist tradition which had gotten underway five or six generations earlier in Germany, and subsequently in virtually all other countries in which Jews lived. Assimilation has suffered a bad press in recent decades, but it is useful to remember that it was a perfectly natural process. Traditional Judaism had become irrelevant, certainly for the educated Jews. There was no Jewish culture outside religion, which put greater emphasis on ritual than on anything *else.* Life in the ghetto had not been as good as it is now sometimes made to appear; if it had been so warm, cozy, and inspiring, Zionism would never have arisen. But Klemperer did not like the Zionist response either; he repeatedly observed in his diary that he hated Zionism as much as Nazism.

If Klemperer acquired a Jewish education of sorts it was late in life, while waiting to be deported. He read Shmaryahu Levin with great interest, but was not attracted by Buber. He was fascinated by Herzl's *Zionist Writings.* How prophetic Herzl had been (Klemperer wrote) and yet he had been wrong with regard to those (like Klemperer) who belonged to another nation; to pretend that this was not so would be a comedy and a lie. In Jerusalem, Klemperer would be considered a renegade and a traitor. To study Hebrew, as some of his acquaintances did, seemed a waste of time and he wrote with disdain about a couple from Dresden who, living now in Haifa, were confined to a three-room apartment. Soon Klemperer would live in one room and constantly complain about "promiscuity." Herzl and the Zionists had caused great harm, politically and philosophically, and in the middle of the war Klemperer played with the idea of writing a polemical book defending (spiritual) Germany against "Zion." He expressed a certain sympathy with the Arab rising against the British and the Zionists in 1936. But he also attacked the German Jews who found Nazism (minus anti-Semitism) acceptable. As early as March 1933, he wrote in his diary, "Never again shall I have confidence in Germany." Later on, during the war he jotted down that "if I *hope* to be a nationalist I might as well be a Jewish nationalist." But he still thought that those emigrating to Palestine were merely exchanging nationalist narrow-mindedness in one country for the same aberration in another.

In this account there is an eerie quality of almost total hopelessness from beginning to virtually the end. Typical is the surrealist scene worthy of a Beckett or a Dürenmatt, the ex-surgeon, the former textile merchant, and the erstwhile traveling salesman engaged in their unending card game on the Jewish cemetery, forever afraid that someone would surprise them. This was the unofficial information center and Klemperer frequently went there to hear the most recent rumors. And there is the grand finale, the *Götter-dämmerung*, the ocean of flames engulfing Dresden following the great air raid in February 1945 in which the city was destroyed, but which saved the Klemperers. His shelter was hit, the whole neighborhood was on fire, a dazed Klemperer, swallowed by the stampeding crowd, went to the Bruehl terraces on the shores of the river Elbe in search of his wife. He found her, lost her again, found her a second time, a battlefield scene worthy of a Stendhal or a Tolstoy. At last he removed his *Judenstern* and, together with Eva, set out on another odyssey through Germany to a small Bavarian village where he witnessed the liberation of his country by the Americans. Even in that village, he notes, they had heard about the death camps.

Klemperer was not a man at peace with himself. He despised himself for being useless, for having become cold and unfeeling—news about the death of friends and relatives no longer registered. On the contrary, there was perhaps satisfaction that he was still alive. He despised himself for not having written better books, for being impractical and weak and ill, for his frequent hysterical outbursts, for his inability to help his wife, for stealing a little food from a neighbor who, he had persuaded himself, needed it less than he did. He derided the constant Jewish fear of the Gestapo, yet he was not less fearful, aware that each moment could be the last. The idea of suicide must have occurred to him. And yet, every now and then, the obstinacy would return, precisely because so few would survive: was it not his duty to bear witness up to the last moment? However unlikely, perhaps Hitler would not win the war and Klemperer's diary would survive to tell later generations what it really was like.

What did Klemperer know about the fate of the Jews and when did he know it? He was almost totally isolated from the beginning of the war, he did not belong to any network, Berlin seemed millions of miles away, and the Jews remaining in Dresden did not even know, for want of a Jewish Calendar, the date of Rosh Hashana and Yom Kippur. And yet even this ivory-tower intellectual in the *Judenhaus*, privy neither to Jewish nor Christian confidences, had few doubts. In December 1940, before the mass deportations had even started, he noted in his diary that "we shall be deported or slaughtered." On January 13, 1942, shortly before the Wannsee Conference, he wrote that he had heard from several sources that the Jews deported to Riga from Dresden had been shot next to the railway lines within a week of their arrival. This is all the more astonishing since the first deportation from Dresden had taken place only a few weeks earlier. There are entries in the diary about mass graves of Rumanian Jews (1942), about railway transports to Poland taking eight days, and to the effect that all the deportees were killed; he specifically mentioned Auschwitz in October 1942.

Following speeches by Hitler and Goebbels he noted in February 1943 that there was no reason to assume that any Jew would ever return from Poland. There are entries about the Warsaw Ghetto uprising (June 1, 1943), and stating that the majority of those taken to Theresienstadt were eventually brought to Auschwitz. As the crow flies, Terezin is less than fifty miles from Dresden; Klemperer first heard about it in April/May 1942, that it to say in the very early period of this *Musterghetto*. He had no illusions: there was no room in the little Czech town for the many concentrated there, so people were killed in Terezin (September 1942) or dispatched to their death elsewhere.

Countless such entries show that the mass murder in Eastern Europe was no secret among Jews and non-Jews alike. He even knew by August 1944 that a transport of Hungarian Jews had been permitted to leave for Switzerland. There were fairly accurate figures about the total number of victims. In 1944 Klemperer reports on the authority of a Jewish acquaintance, that "we shall not see again any of those who have left; of the fifteen million Jews, six to seven have been slaughtered, gassed and shot." His source was neither an intelligence officer nor a professional demographer, but Mr. Konrad, formerly a well-known butcher in Dresden. Details were, of course, unknown but even in the *Judenhaus* in Dresden cut off from the outside world it was known as early as January 1942 that deportations to the East meant death sooner rather than later. And it ought to be recalled that this was well before the gas chambers at Auschwitz, Majdanek, and Sobibor began to operate.

Klemperer frequently writes about the attitude of the non-Jewish population, especially after the introduction of the *Judenstern* in 1941. There were many manifestations of sympathy. Dozens apparently knew about the existence of his diary and the work in progress, yet no one gave him away and a few offered their help hiding it. One of them was Dr. Fetscher; a local physician, the father of Irving Fetscher, a well-known German sociologist (Fetscher, the father, was killed by the S.S. during the last days of the war.) The German women married to Jews, with a few exceptions, stuck with their husbands despite the constant pressure to divorce them. At one stage there was a rumor that the Aryan spouses would be faced with the alternative of either divorcing their husbands or joining them on the road to Poland. In this case, Klemperer wrote, they should divorce them, for nothing could be gained if the spouses were to share their fate.

Klemperer experienced correct behavior on the part of the physicians he had to consult, and, on occasion, shopkeepers would give him food over and above the miserly Jewish rations. In the cover of darkness, he would be approached by strangers who told him that they condemned the Nazi policy vis-à-vis the Jews, that he should not lose courage because better days would come again. He even reports that the gruesome shouts of the Gestapo and the savage beating were usually for show, meant to impress their colleagues rather than to hurt. And yet, each time a school child would call him "dirty Jew" he would carefully note it and remain deeply hurt; he could not accept such behavior in the land of Goethe.

The last Dresden Jews, including seventy bearers of the *Judenstern,* had been informed that they would be deported on February 16, 1945, but three days earlier the city was destroyed. Thus began the last act in Klemperer's Odyssey. He and his wife sought refuge with their former Sorbian domestic in a small place not far from Dresden. This village girl was attached to the Klemperers and had shown more foresight than the professor when she left the family in 1933, arguing that soon the professor would no longer be able to afford her. They were now welcomed with open arms but still could not stay, because all *the* villages were overcrowded with refugees from the big cities and also from Silesia, where the Russians were advancing. So they went on walking, a sick, elderly couple, hitchhiking trough Saxony into Bavaria. They had a few names and addresses; usually they could stay for a day or two but not longer. They were still afraid of being caught; how often during the war had they thought that liberation was just around the comer, and then, inexplicably, the Allied offensive had come to a halt. But no Nazi miracle weapon appeared in 1945 to stem the tide and thus, inevitably, the end approached fast.

Klemperer knew no English and had difficulties explaining to the Americans who he was; they would mix him up with his famous cousin, the conductor, which probably helped. The Russians were impressed by the fact that his brother had been Lenin's doctor. And so the Klemperers made their way back to Dresden, which took another few weeks, since public transport did not yet function. Klemperer had vision with regard to his future. He thought he would again receive his chair, become president of a university, and perhaps even be appointed to a more important position. He was again made a professor, at first in Greifswald, later in Berlin, and even became a member of the prestigious Academy of Sciences. But beyond this the new authorities had no use for him.

A few months after his return he joined the Communists, the new state party, even though in the past he had tended to equate Communists and Nazis. In a diary which he continued for a few months after the war, and which has now been published separately (*"Tagebücher"* June–December 1945 in *Dresdener Hefie,* 1995), he noted that there were considerable similarities between the language used by the old masters and the new.

So much then about a diary, honest and annoying in equal measure, powerful, difficult to read not because it is badly written but because of the deep despair permeating it. As early as 1936, he wrote in his diary, "I am the last of our family, I shall stay here and I shall perish." Of course, it was not a typical account, even though there were thousands who felt like Klemperer did and shared the same experiences; they lacked the facility to express their feelings and thoughts, the impulse to write, the opportunity to hide. As a source of conveying what it was like to belong to the victims in the Third Reich it is worth whole libraries.

***

Is Klemperer's case unique, is this diary, having miraculously survived, the last to be expected? I know of other hitherto untapped sources, and I am sure there must be more. When I went to school in Breslau (now Wroclaw) in the 1930s, there was a history teacher named Willy Cohn, irreverently known as W.C., in contradistinction to A.C. (Alfred Cohn), a teacher of Latin, Greek, and philosophy. In fact, Willy Cohn was a graduate of the school at which he was teaching. W.C. was also known as *der Normannen Cohn*; having written an important monograph on the thirteenth century fleet of the Norman kingdom in Sicily, he continued to study and publish in the field. In other circumstances he would have become a professor of history but there were very few chairs in Germany at the time, and since he liked teaching school children as much as adult education, he became and remained a schoolteacher.

Having left Germany, I lost track of him, though I did hear that he was among the first to be deported, but that the three children from his first marriage survived, of whom two lived in a kibbutz in Israel. In the 1970s, a little book was published under his name—fragments from a diary during the Nazi period. Last year a huge volume followed, *Verwehte Spuren* (Cologne: Bohlau, 1995, 776pp.), Willy Cohn's autobiography up to 1933 as dictated to his wife. But in addition Cohn, like Klemperer, wrote a diary consisting of thousands of pages, leading up to November 17, 1941; four days later he was deported with his new family and murdered after arrival in Kovno by Lithuanian hired killers under German command. The manuscript was smuggled to a mixed couple in Berlin where it survived; when the son arrived in Berlin in Allied uniform he found the manuscripts intact.

There is a surprising similarity over wide stretches between the biography of Klemperer and Willy Cohn. They were men of the same generation; Cohn was born in 1888 to a well-to-do merchant family in Breslau slightly less assimilated than the Klemperers. He graduated from a German university before 1914 and served in the war on the French front; like Klemperer, he was critical of the *Ostjuden*. He almost died of the Spanish flu at the end of the war. But unlike Klemperer, he became a Zionist and social democrat after the War. His ambitions were educational rather than political. He wrote widely, including popular biographies of Lassalle and other socialist leaders. Above all, he was a passionate speaker; he would regularly visit small and very small Jewish communities all over Germany and give lectures on historical topics. He regarded this as a vocation rather than a source of income; the fees on these occasions were miserly. His political assessment of the situation was a curious mixture of astute foresight and tragic misreading. In his autobiography he compares the mood in 1932, even before Hitler had seized power; with the situation on the eve of the expulsion of the Jews from Spain. In 1937 he visited Palestine, but returned to Germany, there were not many German Jews who would have behaved in a similar way that year. Despite being a staunch Zionist, he did not want to forsake the small Jewish communities in Germany: *this* would have been "desertion." Does this make sense from a Zionist or any other perspective, did he truly believe that this place was with a community which was doomed? Or did he perhaps rationalize a difficult personal situation, the fact that he left his wife and their two small children behind when he toured Palestine in 1937?

Breslau had been one of the largest and most important Jewish communities in Germany; when war broke out some eight thousand were still there. What happened to them, how they were treated, how their leadership reacted is described in minute detail in this diary of a professional historian, which, in view of its very length, may never appear in print. (Correction 2010: It was eventually published.) It is less introspective than Klemperer's diary and also a trifle more cautious, but it still represents a monumental potential addition to our knowledge.

***

A similar source is the autobiography and letters (more than a thousand) of Richard Koch and his family, which cover the period between 1937 and 1973. Richard Koch, born in Frankfurt in 1882, belonged to the same generation; he too was an academic, a physician, and, at Frankfurt, a professor of the history and philosophy of medicine. Students of the history of medicine know him as the author of works on Paracelsus, on the theory of medical diagnosis, and on other topics; on the occasion of Koch's hundredth anniversary, there was an international conference in his honor. Students of Jewish thought know him as one of the founders of the Frankfurt *Lehrhaus* (together with Martin Buber and others), as the friend and physician of Franz Rosenzweig, and as a thinker in his own right. Like so many others, Koch lost his job in 1933, and in 1936, having been warned of impending arrest, escaped to Belgium. He had been one of the very few thinkers in Germany, or indeed anywhere, who had considered the possibility of a holocaust. Back in 1923, welcoming the inauguration of the leading institution of Jewish adult education in Frankfurt, he had written, "If our historical suffering should recur one day, then we want to know why we suffer; we do not want to die like animals but like humans, who know what is good and what is best."[7]

At this stage (in 1936), his life took an unexpected turn, probably unique in the history of Jewish emigration from Germany. Following a special invitation, together with his wife and two children, he accepted Soviet citizenship and went to Moscow in 1937. Koch was not a Communist; in fact, his political interest was strictly limited. The Soviet Union was not known for accepting foreign immigrants at the time of the great "purge"; it certainly was a unique case inasmuch as he was never arrested and that throughout the Stalinist period, the war, and the Cold War, he kept writing regularly long letters to his family and some of his friends abroad: fellow students of Soviet affairs have assured me that they know of no other such case. It may have helped that soon after their arrival the Kochs left Moscow and settled in Essentuki, a Caucasian resort not far from the scenes of the present fighting and where some of the grandchildren and great-grandchildren still live.

Soon after his arrival in Moscow, Richard Koch with his son Friedrich, aged fifteen at the time, went to the local ("choral") synagogue. They were received in a friendly fashion but the overall impression was one of great sadness. Only elderly people were present, for it seemed only a question of time until Soviet Jewry would disappear. Richard Koch was neither an observing Jew nor a Zionist. Over the years he had constructed his own religious belief system, a positive approach to Judaism. He even believed in a special Jewish ethical mission, but all this very much in a personal vein. Philosophically, he was a believer in German idealism, hence the "difficulties in the realm of spirit with official Soviet ideology" he mentioned in his letters. He had to subscribe (as he wrote) to Soviet theory and practice; he even accepted the idea that with the building of a perfect society, religion, philosophy, and even injustice would disappear. Yet at the same time he could not abjure, but had to cherish and develop the views and ideals he had previously held.

This would have amounted to a philosophical synthesis of liberal Judaism, German idealism, and Marxism-Leninism in the Stalinist version, which was of course impossible. But Richard was no uncritical admirer and he stressed that "no state, no new creed could permit itself the luxury to take into account that it too, would one day disappear." These were prophetic and heretical words at a time when Stalin and his state were considered immortal.

Richard returned to the subject of Judaism and the Jews very frequently in his letters. His interest in things Jewish grew as the anti-Jewish persecutions spread, a fact of which he was well aware despite Soviet censorship. He learned Hebrew and began to read the Bible in Hebrew without the assistance of a teacher. All in all the pre-war years in Essentuki (which he compared to Baden-Baden) were peaceful; he had found food, shelter and rewarding work at a time when few Jewish refugees had been equally lucky. Even after World War II had broken out it seemed almost unreal from far-away Essentuki. Intellectual isolation had been one of the major drawbacks facing the family, but with the evacuation to Essentuki of many Leningrad academics in 1941, Richard made new acquaintances, educated men and women steeped in Russian as well as European culture, among them many Jews. Even during that winter of 1941/2 the front seemed far away and there was the feeling that it would never reach Essentuki.

But it did: the Kochs, or to be precise, their hospital was evacuated from Essentuki on August 4, 1942 with the German motorized columns always a few days behind. They were taken to a little resort named Zelob Anba in Georgia, not far from Tbilisi. It took them twenty days to reach their destination; Richard, who had a game leg, had to walk for seven days. Living conditions in Georgia were unspeakable, and the attitude of the local population towards the evacuees was anything but friendly. The Kochs lived in a miserable hovel and starved. They had no clothes and shoes. But they survived.

All this time no one of the family and friends knew of their fate. For a year there was no message. Only in mid-June 1943 did a letter arrive from Essentuki, reoccupied by Soviet forces, which began with the words: *Wir sind also dem Verderben entronnen* (We have escaped the disaster). It said that in Essentuki the Germans had committed unspeakable atrocities; three thousand people had been killed, about half of them Jews, among them many of their friends and acquaintances: "we now live in the shadow of the death." The total number of those murdered in the resort region was considerably higher. The victims were buried in a mass grave in a ravine one kilometer long near Mineralnye Vody, the railway station, and the airfield. The murder was perpetrated by Einsatzgruppe D under Colonel Bierkamp (no trace of whom was found after the war). "Of course we lost everything," Richard wrote, "all we found was a detailed list of the things that had been taken." They were now desperately poor, lacking clothing, furniture, the most essential things. But their personal misfortune was overshadowed by the general tragedy; "Coolly, methodically, in a satanic way the Germans had killed children, women, old people, they had been shot or gassed, according to plan; no one had escaped, except a few by sheer luck" Richard, the lifelong humanist, now wrote that the "blood of those murdered, not yet avenged, was crying to high heaven." Nor was the reception by the local population cordial; the major collaborators had fled with the Germans, but many others had benefited from the looting and the general lawlessness during and after the German occupation. Every returnee meant that there would be less food and housing for those who had stayed behind.

During the war years that followed, Richard Koch, starved and freezing, surrounded by death and destruction in circumstances not dissimilar to those of Klemperer, occupied himself by concentrating on issues unconnected with the sad present-day realities. Somehow he found sufficient paper (admittedly of horrible quality) to write his long autobiography and to continue writing his letters abroad. Whether out of boredom, laziness or compassion, no Soviet censor ever interfered with these letters. And so it happened that fifty years after the event the retyped autobiography was found and first used by a young generation of intrepid scholars. The letters, as yet in private hands, remain to be discovered as a unique source on the first half of the twentieth century.[8]

Three witnesses of the tragic events of the 1930s and 40s, born within a few years of each other, whose formative years—family, school, university—were quite similar, their interests and outlook as young men hardly distinguishable. Yet how different their subsequent fate, how different their perspectives and reactions facing the disaster! They still have this in common: they all left a huge body of evidence which must be studied by subsequent generations eager to understand what really happened in those dark times and how contemporary witnesses saw it and explained it.

***

Since we have many eye-witness accounts, has the time not come to concentrate on writing history, that is to say on generalizing rather than dealing with the experience of individuals which might add a little to our knowledge and understanding? Generally this would be, of course, perfectly correct. But it is also true that there cannot be too many personal accounts. And I must confess that almost always I have found something of interest in the stories, often unpretentious and artless, of survivors in various parts of Europe.

I fear one cannot say the same with regard to all general works in recent years, especially those strong on innovation and new theories. We have been told that Hitler's anti-Semitism was merely a function of his anti-Communism; others have explained the Holocaust as the result not of ideological motives but of the blueprint of German town and country planners for the postwar period. The postmodernists have tried to come to terms with the Holocaust, and Professor Daniel Goldhagen has developed his new theory of anti-Semitism. It is my job at the present time to read most of the current literature on the Holocaust, but if someone had the time and the inclination to read only one book published recently, I would not recommend any of these studies but choose without hesitation a small book which appeared last month in England and will be published eventually in the United States too. It offers no new concepts and generalizations: its purview is far more modest. It is the account, partly narrative, partly in the form of letters, of a German-Jewish girl aged fifteen when the war broke out, who describes in simple language what life was like in those days, first at school, later, after the deportation of the parents, in an orphanage, then as forced laborer in an ammunition factory, and later yet in prison, for Anita and her sister forged documents to help French prisoners of war to escape. Released from prison, they went to Auschwitz, and since the young lady was an accomplished cellist, she was co-opted into the famous orchestra. Once Auschwitz was evacuated the two girls were brought to Bergen-Belsen where they just barely survived.

Again I must admit that I have a certain personal interest in this story. For I had known the two girls in my hometown, where we had belonged to the same youth group and moved in the same circles. I had the good fortune to leave in time; they had not, and I believed they had perished like so many cithers. And I well remember that day in April 1945 listening to the British Broadcasting Corporation war correspondent with the forces that had just liberated Belsen desperately looking for someone speaking English. And whom should he bring to the microphone but the Lasker sisters? I may be prejudiced, but it is precisely as a historian that I recommend this account, because it is all there: the nasty yellow mud of Auschwitz, the quarantine bloc, the stench, the smoke, the hunger and the despair, the screaming, the Muselmanner and Kanada, and playing Schumann's "Traumerei" for Dr. Mengele.[9]

I do not want to argue that history can be written only by those who had been there, for this would make most of the writing of history impossible. But there are certain situations which were so extreme that an extraordinary effort is needed to grasp their enormity, unless one happened to be present.

Notes

1. The Weissman biography includes an excellent bibliography of Victor Serge's writings; the French collection of his writings edited by Jil Silberstein has notes about events and personalities mentioned in Serge's books and articles that are a model of their kind.

2. During the last year, there has been a dozen of new books on the history of Trotskyism which show this enormous turnover in their ranks—most notably Christophe Nick, Les Trotskistes. Fayard Paris, 2002, pp. 616 and Edwy Plenel, Secrets de Jeunesse, Paris 2001, pp. 252.

3. These letters appear in the collection of Serge's writing edited by Ms. Silberstein. They seem not to have been at the disposal of Susan Weisman who does not mention them.

4. A version of this article was originally presented as the Joseph and Rebecca Meyerhoff Annual Lecture at the United States Holocaust Memorial Museum on June 18, 1996. This lectureship has been endowed by a grant from the Meyerhoff family to the Research Institute of the Museum in order to promote excellence in and to disseminate Holocaust research.

5. Peter Heyworth, *Otto Klemperer, His Life and Times, 1933–1973* (Cambridge: Cambridge University Press, 1996), Vol. 2, *passim.*

6. I must confess personal interest since I write about my father-in-law, nonetheless, I think I can muster sufficient objectivity to judge their wider interest. Willy Cohn was my teacher in school for a year or two.

7. R. Koch, "Das Freie Judische Lehrhaus in Frankfurt am Main," *Der Jude* 7 (1923): 116–20, quoted in Michael Brenner, *The Renaissance of Jewish Culture in Weimar Germany* (New Haven: Yale University Press, 1996).

8. See Brenner, *passim*. On Koch's contribution to medical thought Gert Peiser, ed., *Richard Koch und die Aerztliche Diagnose* (Hildesheim: Georg Olms, 1988). Koch's autobiography has been published in part since these lines were written.

9. Anita Lasker-Wallfisch, *Inherit the Truth 1939–1945* (London: DLM Publishers, 1996).

Index

Abdul Hadi, Sleiman, 20
Abu Taleb, Ahmed, 121
Addison, Joseph, 192
Admor of Sadagora, 17
Adrian, Leopold Baron von, 222
Afghan war, 90, 163
Ahmadinejad, Mahmoud, 83
al Husseini, Haj Amin, 126
Alexander, Edgar, 126
Ali, Mehmet, 9–10, 11, 14
Alkalai, Yehuda, 13, 15
Allison, Graham, 166
Alon, Yigal, 30
al-Qaeda, 118, 149, 150, 164, 171,
   178, 181
Alroy, David, 7
Alterman, Nathan, 63
Altneuland (Herzl), 35–36, 40
Amir, Yigal, 139
Andropov, 76, 80, 81
Animal Farm (Orwell), 23
Annan, Kofi, 179
Anstrutter, Lady, 6
anti-Americanism, 76–77, 100
   see also anti-Westernism
anti-Arab sentiment, 29–30
   see also Danish cartoon affair
anti-Semitism, 3–6, 132–133, 201,
   223, 225–226
anti-Westernism, 84–85
   see also anti-Americanism
apocalyptic movements, 142–143
Arab-Israeli conflict
   importance of, 25–26
   literature on, 26–27
Arafat, Yasir, 91, 139
Arendt, Hannah, 61, 62–63, 89
arms sales, 90–91

Arrival and Departure (Koestler), 207
Arrow in the Blue (Koestler), 207–213
Arthur Koestler (Buckard), 207–213
Ashton, Cathy, 114
Assad, Hafez el, 25, 156
assassinations, 137, 139
asymmetric warfare, 155–157, 181
atomic bomb, 20, 166
   see also Manhattan Project;
      nuclear weapons
Atta, Muhammed, 178
Auden, Wystan Hugh, 210
Aum Shinrikyo, 141, 142, 143
Auschwitz, 47–48, 49–53, 54, 238, 244
Austen, Sarah, 6–7

Bakunin, Mikhail, 8
Balfour declaration, 28, 57
bande Bonnot, 215–216
Bankier, David, 48
Basque Homeland and Liberty
   (ETA) movement, 138, 145
Bek, Kazem, 205
Ben Ami, Shlomo, 26
Ben Gurion, David, 28–29, 41, 43, 62
Berenbaum, Michael, 48
Berlin, Isaiah, 210
Bey, Kurban, 205
Bierkamp, Colonel, 243
bin Laden, Osama, 19, 119, 149, 151,
   158–159, 164, 172, 173, 180, 181
binational state, feasibility of, 30–31
biological weapons, 140–142
Bion, Wilfred Ruprecht, 62
birth rates, 22, 32, 34, 58, 75, 119,
   120, 124, 175
Bischoffsheim, 10
Bismarck, 112

Blood and Oil in the Caucasus
  (Bey), 203
Bloom, Harold, 210–211
Boumediène, Houari, 119–120
Breitman, Richard, 48
Brezhnev, 89, 106
BRIC, 77
Buber, Martin, 61, 236, 241
Buchanan, James, 76
Buckard, Christian, 207–213
Buelow, Heinrich von, 8–9, 10
Bunn, Matthew, 166
Burckhardt, Jacob Carl, 221–226
Bush, George W., 94, 163
Byron, George Gordon 9

Cambridge History of the Cold War,
  103–108
Canning, Stanford, 9–10
Carter, Jimmy, 26
The Case for Israel (Dershowitz), 63
Case of Comrade Tulayev (Serge), 219
Center on European Reform, 114
Cesarani, David, 208
Cesari, Jocelyne, 118
Chaadayev, Pyotr, 88, 95–96
Chamberlain, Neville, 49
The Changing Face of Antisemitism
  (Laqueur), 132
Chavez, Hugo, 83
Chechen wars, 90, 93
chemical weapons, 140–141
Chukovsky, Kornei, 232
Churchill, Winston, 51, 55, 104, 224
Ciano, 232
Clausen, Jytta, 118–119
Clemenceau, Georges, 117
clerical fascism, 125
Clinton, Bill, 137, 163
The Clock is Ticking, 166
Cohen, Job, 121
Cohn, Willy, 240–241
Cold War, 99, 103–108, 158, 165,
  218–219
conspiracy theories, 5–6, 82, 158,
  167, 180
Contarini, 7
Conzen, Peter, 183–186
Coughlin, Father, 127
Croce, Benedetto, 232
cultural propaganda, 105
Curriculum (Klemperer), 233

cyberwarfare, 144–145
Czemiakow, Adam, 232

Daguerre, Louis, 18
Damascus scandal, 228
Dangerous Games (Macmillan),
  69–71
Danilevsky, Nikolai, 108
Danish cartoon affair, 118
Darkness at Noon (Koestler), 208,
  209, 211, 213, 219
Das Kapital (Marx), 119
David, King, 40–41
de Beauvoir, Simone, 207, 208, 209
Dead Souls (Gogol), 75
Papalagi (Scheurmann), 192
Dershowitz, Alan, 63–64
détente, policy of, 78–79, 81,
  83–85, 106
Dialogue with Death (Koestler), 210
Dimitrov, Georgi, 104
Dirksen, Giselher von, 20
Disraeli, 6–7, 11, 13–14, 15, 16, 19
Disraelia, 17–23
Doenhoff, Marion Countess, 224
Dostoevsky, Fyodor, 85, 108
drug problem, in Russia, 78
Dufresny, 192
Dugin, Alexander, 96–97, 101

economic situation, 3, 38, 77, 165
Ehrlich, Paul, 17
Einstein, Albert, 161
Eitan, Walter, 46
el Sibai, Youssef, 26
emigration
  arguments against, 13–14
  feasibility of, 11–13
  industry and, 17–18
  promotion of, 8–9, 10–11
  restrictions on, 28
  results of, 17–18
  start of, 15–16
  support for, 14–15
  see also immigration
Emmerich, Edgar Alexander. *see*
  Alexander, Edgar
Engel, David, 48
environmental concerns, 143,
  193–194
Erdheim, Stuart, 53
Erikson, Erik, 183

Eshkoli, Chawa, 48
Essad Bey, Mohammed, 203–206
ethnic cleansing, 27, 28
Etter, Philip, 222, 225
Eurabia, 117, 119
Eurooptimists, 111–112, 113
European unity, 114–115
European welfare state, 111–112
Europe's Promise (Hill), 111
Europessimists, 111, 114

The False Messias (Weinstock), 201
fanaticism, 183–186
Fanatismus (Conzen), 183–186
fascism, 125–130, 199, 202
Fascism: Past Present Future, 125
Fatah, 29
Faust, 193
Favez, Jean Claude, 226
Feingold, Henry, 48
Festinger, Leon, 152
Fetscher, Dr., 238
Fetscher, Irving, 238
Fichte, Johann Gottlieb, 4
Finkelstein, Juan, 21, 63–64
Forebodings of a New Cold War
    (Prokhanov), 108
Foucault, Michel, 127
Fould, Achille, 7, 10, 15
Fourier, Charles, 5
Franco, 127, 211
Frank, Anne, 232
Franklin, Benjamin, 98
Frederic II, 192
Freedman, Lawrence, 26
Fremdenlegionaer Kirsch (Paasche), 197
French riots (2005), 118–119
Freud, Sigmund, 62, 161
Friling, Tuvia, 48
Frost, Robert, 21
Fry, Varian, 54–55, 217
fundamentalism, 125, 129

Gaddafi, Colonel, 119
Gainutdin, 97
Gandhi, Mahatma, 61
Gandhi, Rajiv, 139
Gasprinski, Ismail, 88
Gaza strip, 25, 29, 30, 34, 58–59, 90
gender equality, 122
Geneva Conventions, 156
genocide, 113

Gentile, Giovanni, 205
George, Stefan, 221
German Reform Movement,
    192–194
German Youth Movement, 191,
    194–195, 197
ghettos
    closing of, 3
    reconsideration of, 5
The Gladiators (Koestler), 207
Goebbels, Joseph, 47, 133, 232, 238
Gogol, Nikolai, 75, 85
Goldhagen, Daniel, 244
Goldsmith, Oliver, 192
Gorbachev, Mikhail, 75, 91
Gorenberg, Gershom, 26
Graetz, Heinrich, 3
Graffigny, Francoise de, 192
Grant, Charles, 114
Great Depression, 49
Green, Abigail, 227–229
Griboedov, Aleksander, 88
Guantanamo Bay, 163
Guardian, 113
guerrillas, 137, 138, 155
Guevara, Che, 19
Guggenheim, Paul, 224

Haifa, 31
Halpern, Manfred, 128–129
Hamami, Said, 31
Hamas, 29, 91, 99, 138, 139, 178
Hamilton, Ian, 208
Hammerstein-Equord,
    General von, 198
Harden, Maximilian, 197
Harpprecht, Klaus, 224
Harun al Rashid, 154
Hassan I Sabbay, 143
Havel, Vaclav, 62
Heggy, Tarek, 26
Heidegger, Martin, 20
Heine, Heinrich, 4, 15–16
Heinzen, Karl, 160
Helmut Harringa (Poppert),
    194–195
Hep Hep riots, 4
hero worship, nationalist, 63
Herzen, Alexander, 76
Herzl, Theodor, 28, 35–36, 37, 40, 42,
    58–59, 60, 61, 62, 200, 209, 236
Hess, Moses, 7–8, 23

Hezbollah, 29, 91, 99, 139, 181
hijackings, 138
Hill, Steven, 111
Hirsch, Baron de, 10, 15
Hirsi Ali, Ayaan, 117
historian's dispute, 199
History of Russia (Zubov), 103–108
Hitler, Adolf
  anti-Semitism of, 244
  assassination attempt and, 52
  Burckhardt and, 221, 223, 225–226
  Chamberlain and, 49
  defeat of, 53
  Dirksen and, 20
  Essad Bey and, 205
  fanaticism and, 184
  fascism and, 129
  Klemperer and, 238
  lifestyle of, 195
  Lloyd George and, 70–71
  Nolte and, 199
  Petukhov and, 96
  speech of, 48
  Stalin and, 87
  Zionism and, 61
The Hitler Mythos (Alexander), 126
Hizb al Tahrir, 89, 95, 126
Hoepp, Gerhard, 206
Hofmannsthal, Hugo von, 221, 222, 225
Hölderlin, Friedrich, 177
Holocaust, 46–47, 48, 199, 223
  see also Auschwitz; Cohn, Willy;
    International Red Cross;
    Klemperer, Viktor; Koch,
    Richard; Lasker sisters
Homer, 178
Horace, 177–178
Horstenburg, General von, 20
Howe, Irving, 217
human rights, 113, 116, 159
Hussein, Saddam, 26

Ichkeria, 90
immigration
  demographics and, 119–121
  integration and, 113, 118, 121–123, 153, 174
  from North Africa, 36–37
  objections to, 28–29
  from Russia, 37
  terrorism and, 153–154

xenophobia and, 132
  see also emigration
indoctrination, 179–180
industry, emergence of, 17–18
Indyk, Martin, 26
infoterrorism, 144–145
Institute of Advanced Philosophical Studies, 19–20
International Atomic Energy Agency, 141
International Red Cross, 47, 48, 221–222, 224, 225, 226
The Invisible Writing (Koestler), 207–213
Iraq war, 91
Irish Republican Army (IRA), 138, 145
Islam
  in Central Asia, 94–95
  in Russia, 83, 87–101, 123
  see also Muslims, in Russia
Islamic Challenge (Clausen), 118
Islamic Movement of Uzbekistan (IMU), 95
The Islamisation of Russia, 123
Islamism, 199–200, 202
Islamist terrorism, 150–152, 153, 172
Islamofascism, 125, 127, 129–130, 133, 202
Islamophobia, 90, 131–133
Israel
  achievements of, 35
  establishment of, 29, 57–58

Jabotinsky, Vladimir, 38, 209
Jerusalem, Zionism and, 42–43, 61
The Jewish Century (Slezkine), 65–67
John Paul II, 107
Johnson, Dr., 166
Jones, Felix, 11
Judenstaat (Herzl), 28, 35, 61
Judt, Joel, 21
Jünger, Ernst, 181

Kadyrov, Ramzon, 93, 94
Kalischer, Zvi Hirsch, 13
Kaplan, Chaim, 232
Karski, Jan, 46
Katyn, 79
Kennedy, John F., 106
Khalidi, Rashid, 26
Khan, Ayub, 152
Khatami, Ahmad, 127

Khomeini, Ayatollah, 19
Khomyakov, Alexei, 88
Khrushchev, Nikita, 96, 106
Kibalchich. *see* Serge, Victor
Kim il-Sung, 104
Kissinger, Henry, 106
Klemperer, George, 232, 233, 239
Klemperer, Otto, 232
Klemperer, Viktor, 51, 232–240
Koch, Richard, 241–244
Koerner, Theodor, 177
Koestler, Arthur, 207–213, 219
Kohl, Helmut, 119
Kohn, Hans, 89
Kolarz, Walter, 89
Korean War, 103, 104, 105
Koresh, David, 143
Kos, 47–48, 52–53
Kramer, Martin, 128
Kristeva, Julia, 185
Krivitski, Walter, 216
Krueger, Alan, 147
Ku Klux Klan, 125
Kurdish Workers Party, 145
Kurtzer, Daniel, 26

Lacan, Jacques, 61
Lamblin, Bianca, 208
Landau, Ludwik, 232
Laqueur, Walter, 22–23
Larssen, Rolf Mowatt, 166
Lasalle, 8
Lasker sisters, 244–245
Last Days of Europe (Laqueur),
    117, 119
Laval, Michel, 207–213
Lavrov, Serge, 84
Le Vernet, 212–213
League of Nations, 28
Lebensreform, 193–194
Leff, Laurel, 48
Lehrer, Tom, 105
Leibowitz, Y., 62
Lend-Lease Act, 51
Lenin, Vladimir, 43, 96, 232, 239
Lermontov, Mikhail, 88
Les Juifs, rois de l'epoque
    (Toussenel), 5
Lettres Persanes (Montesquieu), 192
Levin, Shmaryahu, 236
Lewandowski, Jozef, 48
Lewis, Bernard, 117

L'homme sans concessions (Laval),
    207–213
Liebknecht, Karl, 197
life expectancy, 3
Lisbon treaty, 113–114
Litvinenko, Alexander, 78
Lloyd George, David, 70–71
Lohengrin, 61
London bombing, 122
Longerich, Peter, 48
LTI (Lingua terti imperii)
    (Klemperer), 233
Lucas, Edward, 108
Ludendorff, Erich, 192
Luettwitz, General, 198
Lukanga Mukara (Paasche), 189,
    190–191
Luxemburg, Rosa, 197
Luzhkov, Yuri, 93

Macdonald, Nancy and Dwight, 217
Macmillan, Margaret, 69–71
Madrid bombing, 122
Mahbubani, Kishone, 116
Malashenko, Aleksei, 87, 99
Maleckova, Jitka, 147
Manhattan Project, 51
    see also atomic bomb; nuclear
    weapons
Marr, Wilhelm, 4, 7, 8, 132
martyrdom, 181–182
Marx, Karl, 7–8, 16, 96, 156, 164
Marx, Emanuel, 19
Maslow, Arkadi, 198
Massad, Rashid, 21
Mazzini, Giuseppe, 64
Mecid, Abdul, 9
Medvedev, Dmitry, 76, 79, 93, 94, 103
Mein Kampf (Hitler), 61, 126
Melkov, 98
Memoires d'une jeune fille derangée
    (Lamblin), 208
messianism, 60–62
Metternich, Klemens von, 8, 10
Meyerbeer, Giacomo, 222
Michman, Dan, 48
Midnight in the Century (Serge), 219
migration, 3
Miller, Aaron, 26
Miller, Rene Fülöp, 205
Moltke, Helmuth von, 11
Mongols, 97

Monnet, Jean, 115
Montefiore, Moses, 10–11, 13, 16, 227–229
Montesquieu, Charles Louis de Secondat, 192
Morris, Benny, 27–28, 29–30, 31, 34
Moses Montefiore (Green), 227–229
Mosley, Oswald, 127
Mossad, 158, 167, 180, 201
Mounier, Emanuel, 219
Mount Carmel, 19–20
Musharraf, Pervez, 152
Muslim Brotherhood, 25, 99, 128–129, 138, 156
Muslims, in Russia, 89–90, 91–94, 99–100
Mussolini, 54, 129, 156, 202, 205

Napolitano, Janet, 163
Nashashibi, Fakhri, 31
Nasser, Gamal Abdul, 41, 59, 128
National Socialism (Nazism), 126–127, 130, 178, 184, 195
nationalism, 125–126
NATO, 77–78, 79, 84, 95, 124
Nesselrode, Carl, 8–9
Neufeld, Michael, 48
The New Cold War (Lucas), 108
Nicholas I, 228
Nietzsche, Friedrich, 181
9/11, 165, 167, 171, 173–174, 200–201
Nixon, Richard, 106
Nobel, Alfred, 151, 173
Nolte, Ernst, 199–202
Nordau, Max, 60
Norwegian model, 111
nuclear weapons, 140, 166
    see also atomic bomb; Manhattan Project
Nussimbaum, Lev. *see* Essad Bey, Mohammed
Nye, Joseph S., 158

Obama, Barack, 108, 112, 163, 166, 167
occupied territories, possible surrender of, 32
Ofer, Dalia, 48
Office of War Information, 55
oil
    Arab-Israeli conflict and, 164
    European dependence on, 113, 114

In Iraq, 148
    in Russia, 76, 80, 81, 87
    terrorism and, 164, 171
Oklahoma City bombing, 144
One State Two States (Morris), 27
Oppenheim, 10
Organization of African States, 114
Organization of Islamic Conference (OIC), 123
Organization of Islamic States, 90
The Orientalist (Reiss), 203–206
Orwell, George, 207
Ostjuden, 235–236, 240
Ostrower, Hirsch, 17

Paasche, Hans, 189–198
pacificism, 195–196
Pale of Settlement, 3
Palestine Liberation Organization, 29
Palmerston, Lord, 9–10
Pamyat, 96
Panarin, Igor, 96–97
Pape, Robert, 164
paranoia, 186
Paskevich, General, 11
Pasternak, Boris, 105, 232
Pasteur, Louis, 17
peace negotiations, 26, 29
Peel Commission, 28–29
Peres, Shimon, 139
Peron, Juan, 127
Peters, Joan, 64
Petukhov, Yuri, 96
Philippson, Ludwig, 13–14
Philosophical Letters (Chaadayev), 95
photography, development of, 18
pilgrimages, 89
Pius XII, 55
pogroms, 4–5, 6
polarization, 38
Politics of Social Change in the Middle East and North Africa (Halpern), 128
Poppert, Hermann, 194–195
Porat, Dina, 48
post-Zionism, 39–41
    see also Zionism
Pound, Ezra, 205
poverty, terrorism and, 147–148, 170–171, 179
Primakov, Evgeni, 90
Prokhanov, Alexander, 98, 108

propaganda, 158
The Protocols of Satan and the Sanhedrin, 5
psychoanalysis, 62
Pushkin, Alexander, 76, 88
Putin, Vladimir, 76, 77, 79, 80, 82, 84, 93, 96, 107

The Question of Zion (Rose), 60
Qutb, Sayed, 131, 183

Rabin, Yitzhak, 139, 143
racism, 131–132
radicalism, 121
RAF, 184
Rafsanjani, Ali Akbar Hashemi, 140
railways, 5–6, 7, 50, 52
Rakhomov, Murtaza, 92
Ranke, Leopold von, 49
Reagan, Ronald, 107
Red Cross. *see* International Red Cross
Reiss, Ignaz, 216
Reiss, Tom, 203–206
Reshid, Mustafa, 9–10
Reshid Pasha, 14–15
Resolution *3379*, 43
Reuter, Christoph, 177–182
Rhodes, 47–48, 52–53
Riegner, Gerhard, 46
RIKI countries, 98
Rilke, Rainer Maria, 221
Ringelblum, Emanuel, 232
riots
    in France (2005), 118–119
    Hep Hep riots, 4
Ritzen, Debray, 208
The Road of Allah's Warriors (Zhuravlyov, Melkov, and Shershnev), 97–98
Rodinson, Maxime, 127–128
Rogers, Barbara, 48
Rolland, Romain, 216
Rompuy, Herman van, 114
Roosevelt, Franklin Delano, 51, 55
Rose, Jacqueline, 60–62
Rosenthal, Rubik, 60
Rosenzweig, Franz, 241
Ross, Dennis, 26
Roth, Leo, 198
Rothschilds, 8, 10–11, 15, 17
Rowley, Hazel, 208

Runnymede Trust, 131
Russia
    Central Asia and, 94–95
    doctrines of, 95–98
    East and, 83
    foreign policy of, 78–79, 82–85, 99–100
    future of, 75–85
    Islam and, 87–101, 123–124
    as mediator, 91
    modernization and, 78–82
    Muslims in, 89–90, 91–94, 99–100
    raw materials and, 76, 81, 87
    revolution in, 66
    technology and, 80–81
    U.S. relations with, 75, 84, 99–101, 107–108
    West and, 82–83
    see also Soviet Union
Russian Academy of Science, 81
The Russian World Order (Petukhov), 96
Ruthven, Malise, 127–128

Sabuni, Nyamka, 121
Sadat, Anwar, 26
Sageman, Marc, 183–186
Samuel, Viscount, 30
Sartawi, Issam, 31
Sartre, Jean Paul, 207–208, 209
Scammell, Michael, 208
Scherl, August, 197
Scheurmann, Erich, 192
Scholem, Gershom, 61
Scholem, Werner, 198
Schopenhauer, Arthur, 4
Schulte, Eduard, 46
Scum of the Earth (Koestler), 210
secularism, 122
self-hatred, 62
Serge, Victor, 215–220
settlements, 26, 30, 34, 42, 59
Shaimiev, Mintimer, 92
Shamil, Imam, 94
sharia, 93, 98, 122–123, 152, 171, 173
Sharon, Arik, 30
Shershnev, 98
sho'ah. *see* Holocaust
Shoko Asahara, 143
shuttle bombing, 51
Simmel, Georg, 65
Since Time Immemorial (Peters), 64

Six Day War. *see* War of 1967
Skolkovo, 81
Slezkine, Yuri, 65–67
Smith, Gerald, 127
socialism, fear of, 112
societal bonds, 186
soft power, 157–158, 167
Soloviev, Vladimir, 88
Solzhenitsyn, Alexander, 19, 96, 106
Sombart, Werner, 65
Soviet Union, 45, 66, 242
    see also Russia
Spanish Testament (Koestler), 210, 211
Squire, Paul, 224–225
stagnation, 89
Stalin, Josef, 51, 66, 76, 77, 87, 96, 103, 104, 105, 203, 205, 216, 219, 232
Stark, Freya, 128
Stauffer, Paul, 222, 223, 225
Sublime Porte, 9, 10, 18, 228
suicide terrorism, 138–139, 151, 164, 173, 177–182
    see also terrorism
Summers, Lawrence, 112
Surkov, Vladislav, 79, 80, 96
Swedish government, 47
Syed, Ajaz Saka, 120

Tadjik civil war, 91
Taha, Sami, 31
Talbot, Fox, 18
Taliban, 95, 124, 152
Tamil Tigers, 138, 139, 145, 178, 179, 181
Tanner, John, 76
Tanner, William, 11
temperance movement, 193, 194–195
Tennyson, Alfred Lord, 116
The Terrible Secret, 48, 51
terrorism
    apocalyptic movements and, 142–143
    changes in, 137–139
    effects of, 139–140
    in Europe, 152–155, 173–175
    future of, 172–173
    Islamist, 150–152, 153, 172
    literature on, 183
    local conflict and, 149–150, 171
    misconceptions and, 169–172
    opposing, 155–157
    political context and, 163–165

poverty and, 147–148, 170–171, 179
    technology and, 144–145
    weapons and, 140–142, 166–167, 181
    see also suicide terrorism
Tete a Tete (Rowley), 208
Thirteenth Tribe (Koestler), 210
Three Faces of Fascism (Nolte), 199
Tindemans, Leonard, 119
Tiso, Monsignor, 127
Tocqueville, Alexis de, 77
Tolstoy, Lev, 88
Toussenel, Alphonse, 5
Trotsky, Leon, 19, 203, 216–217, 218
Trumpeldor, Josef, 41, 63
Tucholsky, Kurt, 197

ultra-orthodox community, 39
Umland, Andreas, 97
UN Special Committee on Palestine, 31
Unabomber, 144
Understanding Terror Networks (Sageman), 183–186
United Nations, 21, 113, 149
Ushakov, Yuri, 79

Vaisse, Justin, 117–118
van Gogh, Theo, 122
Vatican, 45
Vavilov, Alexander, 98
Verwehte Spuren (Cohn), 240
Victor Serge (Weissman), 215–220
Vienna Jewish Congress, 15
Viereck, George Sylvester, 205
Vietnam War, 106
von Hundsfott, 6
Von Ossietzky case, 224
Vortrupp, 191, 194
Vorwaerts, 191
Vrba-Wetzler report, 51

Wałesa, Lech, 43
Wannsee Conference, 237
War of 1967, 31–32, 38, 42, 59–60
Warburg, Moses, 10
Warsaw Ghetto uprising, 238
weapons of mass destruction, 140–142, 144, 151, 160–161, 165–167, 172, 173, 181
Weber, Max, 98

Wegner, Armin T., 205–206
Weinstock, Nathan, 201
Weissman, Susan, 215–220
Weitling, Wilhelm, 7, 8
Weitz, Michael, 48
Weizman, Chaim, 42–43, 200
welfare state, European, 111–112
West Bank settlements. *see* settlements
Wiskeman, Elizabeth, 222
Wittgenstein, 20
Witting, Richard, 189, 196
World at Risk, 166
World Jewish Congress, 46
World War I, 18–19, 28, 70
World War II, 22–23, 36, 41, 53–54, 96
    see also Auschwitz; Cohn, Willy; Hitler, Adolf; Holocaust; Klemperer, George; Koch, Richard; Lasker sisters

Year One of the Russian Revolution (Serge), 216
Yeltsin, Boris, 75

Ye'or, Bat, 117
Yevkurov, Yumusbek, 94
Yom Kippur war, 32

Zahar, Mahmud, 91
Zborowski, Mark, 216
Zertal, Idit, 26, 62–63
Zetkin, Clara, 197
Zhuravlyov, 98
Zionism
    antagonists to, 39–40
    Cohn and, 240–241
    definition of, 60
    establishment of Israel and, 35–37, 41
    extremism and, 38
    holocaust and, 57–58
    international opposition to, 43–44
    Jerusalem and, 42–43
    Klemperer and, 236
    Koestler and, 209, 210
    in Northern Caucasus, 94
    opposition to, 57, 60, 62–64
Zionist Writings (Herzl), 236
Zvi, Sabbetai, 60